James Murphy

**Travels in Portugal**

James Murphy

**Travels in Portugal**

ISBN/EAN: 9783337764104

Printed in Europe, USA, Canada, Australia, Japan

Cover: Foto ©Andreas Hilbeck / pixelio.de

More available books at **www.hansebooks.com**

# TRAVELS

IN

# PORTUGAL;

THROUGH

The PROVINCES of *ENTRE DOURO E MINHO*, *BEIRA*, *ESTREMADURA*, and *ALEM-TEJO*,
In the Years 1789 and 1790.

CONSISTING OF

OBSERVATIONS on the MANNERS, CUSTOMS, TRADE, PUBLIC BUILDINGS, ARTS, ANTIQUITIES, &c. of that Kingdom.

By JAMES MURPHY, Architect.

---

Illustrated with PLATES.

---

LONDON:
Printed for A. STRAHAN, and T. CADELL Jun. and W. DAVIES (Successors to Mr. CADELL) in the Strand.
1795.

TO

HIS ROYAL HIGHNESS

# DON JOHN, Prince of *Brazil.*

MAY it pleaſe your ROYAL HIGHNESS to permit me to lay at YOUR Feet this Work, being a Part of my Reſearches in the Kingdom of YOUR ROYAL HIGHNESS; and to expreſs my Wiſhes, at the ſame Time, that Portugal, the benign Mother of glorious Diſcoveries, may rival her ancient Greatneſs, under the auſpicious Reign of KING JOHN THE SIXTH.

YOUR ROYAL HIGHNESS's

Moſt obedient,

and moſt devoted Servant,

LONDON,
May 30, 1795.

*James Murphy.*

A VIEW OF THE BRITISH FACTORY HOUSE at OPORTO.

Plate II.

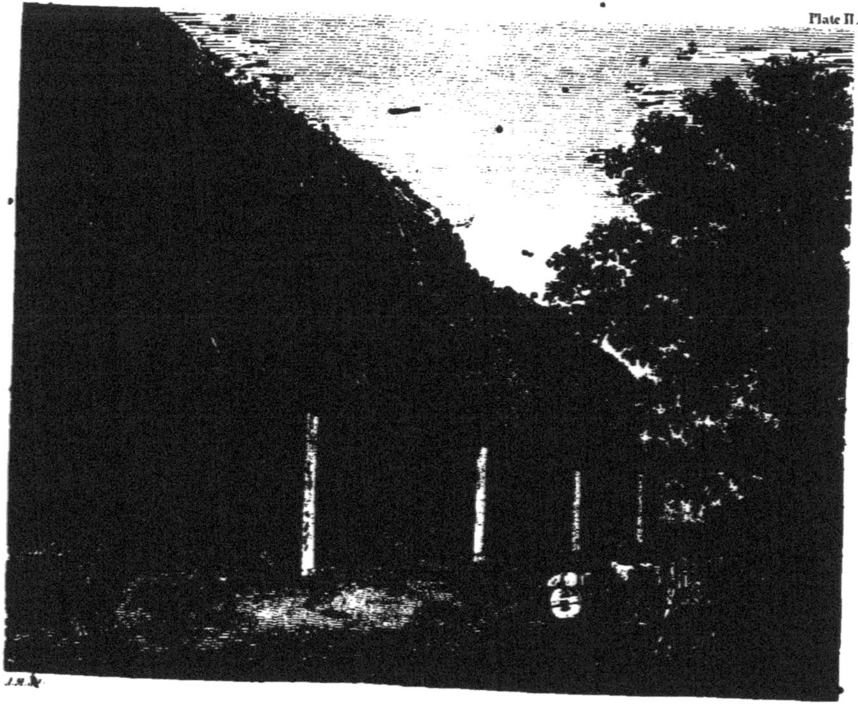

J. H. del.

Lehman & Lowry, Sculp.

A VIEW OF THE CARAVANSARY OF THE OAKS

Plate III.

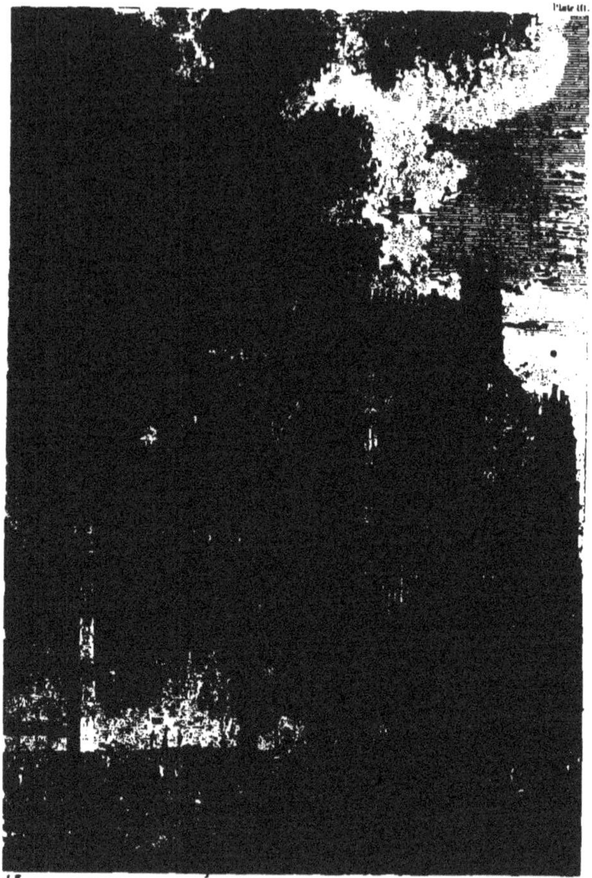

J. M. — Milton Sculp.

A VIEW OF THE CHURCH OF BATALHA

Plate V

A REPRESENTATION OF THE PRINCIPAL MODERN STREETS OF LISBON.

Plate VI

J. Murphy del. Walker Sc.

A VIEW OF THE CUSTOM HOUSE and ROYAL EXCHANGE at LISBON.

Publish'd May 1st 1795 by Cadell and Davies in the Strand

E

D

مولانا سلطان سلاطين الزمان المحيي بني لست
الرحمان المجاهد في اعلاء اوامر القران
القامع اساس اهل الطغيان القالع ديار عبدة
الاوثان الغالب في يوم التقى الجمعان الوارث لملك
سليمان الواثق بالله المنان مالك الفضايل
بساهد شاه السلطان ٭ هذا المدفع صنع في خامس
من ذي القعدة بسنة تسع وثلثين وتسعماية ٭ يتبي

[illegible]

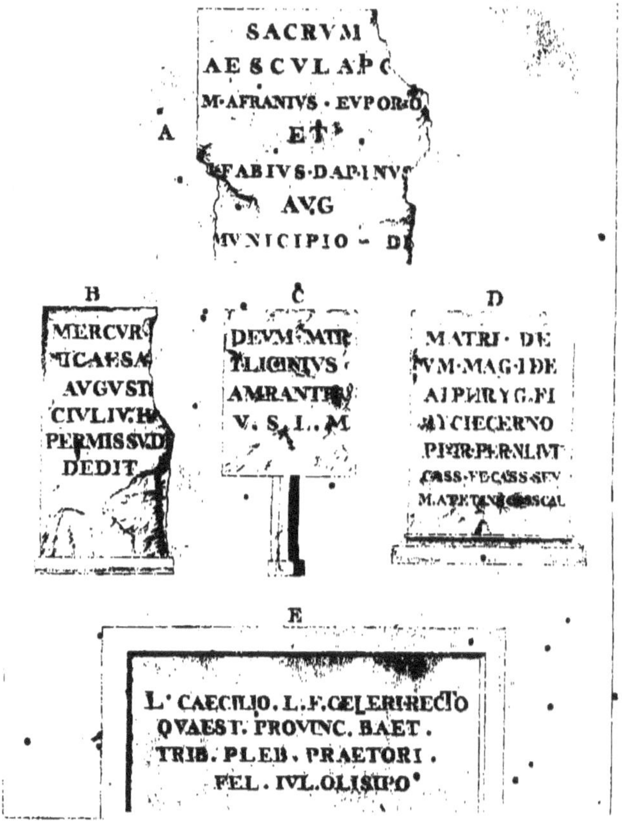
A
SACRVM
AESCVLAPC
M·AFRANIVS · EVPORIO
ET
FABIVS·DAPINVS
AVG
MVNICIPIO — D
B
MERCVR
CAESA
AVGVST
CIVLIV
PERMISSV.D
DEDIT
C
DEVM·MATR
LICINIVS
AMRANTI
V. S. L. M
D
MATRI · DE
VM·MAG·IDE
AI PHRYG.FI
CIECERNO
E
L' CAECILIO. L. F. CELERI RECTO
QVAEST. PROVINC. BAET.
TRIB. PLEB. PRAETORI.
FEL. IVL.OLISIPO

C — A — B

A PEASANT OF ALENTEJO — A LISBON FRUIT WOMAN — A WOMAN OF BEIRA

London Published [illegible] Strand.

J. M.    J. F. Clemens Engraver to the King of Denmark Sculp.

A PORTUGUESE MERCHANT with HIS WIFE and MAID SERVANT

J.M. — J. Heath Engraver to the King, Sculp.

THE FANDANGO DANCE

Plate XII

J. M. del.

Lowry Sculp.

Plate XIV.

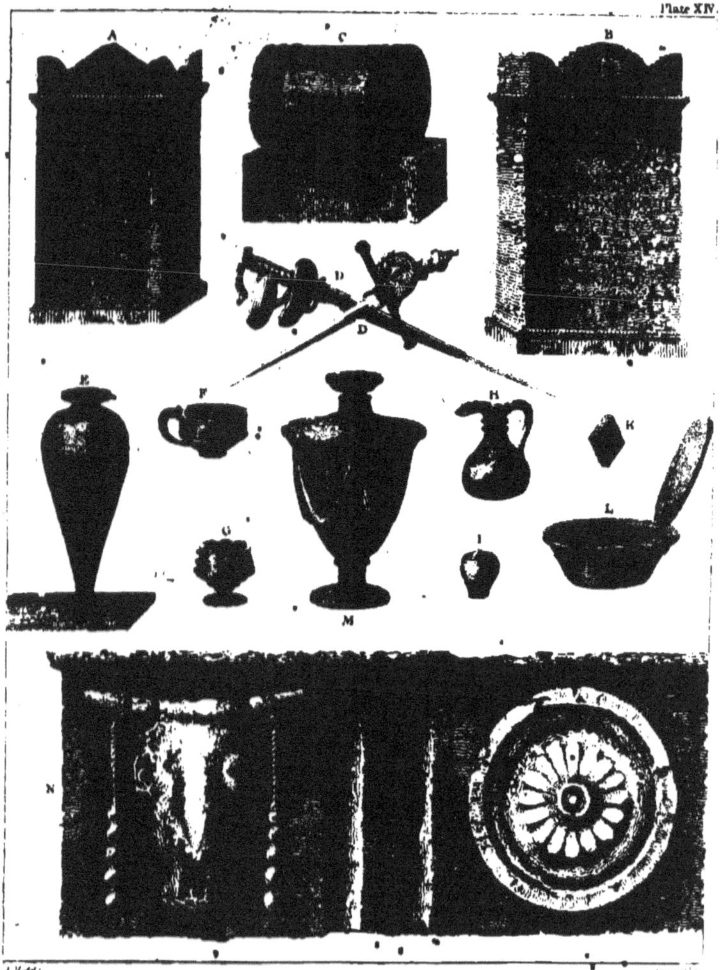


*FRAGMENTS OF ROMAN ANTIQUITIES FOUND AT BEJA & EVORA*

London: Published ... by Cadell & Davies, Strand

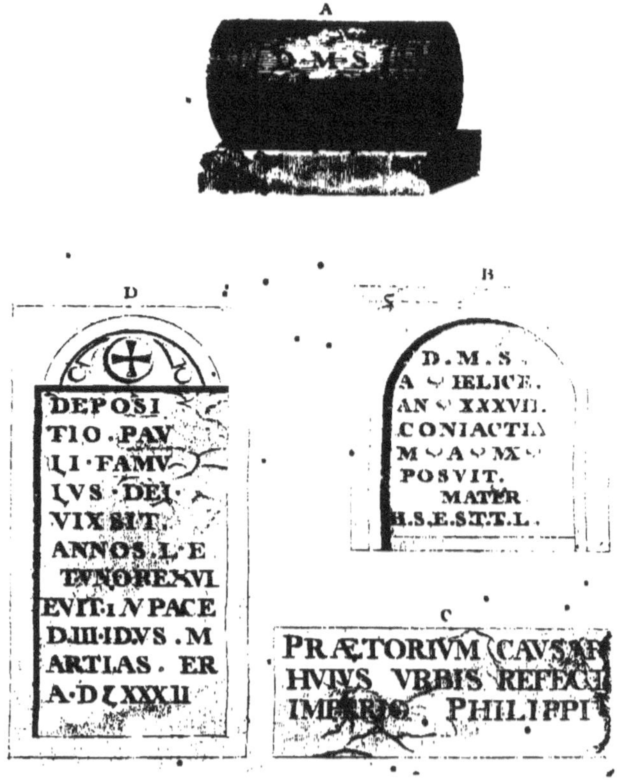
A
D.M.S.
B
D.M.S.
POSVIT.
MATER
H.S.E.S.T.T.L.
C
PRÆTORIVM CAVSAR
HVIVS VRBIS REFECI
PHILIPPI
D
DEPOSI
TIO.PAV
LI.FAMV
LVS.DEI
ANNOS.L.E
D.III.IDVS.M
ARTIAS.ER

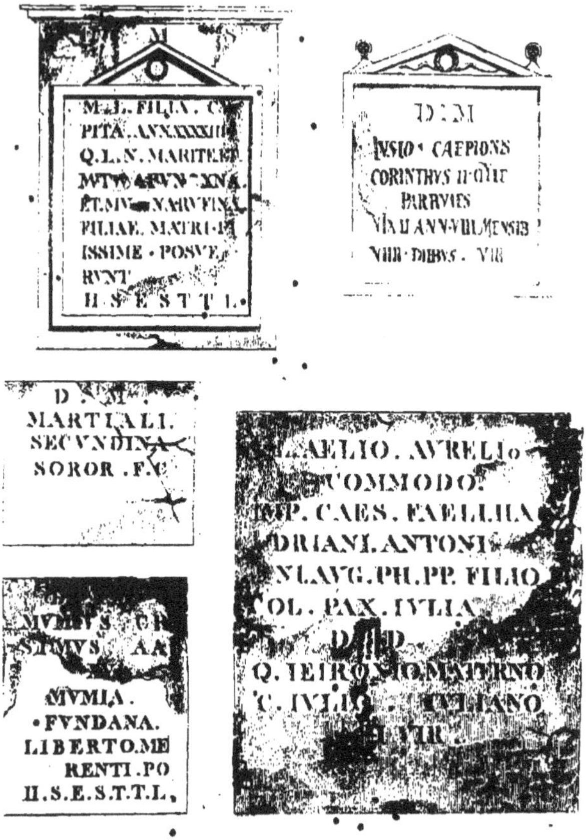


Published May 1st 179? by Cadell and Davies in the Strand

J. Murphy del. Lowry Sc.

A VIEW OF THE AQUEDUCT OF Q. SERTORIUS at EVORA.

Plate XVIII

*A VIEW OF THE CASTELLUM OF Q. SERTORIUS at EVORA*

*Publish'd May 1 1793 by Cadell and Davies in the Strand*

Plate XIX

Murphy del. — Lowry Sculp.

A VIEW OF THE TEMPLE OF DIANA at EVORA.

D

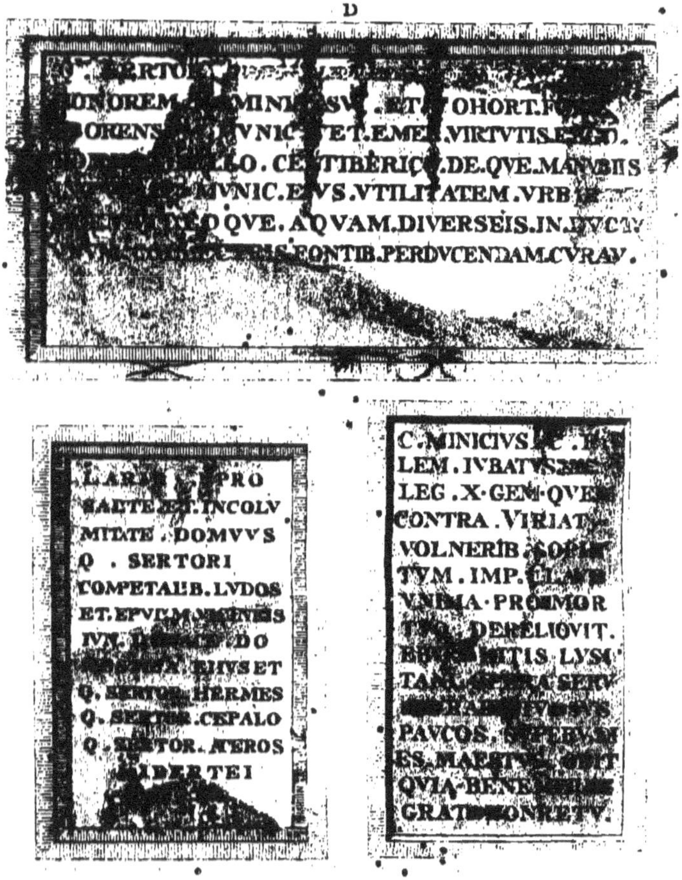
C.MINICIVS
LEG.X.GEM.QVE
CONTRA.VIRIAT
MITATE.DOMVVS
Q.SERTORI
Q.SERTOR.HERMES
PAVCOS

MANILIA . M . F .
MAXVMA . AN XII
H. S.E. S.T.T.L .
C. VIBIVS . TANCI
NVS . COGNATAE
SVAE . F . C .

D . M . S .
C . ANTONIO . C . F. FLA
VINO . VI . VIRO . IVN .
HAST . LEG. II. AVG. TORQ .
AR . ET. AN . DVPL. OB. VIRT.
DONATO . IVN . VERECVN
DA . FLAM. PERP. MVN. EBOR
MATER . F . C .

DIVO . IVLIO .
LIB . IVL . EBORA .
OB . ILEVS . IN . MVN .
E . MVN . LIBERALI
ATEM . EX . D . D . D .
QVOIVS . DEDICATIO
NE . VENERI . GENE
TRIC . DONVM . MA
TRONAE . CESTVM .
TVLERVNT .

I . O . M
OB . PVL . SOS . A . Q . SERTOR
METEL . ADQ . POMPE . IVN .
DONACE . CORONA . ET . SCEP
TR . EX . ARG . MVNVS . ADTVLIT
FLAMIN . PHIALA . CAELATAM .
HIERODVLIS . COENAM . D . D .

[illegible]CILIO . Q . [illegible]
VOLVS [illegible] AE[illegible]
COH . I . G . R . SEX[illegible]
PROVOC . VICTORI .
DON . DONATO . AB
IMPER[illegible]II . HAST .
PVR . III . VEXIL . [illegible]
[illegible]CIVIC . I . MVR .
IIII . OBSIDIONIB[illegible]
HIS . IN . RES . P . S . FVNC[illegible]
EBORENS CIVI . OPT .
[illegible]MERITA . EIVS . IN .
MVNIC . MARMOR
BASI . AENE [illegible] . D

Published [illegible] by Cadell and Davies in the Strand

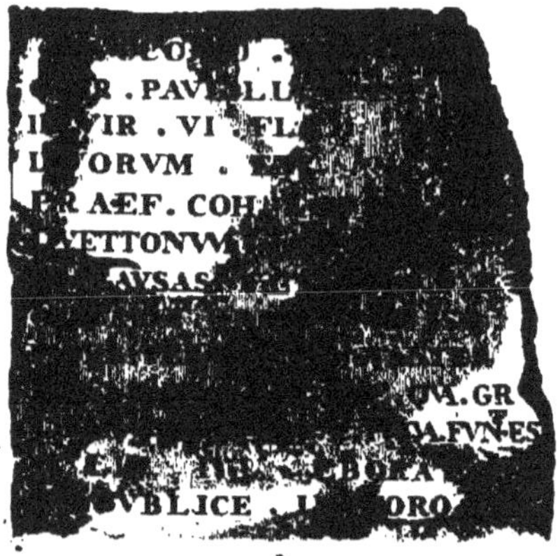


IOANNES III LVSITAN · INDIAR · ET · IN · AFRICA · REX .
CELEBREM · AQVÆ · ARGENTEAE · DVCTVM · A · Q ·
SERTORIO · AN · LXXV · ANTE · D · CHRISTVM · NATVM ·
EXTRVCTVM · BARBARIE · ET · ANTIQVITATE · FVNDE
TVS · DEMOLITVM · NOVA · FORMA · LIBERALI · IMPEN
SA, MAIORI · AQVARVM · COPIA · ADIECTA · XVII · MIL.
PASS · DVCTVI · VERVS · P · P · IN · VRBEM · REDVXIT.
ANN · SOLVTIS · MDXXII ·

PHILIP . II · AQVAM · A · Q · SERTORIO · AB · AN
OLIM · DIVORVM · NVNC ; ODIVOR · PERDVCT
ET . IOANNE · III · RESTITVTAM · REGNI · ET ·
TATIS · HÆRES · MVNIFICENTIA · REGIA · CON
ERVANDAM · CVRAVIT · BENEFICIS · BENEFIC
PONI · STATVIT · CEPPIS · EBORENS · ANTIQVAM
NOBILITATEM · ATTESTANTIBVS · FORVM
ILLVSTRAT · ANNO · DOM · MDCV ·

Plate XXIII

J. Murphy Delin. — Sculp.

A COPY OF AN ARABIC INSCRIPTION at EVORA.

Plate XXIV

J. Murphy del. Fond. Sc.

AN INTERIOR VIEW OF A CHARNEL HOUSE at EVORA.

# CONTENTS.

## DIRECTIONS to the BINDER for placing the PLATES.



---

## ERRATA.

Page 274. line 6. For *the Duke de Bragança* read *Don Conſtantino de Bragança.*
277. — 8. For *renders* read *render.*

# PREFACE.

MOST of the travellers who have hitherto obliged the world with their obſervations on Portugal, repreſent it as a barren inhoſpitable field for information, without allowing it to poſſeſs ſcarcely an object worthy to arreſt the attention of the Philoſopher, the Antiquary, or Artiſt; and, indeed, the contents of their pages appear to corroborate the repreſentation.

Truth, however, will not allow me to plead the ſame apology for the want of intereſting matter in this work; if it fall ſhort of the end propoſed, the fault is not to be aſcribed to that fertile country, but to the want of talents or induſtry on my part.

A nation once celebrated in every quarter of the globe for its diſcoveries and conqueſts, that abounds with the moſt valuable mineral and vegetable productions, that carries on a trade of the greateſt extent and importance, and poſſeſſes many of the moſt valuable colonies in the world, muſt furniſh an innumerable ſeries of objects for the

 conſider-

consideration of the Historian, the Naturalist, and Statesman.

Leaving these momentous subjects for the investigation of more enlightened travellers, I have contented myself with giving only such casual remarks as came within the contracted sphere of my observation, and these I have thrown together with very little art or arrangement.

Whether I have been more or less successful in noting or recording whatever occurred, than my predecessors who have traversed the same ground, the public will best determine. I shall only observe, that there is not an article in this work they have anticipated, nor a Plate with which it is embellished or illustrated (except one *) has ever been engraved before, as far as my inquiry has extended.

The extracts inserted are chiefly from the Portuguese writers, whose names are mentioned, with very few exceptions; and wherever any omission of that nature occurs, it happened through mistake or failure of memory, and not with a view to usurp the merit of the author.

When first I collected these fragments, it was not with an intention to publish them; but in order to obtain some knowledge of the manners and customs, the ancient and

* The Plan of Lisbon.

present

present ſtate of Portugal. My friends, however, at length intreated me to commit them to the preſs; aſſuring me that I would meet with the ſame indulgence which artiſts uſually claim, and generally receive from the public, whenever they attempt any literary performance.

Encouraged by this circumſtance, I have complied with their requeſt, from a conviction of having faithfully repreſented whatever came within my view, and correctly reported the ſubjects that were verbally communicated to me. But at the ſame time, not conſidering myſelf as reſponſible for the authenticity of ſubjects thus collected; ſince I am but the humble organ through whom they are conveyed; and as a ſtranger to the country, without an opportunity to compare, variety to furniſh ſelection, or the means of inveſtigating the truth by a number of collateral evidences.

Having taken a review of the whole in arranging it for the preſs, I found many paſſages that ſtood in need of emendation, and others that required to be purged of their exuberance or expunged; but thinking it might not be unacceptable to the reader to behold the irregular ſallies of one unaccuſtomed to write, I have ſuffered them to remain unpruned, like ſuperfluous branches ſhooting from a ſtock.

As it was principally through the munificence of the Right Honourable William Burton Conyngham, that I have been enabled to collect the materials of this work, as well as those relating to my description of the Royal Monastery of Batalha, I feel it my indispensable duty most gratefully to acknowledge the many obligations I owe to his constant patronage and friendship.

# TRAVELS

IN

# *PORTUGAL.*

ON the twenty-feventh of December, one thoufand feven hundred and eighty-eight, I failed from the port of Dublin, on board a trading veffel bound to Oporto. On the morning of the feventeenth day after our departure, we defcried the mountains of Vianna, which rife at the Northern extremity of Portugal. A few miles to the South of thefe mountains, appeared *Villa do Conde*; here our Captain pointed to a feries of arches, the remains of an ancient aqueduct; the number we could not afcertain with the motion of the fhip, but the Captain affured us that they exceeded three hundred, and their apparent extent feemed to juftify the affertion.

On the evening of the fame day, we approached the bar of Oporto, and made the ufual fignal for a pilot. An eight-oared barge, equipped with a white and black crew, ſoon arrived, with two commiſſioned pilots, who informed us, much to our regret, that we muſt put to ſea till the next day, as it was too late to paſs the bar. In the mean time, a heavy gale aroſe which ſwelled the ſea mountain-high. One of the pilots who continued on board, ſeeing the ſtorm increaſe, conducted us to the bar early the following morning, when ſeveral boat-men came to our aſſiſtance.

Nature has almoſt cut off all communication between this city and the ſea; the channel, in ſome parts, being not more than double the breadth of a ſhip, and ſo full of windings, that it requires the utmoſt ſkill to paſs it with ſafety, even in a calm day, but in a tempeſt like this, the ſcene is tremendous, and called forth the united efforts of the crew, to obviate the danger of the rocks, ſands, and waves, which oppoſed our entrance. The river Douro alſo increaſed the difficulty, as it now ran with the velocity of nine miles an hour, in conſequence of being ſwelled beyond its uſual bounds by a ſucceſſion of rainy days. It is eaſier to conceive than deſcribe the conflict which enſued between this current and the waves of the Atlantic, as they met in a narrow channel at the mouth of the river.

About five in the evening, we paſſed this Charybdis, with only the loſs of an anchor, and arrived oppoſite to a con-

vent

vent belonging to the order of Saint Anthony, about a mile up the river. A ſhip from Greenock, in attempting to follow our example, was daſhed to pieces almoſt in our view, but fortunately the hands were ſaved, though with much difficulty.

## *The River* DOURO.

The Southern banks of the *Douro*, as far as the eye can reach, is diverſified with convents, and villas, the occaſional retreat of the wealthier citizens. The groves and gardens that accompany them have a charming effect on the eye of a Northern viſitant, as the ravages of Winter have not ſtripped them of their verdant foliage. The orange-tree, which may be juſtly conſidered as the emblem of gratitude, here ſurpaſſed in beauty all the reſt;

> " Flowers and fruits at once ſhe ſhewed,
> " And as ſhe paid, diſcovered, ſtill ſhe owed."

The beauty of the proſpect, and the ſerenity of the air, when compared to the naked trees and piercing winds of the country from which we had lately departed, rendered the tranſition enchanting.

The Douro is the largeſt river in Portugal, except the Tagus; it takes its riſe near *Sória*, in Old Caſtile, and having traverſed a tract of about an hundred and twenty leagues, is loſt in the Weſtern Ocean. As it approaches the ſea, it winds its courſe in a vale formed by two immenſe and oppoſite mountains, where it is of depth ſufficient for the largeſt trading veſſels to anchor along the banks on either ſide. During three days the rapidity of the current prevented our receiving the cuſtomary viſits, without which none dare attempt to go aſhore, under pain of impriſonment. The object of theſe viſits is twofold, the one to ſearch for contraband goods, the other to examine and report the ſtate of the paſſengers health. On the evening of the fourth day, three officers came aboard, accompanied by an interpreter, who, in the lofty tone of authority, commanded thoſe who had either tobacco or ſoap * in his poſſeſſion, to bring forth the ſame: his mandate was immediately obeyed; but as the Captain was aware of the laws of the country, he ſuffered no prohibited goods on board, except a ſmall quantity of the above articles for private uſe, and theſe were not ſeized.

We muſt declare, in juſtice to theſe officers, that they performed their duty with ſo much politeneſs, that it carried more the appearance of a friendly viſit than an official ſearch. Thoſe who have witneſſed the viſits of Britiſh cuſtom-houſe officers, upon ſimilar occaſions, will ſcarcely believe that ſo much urbanity exiſts among men of that claſs. The late Marquis de Pombal, on his arrival as ambaſſador to the Britiſh court, was ſo rudely treated by a group of theſe gentry, that it impreſſed him, ever after,

* The importation of theſe articles is prohibited even in the ſmalleſt quantity.

with

with an unfavourable idea of the execution of the revenue laws of this country. And it is generally ſuppoſed, that this circumſtance alone operated as the cauſe of the regulations which he afterwards eſtabliſhed relative to the wine-trade of Oporto, regulations not very friendly to the intereſt of the Britiſh factory of that city.

After the viſitation of the above officers, we were in expectation of that of the phyſician; but as his perſonal attendance was prevented by indiſpoſition, he diſpatched a certain deputy to ſupply his place. This illegitimate ſon of Eſculapius commanded every perſon on board to appear on the deck, whilſt he ſurveyed them from the oppoſite ſhore, at the diſtance of about two hundred yards; and indeed I could not help ſurveying him from head to foot, for ſo curious a figure in the medical line never ſtruck my ſight before. To judge of his talents by his dreſs, (the modern criterion of merit,) little was to be expected, for he appeared to deſpiſe all the formal trappings of the faculty, ſuch as the ſable drapery, the broad-brimmed beaver, the full-bottomed wig, &c. his dreſs was rather convenient than otherwiſe, it conſiſted of a red cap, a blue jacket ſomewhat lacerated at the elbows, — — —. Having conſidered a few minutes, he took a pinch of ſnuff, then nodding his head, pronounced a few words to this effect: *I certify that ye are all in good health.* Whether he derived his information from intuition, or from the penetration of the viſual organs, or whether it happened merely from chance, he certainly pronounced a verdict which even Hippocrates could not refute.

*Oporto.*

On the evening of the eighteenth of January, one thousand seven hundred and eighty-nine, the passengers, consisting of two students, appointed for the university of Salamanca, and myself, were conducted to Oporto, and recommended to an English tavern, where we took up our residence. The first thing that strikes the mind of a stranger, on his arrival here, is the devout appearance of the inhabitants. Religion seems to be their only pursuit. The clattering of bells, the bustling of processions, and the ejaculations of friars, engage the attention by day, whilst every part resounds by night with the chaunting of hymns.

Oporto is the second city in Portugal, in point of extent, population, and trade. It is seated about a league and a half from the sea, upon the declivity of a hill, on the North side of the river Douro. The houses rise gradually one above another, like the seats of a theatre. The majestic river which flows in the vale, covered with ships and boats, may be compared to a stage, on which, thousands of actors are seen daily engaged in the busy drama of trade. On the opposite side, we behold an immense mountain, which terminates the prospect, and presents this

commercial

commercial theatre with a ſcene highly picturesque, conſiſting of gardens, villas, convents, wine-ſtores, &c. all in the moſt natural ſtyle of perſpective and colouring.

According to ſome antiquaries, the name of this city is derived from *Calle*, the title by which the Romans diſtinguiſhed it. According to others, it is derived from the name of the founder, ſuppoſed to be *Getelus*, the ſon of *Cecrops* king of Attica, after whom it was called *Portus Getelus*, and hence they deduce the word Portu-gal. But the name of the kingdom, as Andrew Reſendius, a man of great learning, makes it appear, is derived from the haven or port of *Gale*, formerly a little obſcure place, ſituated upon a riſing ground on the river Douro. The harbour was at firſt reſorted to upon the account of fiſhing, and being found very convenient for that purpoſe, numbers of people flocked from all parts and ſettled there. In time, it became a rich and populous city, and was called Portugal, a name which has ſince extended to the whole kingdom. This was the opinion of Oſorio, and alſo of Camoens, as appears by the following lines:

> In that proud port half-circled by the wave,
> Which Portugallia to the nation gave.
>
> *Mickle's Luſiad*, b. vi.

As we have ſhewn the reaſon antiquaries aſſign for the kingdom's being called *Portugal*, it may not be improper to obſerve, that, as it includes a great part of ancient *Lu-*

5 *ſitania,*

ſitania, ſo it is often diſtinguiſhed by that name alſo. We ſhall therefore, in the courſe of this work, uſe the names *Portugal* and *Luſitania* promiſcuouſly, as all the writers of that country have done.

Oporto, in common with moſt ancient cities, has the defects of being narrow, and ſo irregularly diſpoſed, that there is ſcarcely a houſe in it with four right angles. Hence, a ſtranger would be led to ſuppoſe, that the forty-ſeventh propoſition of the firſt book of Euclid had not yet found its way thither. The corner-houſes of the ſtreets in general, being obliquely diſpoſed, render the adjoining houſes of the ſame figure, as every one follows the crooked plan of his next neighbour. Thus all become rhomboids and trapeziums, defects which at firſt might have been avoided by relinquiſhing a little ground; but there are very few in commercial cities, who would ſacrifice a few feet of their property, even for what Pythagoras ſacrificed a hecatomb.

Many of the ſtreets are ſo ſteep, that a man may be ſaid rather to climb than walk them. But this defect is compenſated by their cleanlineſs, which they owe more to nature than police; for as often as it rains, the floods of the adjoining mountains ruſh down in torrents, and ſweep away all the impurities of the town. Lamps have not yet been introduced in the ſtreets, except thoſe which are placed at the *Sacraria* of the Madonas.

The

The houſes, when viewed at a moderate diſtance, have a clean agreeable appearance, owing to the colour of the materials, the lowneſs of the roofs, and their not being disfigured by a multiplicity of chimnies, thoſe vehicles of dirt, which make ſo conſpicuous an appearance in the buildings of Northern climates. Here no apartment is furniſhed with a fire-place but the kitchen, and this is uſually placed in the attic ſtory.

The churches are large, ſtrong, and magnificent buildings, but totally devoid of every thing that conſtitutes ſcientific architecture: theirs is of a ſpecies between the Teutonic and Tuſcan. The materials of which they are formed are excellent, and the maſonry-part not without merit. It is ſcarcely credible what riches are laviſhed on the inſide of them; the altar-pieces, baldachins, &c. however defective in deſign, exhibit a profuſion of gilding. Gold is certainly a very effectual thing to conceal the want of art or ſcience, or ———. And yet the Portugueſe have ſome artiſts not devoid of merit, but unfortunately they are not encouraged. I knew a painter here named Glama, who would do credit to any ſchool in Europe, had he incitement to call forth the latent powers that were impriſoned within him: he was a native of Portugal, and had ſtudied many years in Italy, where he acquired a correctneſs of drawing, and a chaſteneſs of colouring, that indicated uncommon talents. Notwithſtanding, he aſſured me that he could ſcarcely eke out a miſerable

 pittance,

pittance, though he painted every thing that was offered to him, from the ſign-poſt to the apoſtle.

A lady who reſided many years at Oporto, relates the following anecdote of a rich merchant of that city, who intended to embelliſh his apartments with paintings: for this purpoſe he applied to Signor Glama, who happened then to have ſome valuable ancient pictures in his poſſeſſion, which he was commiſſioned to ſell at a very moderate price; but the merchant, who was a better judge of the produce of the grape than of the pencil, ſtarted with ſurpriſe when he demanded twenty moidores for a Corregio, and ſaid, "That he had lately bought two new "pictures of larger dimenſions for the ſame money!"

Signor Glama was one of the artiſts employed by the Right Honourable William Burton Conyngham, when on his travels through Portugal, in making drawings and ſketches of antiquities, &c. which may be ſeen among this gentleman's valuable collection of papers relating to Portugal.

The General Hoſpital, if completed, would be the largeſt building in Oporto. The principal front was intended to conſiſt of an hexaſtyle portico in the Doric order, with a pavilion on each ſide. Although it is upwards of twenty years ſince the foundation of this ſtructure was laid, there is yet but a wing of one of the pavilions covered in; the rest is raised but a few feet above the surface, and is likely to remain in this state, a magnificent modern ruin, and a lasting monument of the folly of not proportioning the design to the public purse. The site is of all others, perhaps, the most ineligible for œconomy, on account of the inequality of the ground, a circumstance which obliged the architect to build walls in the flanks, as massy as the famous wall which separates China from Tartary.

Towards the North West part of the city, upon an eminence, is situated the barrack; it consists of three files of small but clean apartments, of about ten feet in height; opposite to it, is an extensive parade. The whole is encompassed by a wall, and is supposed to contain about five hundred infantry. On entering the gate, it is customary to salute the centinel. Deserters are generally punished, not with stripes, but with servile labour; we met half-a-dozen of these victims chained in pairs, carrying provision on their *backs*, which to a Portuguese is a mark of the greatest ignominy; for, according to their generous sentiments, that part of the human frame, which is never to be seen by the enemy, is not to be degraded by any servile oppression; hence, even the poorest peasant is always found to carry his load, either in his hands, or on his head.

The annexed plate exhibits a view of a building which is nearly completed, and intended principally for the use of the British factory. The ground-story is to be the Exchange; the next (over the mezzanine) the Ball-room, which is fifty-five feet long by thirty broad, and has two tier of windows in the front. The whole is carried on from the designs of William Whitehead esq. the British consul. Over the center acrotoire, on the top of the building, is to be placed a statue, on the subject of which the factory have not yet decided, and in all probability will not for some time, as artists are generally the last who are consulted here on these occasions. We should suppose, that in a commercial edifice like this, taking the country into consideration, a statue of Prince Henry, the Pharaoh of navigation and the source of commerce, would not be unsuitable. He is generally represented as holding a globe in one hand, a chart in the other, and his motto on the pedestal *Talent de bien faire*. The ingenious architect has filled four pages in folio with calculations, which ran to quadratick equations, in demonstrating how much the intended statue should incline forward, so as to appear perfectly erect to a spectator viewing it from the opposite side of the street. History does not inform us, that Phidias required the assistance of algebra in decorating Athens with his graceful statues.

On the South side of the town, near the verge of the river, is an extensive building called the *Serrá*, perched upon the brow of a lofty precipice. Its form and situation convey the idea of a barrack; and indeed I almost concluded it was ſome military ſtructure, upon ſeeing a number of flags diſplayed from the windows: on inquiry, however, I found it was a convent belonging to the order of friars called the *Cruzes*, who this day diſplayed their enſigns, in honour of their patron ſaint. My guide pointed to one of the fathers, dreſſed in a black cloak and ſlouched hat; he was mounted on a mule, according to the rules of his community, which ordain, that they muſt not be ſeen outſide of the boundaries of the convent on foot. Each friar, therefore, is equipped in that manner; ſo that they form, as it were, a ſort of cavalry to the eccleſiaſtick corps, and are, in general, richer and more reſpected, or at leaſt would be thought ſo, than the eccleſiaſtick infantry.

Among the commercial fabrics, the wine-ſtores claim the firſt rank, after the cuſtom-houſe, in point of ſize. One of them, belonging to Mr. Warre, a Britiſh merchant, is an hundred and forty feet long by ninety broad. The inſide is divided into three corridores, by two ſeries of ſtone piers, extending from the one end to the other. Between theſe piers, and next the walls, are placed the wine pipes, two in height. Several coopers and labourers are daily employed in preparing the wine for exportation. We were ſhewn here a ſort of white wine, the produce of the province, which is ſo influenced by the weather, that when it rains it becomes muddy and unfit for uſe.

The

The following recipe, I am informed, is ſometimes uſed by the merchants of Portugal for correcting ſour wine. Fixed alkali, or ſalt of tartar, put into ſour wine, will abſorb the acidity, and give it the taſte and ſmell of new wine. Too much alkali will turn it black and muddy; in order to avoid this defect, a quantity of the acid liquor is mixed with the alkali before it is applied.

In order to give the reader an idea of the annual exports of this city, it may not be unintereſting to annex the following ſtate of the ſame in the year one thouſand ſeven hundred and eighty-nine:

| | |
|---|---|
| 35,600 | Pipes of wine, ſhipped to various parts of Europe and America. |
| 4,989,000 | *Varas* * of linen cloth, the greater part of which was ſent to America. |
| 40,000 | *Varas* of ſtuff, ſent to Brazil and Liſbon. |
| 92,000 | *Covados* † of woollen cloth, baize, &c. manufactured at Oporto and its diſtrict. |
| 110,000 | Dozen of various pieces of pottery. |
| 8,500 | Pipes of oil, part of which was ſent to Brazil. |
| 10,500 | Cheſts of Brazil ſugar. |
| 56,000 | *Arrobas* ‡ of ſumach, tartar, potter's lamina, lemon-peels, and cork. |

* *Vara*, A meaſure nearly equal to a yard.

† *Covado*, A meaſure which contains three quarters of a yard, or a Flemiſh ell.

† *Arroba*, A weight of thirty-two pounds in Portugal.

1,200

1,200 *Quintals* * of bay-berries.
9,000,000 Sweet and ſour oranges.
8,000 Lemons.
500,000 *Varas* of lace, and other ornamental manufactures; ſent to Brazil.
150,000 *Covados* of ſilk, manufactured at Oporto and its diſtricts; ſent to Brazil.

Reſpecting the manners of the inhabitants of Oporto, my ſhort reſidence in this city has enabled me to form but a ſuperficial idea, eſpecially of the females, who are ſeldom obſerved out of doors, except in going to, or returning from church, a place they uſually viſit twice a-day; and then the face is veiled, or half-concealed beneath the folds of a black mantle. The few that I have ſeen unmaſked, had a pale complexion, black ſparkling eyes, and a countenance replete with ſimplicity. In ſtature they are rather low, but of a pleaſing figure, their walk and deportment are eaſy and graceful.

The men are well-proportioned, rather low than tall, have a brown complexion, and reſerved countenance. They are polite to ſtrangers, and reſpectful to each other; even the pooreſt people are treated by their ſuperiors with civility. Their dreſs in Winter is rather warm than elegant; a large *capote* covers all but the feet, and a part of the head.

* *Quintal*, A weight containing four *arrobas*, or 128 lb.

The

The labourers chiefly employed here are natives of Galicia, a province of Spain; hence they are called *Galegos.* Their number is computed at eight thousand in Oporto alone, and the whole kingdom is thought to contain not less than fifty thousand of these industrious adventurers. If this statement be correct, (and I do not give it on light authority,) and that each man lays up, on an average, eighteen pence *per* week, then the most profitable *trade* of Portugal is carried on by the Galicians; for their savings, according to this calculation, amount to one hundred and ninety-five thousand pounds *per annum*, which they carry to their own country. Those who have witnessed their manner of living, will admit that the sum is stated rather below than above the truth; for they are the most œconomic people in the world. They are fed gratuitously at the gates of the convents, lodged in cellars, stables, or cloisters, and clothed in rags, in which they usually repose. Yet many of them possess lands and houses in their own country, whither they return at stated periods to divide their hard-earned pittance with their families; and finally retire, as soon as they have made sufficient to live independent of labour, to spend the evening of life in the simple enjoyment of domestic felicity. To the honour of this industrious race we should not forget to mention, that the allurements of gain have rarely been known to betray any of them to commit a dishonest action.

Here

Here I took leave of my fellow-paſſengers, highly pleaſed with the civility of our hoſteſs, who was a good friendly old woman, though reputed for raiſing her voice at times; but as this proceeded more from neceſſity than choice, it was excuſable in a ſolitary widow like her, contending with adverſity at an age when others ſink into reſt. Her tongue was the weapon ſhe generally appealed to whenever ſhe thought her rights invaded, and the only weapon ſuch a feeble creature was capable of wielding. We aſked her why ſhe did not return to her native country; "Ah! (ſaid ſhe) that country is too cold for one that has "been ſo long accuſtomed to this; but at all events, I "ſhall return thither three months before I die, in order "to leave my bones in old England."

---

*A Journal of ſeven Days Journey from Oporto to Batalha.*

*January* 23. I ſet out for Batalha in a ſmall chaiſe, accompanied by a Portugueſe youth going to Liſbon to be educated for the church. This youth was recommended to my attention by his guardian, an aged prieſt, who, though in no wiſe related to him, maintained and educated him from his infancy, when death deprived him of his parents. The friendly manner in which he embraced him at our departure, and the tenderneſs he expreſſed for him by his tears, impreſſed me with a high

 opinion

opinion of the humanity of those people, and recommended this worthy priest's sanctity and humanity, more than his rosary and reverential habit.

As soon as we crossed the Douro, we were joined by three other carriages returning to Lisbon; two of them were empty, the other was engaged by a gentleman from the province of Minho. This gentleman has been my topographer on the road; and I fear that the names of some places, not to be found in the Portuguese maps, partake of the corrupt orthography of his province, wherein they speak a dialect between the Portuguese and the Spanish languages. We were also accompanied, in the first day's journey, by four Galician labourers, employed by the muleteers for the purpose of assisting them in rescuing their vehicles and mules from the obstructions that lay in the way. It is extraordinary, that so near the second city in the kingdom, there is not a perch of what we should call a road; some efforts, it is true, have been made to form one, but so ill contrived, that the first torrent has swept the greater part of it away. We should not have been able to proceed without the aid of these labourers, as the mules were every moment tumbling, or embarrassed in the mud, where they must have remained but for the united efforts of the company. At four o'clock in the afternoon we reached *Dos Carvalhos* in a miserable plight; mules and muleteers, Galicians and passengers, all in the same livery, bespattered from head to foot.

*Eſtalagem dos Carvalhos*, or the Caravanſary of the Oaks, diſtant about one league from Oporto, which we left at nine o'clock in the morning, cloſed this day's ſtage. Whilſt dinner was preparing, I took a ſurvey of this extenſive Caravanſary, and ſketched the view of the ſame hereunto annexed, (Plate II.) It contains, beſides a number of unfurniſhed apartments, offices for cattle, implements of huſbandry, &c. The moſt commodious part of the whole is the ſtable; but the kitchen appeared to be the moſt entertaining; about the center of it is a circular eſtrade, raiſed about fourteen inches above the floor, on which the fire was placed, and ſeveral earthen pots reſting upon tripods. Here all aſſembled to ſpend the evening. Prieſts, pilgrims, gentlemen, muleteers, and beggars, without diſtinction, ſat round this blazing orb, in ſocial intercourſe; one claſs chaunting veſpers, another reciting roſaries, a third recounting miraculous tales of provincial ſaints, whilſt, at intervals, a well-timed joke ſtole round, which relaxed even the brow of devotion, and ſet the circle on a roar.

When ſupper was ready, the motley ſociety ſat down as promiſcuouſly as before, to a table covered with ſimples, that would ſuit the palate of an Epictetus. This table was placed in a hall, the door of which was ſeldom cloſed by day or night; every one had free acceſs to it, the poor might enter as freely as the rich, and when once entered, all the imaginary diſtinctions which ſeparate man from

 his

his fellow-being vanished. The grave is not a greater enemy to distinctions, than the *Caravansary dos Carvalhos!*

*January* 24. Here our Galicians consigned us to our fate, and returned to Oporto. At five in the morning we continued our journey, amidst incessant rain, to *St. Antonio da Rafana*, where we took up our lodging for the night. Our repast, which included dinner and supper, consisted of bread, wine, dried fish, and oil; the latter I did not taste, as I saw the cruet replenished from the lamp. A Portuguese gentleman who sat next me, cried in broken English, "This is bad fare, Sir, but you "must expect no better till you get to Lisbon."

After dinner, I paid my respects to the family of the house, and found the hostess, with her two daughters, seated on their heels, spinning flax by the light of a lamp. The spindle and distaff supplied the place of the wheel, the use of which, perhaps, is unknown to them. It is much to the credit of the women of Portugal, especially those of the province of Beira, that they manufacture all the linen used in the kingdom, through its various branches; they sow the grain, reap the produce, and hatchel the flax, afterwards they weave the yarn, and make up linen not inferior, perhaps, to any in Europe, for colour, softness, and durability. Every house is supplied with plenty of this linen, however indigent in other respects; even the table of the pooreſt peaſant has a clean cloth and napkin, though his repaſt conſiſted of nothing more than bread and cheſnuts.

*Sunday, January* 25th.) Our muleteers would not depart this morning till they heard divine ſervice. We accompanied them to a ſmall chapel, about half a mile from the village, where a venerable old father celebrated the ſervice of the day with great decency. The auditory had a reſpectable appearance; not one was to be ſeen among them whoſe apparel beſpoke wretchedneſs. This day's journey was more pleaſant than that of the foregoing, as the weather was fair, and the way tolerably clean. Towards the Weſt we had an agreeable proſpect of the ſea; the land bordering on the coaſt appeared in good cultivation, and the ſhelving mountains were planted with trees. At five o'clock we concluded our Sabbath-day's journey, at a little village called *Algarve Veilha*, nine computed leagues from Oporto. We expected our dinner would have compenſated the involuntary abſtemiouſneſs of the two preceding days, on which fleſh-meat was interdicted; but to an Epicure how great the diſappointment! when ſummoned to the board, inſtead of the ſmoking ſirloin, we found but a morſel of beef floating in an ocean of meagre ſoup.

At the commencement of the night a group of ſwains ſerenaded the village, attuning their nocturnal ſtrains to the charms of their favourite nymphs: afterwards they aſſembled

assembled at our inn, and danced with the muleteers, who seemed at every trip to shake off the fatigue of the journey. The village-nymphs were content to remain as spectators, except one, guarded by a toothless duenna, who ventured to join with a spruce city muleteer in a fandango.

*January* 26th. We set out at six o'clock in the morning, and passed through a pleasant country, diversified with hill and dale, clothed with groves of spruce and cork trees. Having crossed the river *Vouga*, we met another, a short distance from thence, properly named *Rio da Bella*. After taking some refreshment at *Sardad*, we passed through *Villa da Bella*, the appearance of which does not justify the name. In every village, we observed that the residence of the lord of the manor was distinguished from the other houses by its magnitude; in the front are ten or twelve apertures without glass; the inside corresponds to the simplicity of the outward appearance, with regard to ornament; and as to furniture, the post-deluvian habitations, perhaps, were not less encumbered. In a country like this, where the mildness of the air, and the verdure of the fields at every season of the year resemble a perpetual spring, the inhabitants, constantly invited abroad, are accustomed to consider their houses as little more than places of shelter by night. Hence furniture is to them of no real use, except the few articles that appertain to the conveniencies of their simple mode of living, and in the choice of these few they are not very scrupulous.

During

During a good part of this day we travelled through a fine level country, but without inhabitants or cultivation, though the ſoil appeared well calculated for every ſpecies of culture. Land is of ſo little value here, that, inſtead of ſquare or triangular diviſions of property, the only ſeparations known are rivers and mountains. A farm-houſe is a novelty, and one might as well ſeek in the deſerts of Lybia for a rick of hay, or a ſtack of corn. *Melhado* cloſed this day's journey; as ſoon as we ſat down, the table was ſpread with bread, honey, fruit, and wine.

*January* 27th offered the moſt ſublime proſpect I ever beheld. We reached the ſummit of the loftieſt mountain in this part of the country about break of day, when a few feeble rays, of a deep purple colour, began to ſhoot along the Eaſtern ſky. Theſe ſhortly yielded to a tranſient cone of rays of a ſaffron hue, which appeared to aſcend like the flames of a volcano; their rapid expanſion inſtantly diſpelled every gloom, and filled the horizon with a blaze of glory. We ſtopped a while, and looked with admiration at the phenomenon, whilſt we reflected on the omniſcient Fiat of the Creator, as delivered by the Divine Hiſtorian, thus in the language of the Poet,

> Light heard GOD's voice, and eager to obey,
> From all her Orient fountains burſt a way.

## *Coimbra.*

At ten o'clock in the forenoon we arrived at *Coimbra*, a city long celebrated as the Athens of Portugal. It is ſituated in 40° 12′ North latitude, about an hundred miles from Liſbon, and built partly on the Weſtern ſide of a ſteep rocky precipice, and partly on a plain contiguous to the river *Mondego*. Notwithſtanding the elevation of its ſite, we did not perceive it till we had almoſt entered on it; when the churches, colleges, and lofty towers broke in upon the view at once, and realized the deſcription of Camoens:

> Here caſtle walls in warlike grandeur lour,
> Here cities ſwell, and lofty temples tower:
> In wealth and grandeur each with other vies;
> When old and loved the parent-monarch dies *.
>
> *Luſiad*, b. iii.

This city formerly experienced all the viciſſitudes of war, and a rapid ſucceſſion of different maſters. Romans, Alans, Moors, &c. ſucceſſively maintained a tranſitory poſſeſſion of it, as may be collected, I am informed, from the remains of various inſcriptions, ſtill to be ſeen on the walls of its ancient ſtructures.

* *Parent-monarch dies*——King Diniz, who founded the univerſity of *Coimbra*.— For brevity's ſake, we beg leave to advert, that the extracts cited in this work from the Luſiad of Camoens, are according to Mr. Mickle's excellent tranſlation of that beautiful poem.

To

To the philosophic mind it must afford a train of pleasing reflections, on considering, that this delightful spot, once the sanguinary theatre of hostile contention, is now become the peaceful retreat of the muses. Its colleges are numerous, and liberally endowed. The number of students in the various classes of literature are estimated at three thousand.

In examining the interesting objects of this city, I had almost forgot to deliver a letter of introduction to the Prior of St. B——. I was conducted to his cell, where he had just sunk into his after-dinner nap; and as the thermometer, to a Portuguese constitution, was rather low, he sat in a two-armed chair, opposite to a window, through which the beams of the sun played on him in all their meridian effulgence. His feet were inveloped in a basket of straw-work, and his body wrapped up in a black mantle lined with flannel. To the wearied forlorn traveller, how happy must such a state of peace and slumber appear, when contrasted with the anxieties attendant on active life. And the effects of this unagitated abstraction seemed impressed on his Reverence's countenance, the plump features of which plainly evinced that he never perplexed his mind in the intricate labyrinth of science. After a few minutes, he consigned me to the care of two young gentlemen, students of the university, who very politely shewed me several of the most striking curiosities of the Museum.

I regretted that time would not permit me to examine sufficiently the fine collection of land and sea animals this Museum contains. Here are also a very extensive series of the various classes in the mineral and vegetable kingdoms, arranged according to the Linnæan system. If we may judge from the capaciousness of the several apartments occupied by these rarities, the Museum of Coimbra is inferior to few in Europe; which is not extraordinary, if we recollect that for ages it has been the repository of the curious productions of nature and of art, pouring in from the Eastern and Western hemispheres. The Library is also very extensive, and stored with an immense number of printed books and manuscripts.

From the many local advantages Coimbra possesses for trade and manufactures, an English traveller is surprised to see how little the inhabitants avail themselves of these favourable circumstances. But that, in a great measure, is owing to their finding an easier mode of subsistence in devoting their time to the service of the university. Its principal factories consist of pottery, of which there are six for red ware, and eleven for glazed. The experience of ages, with the aid of various experiments made in the chymical elaboratory of the university, have contributed to raise this branch to a high degree of perfection. Woollen and linen cloths are also manufactured here, and it supplies the kingdom with *wooden tooth-picks*.

Towards the close of the evening, I walked through some of the ſtreets in the lower part of the town, and found them crowded, as it was market-day. Among the various articles expoſed for ſale, the chief were pottery, honey, wax, and vegetables. The home-conſumption of the firſt article cannot, I imagine, be very great; for, notwithſtanding its fragility, it ſeldom falls a victim to paſſion or inebriety; as perhaps no nation is more exempt from the ſallies of the one, or the exceſs of the other, than the Portugueſe.

One of our Chineſe hiſtorians obſerves, that the people of Canton make the ſale of their brittle ware the barometer of European paſſions; and as often as the ſale augments, they are known to ſay, "The preceding year has "been a paſſionate one in Europe."

A ſhort diſtance from the above ſcenes of frugal traffic, I approached a ſmall aſſembly of men and women beneath a ſhed adjoining to a ſmith's forge; their voices were united in chaunting veſpers, which, however, did not interrupt the courſe of induſtry. The blackſmith, who led the concert, continued to hammer out the horſe-ſhoe, the malleable notes of which were modulated by the ſonorous baſe of a wine-tierce that a cooper was hooping. Every pauſe of the hammer and adze was filled with the ſweet notes of the females, who, without theſe accompaniments, would have rendered juſtice to the ſacred ſong.

In the year one thouſand two hundred and forty-ſix, an inſtance of loyalty occurred in this city, which deſerves to be recorded, as it ſtrongly marks the bravery of the ancient Portugueſe, and their fidelity to their lawful ſovereign. A brave old ſoldier, named *Don Martin de Freitas*, was appointed governor of the town by *Don Sancho* the Second. When his ambitious brother *Alonzo*, who was about to uſurp his crown, had laid ſiege to it, *Freitas*, faithful to his truſt, and ſuperior to bribes or threats, encouraged the beſieged to bury themſelves in the ruins of the fortreſs, rather than yield to a man who could ſtifle the feelings of a brother, and violate the duty of a ſubject. Having ſuſtained the ſiege twelve months, and finding his reſources exhauſted, he repaired ſecretly to Toledo, the laſt aſylum of his unfortunate ſovereign; But, alas! the Prince, weighed down with affliction, a few days before had paid the laſt debt to Nature. The governor, however, was not ſatisfied till he fulfilled the ſolemn vow he made; namely, never to deliver up the keys committed to his truſt, but to him from whom he received them. Accordingly he ordered his ſepulchre to be opened, and put the keys of the city into the cold hand of his generous maſter. Having thus fulfilled his duty, he returned to Coimbra, which ſtill held out by his order, and then ſurrendered to *Alonzo*.

*Don*

*Don Sancho* is allowed by moſt hiſtorians to have been a juſt king, a brave commander, and an affectionate huſband. His queen, *Dona Mecia*, according to the ſuperſtition of the age, was ſaid to have given him an enchanted draught, to incite his amour, which diſturbed his intellects. The clergy, in conjunction with his brother *Alonzo*, Earl of Bologna, were ſuppoſed to have been the propagators of this calumny, and the fomenters of the confuſions which enſued; till at laſt the unfortunate Prince was depoſed by pope Innocent IV. His beautiful queen was torn from him, conveyed away as a priſoner by one named *Raymond Portocarero*, and was never heard of more.

The fate of the above Prince, when compared to that of *Alfonſo* VI. involves a queſtion which the civilians of Portugal can beſt anſwer. The former loſt his wife, his crown, and his liberty, for one of the moſt amiable virtues in private life; namely, loving his wife. Whereas *Don Alfonſo*, in the ſeventeenth century, loſt his liberty, his crown, and his wife, for the very contrary cauſe.

*January* 28th. At day-break we reſumed our journey, and arrived at the village of *Condexa*; in which I do not remember any thing remarkable. *Solgeira* preſented the ſource of a river, which guſhed from the interſtices of a number of ſharp disjointed rocks. At five in the evening we entered Pombal, a city diſtinguiſhed by giving title to the

the late celebrated Marquis *, whofe name will ever found like the departing knell to the difciples of Ignatius Loyola. The remains of that illuftrious ftatefman are depofited in the parifh church of this city; the inhabitants fpeak of him with enthufiaftic refpect.

There are but few objects here to arreft the traveller's attention, except a caftle, placed, as ufual, on an eminence; the dilapidated remains of which are fcarcely fufficient to enable even an artift to form an idea of its former ftate; and it is probable, that in a few years, the remaining fragments will experience the fate of the foregoing, which have been carried away for the pious purpofe of building convents.

Having furveyed thefe veftiges, I returned to the inn, to partake of a fowl boiled in rice; there were alfo fome frefh eggs, and a defert of figs and walnuts; fo that we fared fumptuoufly to-day. But we were not equally happy in a bed-chamber, for the place where we lay was better calculated for dancing than repofe, both from its dimenfions and fituation; it was immediately over the ftable, where there was at leaft a fcore of mules, each furnifhed with a bracelet of fmall bells, which continued tinkling all night with the nodding of their heads, as they contended with knotty ftraw. The floor was compofed of planks, with-

* The Marquis de Pombal.

out

out a ceiling, perforated in ſome parts, and ſhrunk in others, leaving vacuities about the width of the S in the ſounding-board of a guitar; ſo that every tinkle diſtinctly reached the ear. To reſt in a ſituation of this kind was impoſſible; therefore I was under the neceſſity of rouſing the muleteers to proceed on our journey. The miſtreſs of the inn, at our departure, made a handſome apology: "I am ſorry, Senhors, (ſaid ſhe,) that you have not reſted "well; but ſince the muſick was not agreeable, I ſhall "make no charge for it."

*January* 29th. Paſſed through the city of *Leiria*, of which we ſhall have occaſion to ſpeak hereafter. In five hours after, we arrived at Batalha. Here I took leave of my fellow-travellers, with no ſmall ſhare of mutual regret; no perſon in my ſituation could have witneſſed ſo much kindneſs, without bearing teſtimony to the fidelity of my muleteer, who ſeemed anxious to ſupply every inconvenience of the inns, and render the journey as agreeable as poſſible.

*Royal Monaſtery of Batalha.*

The ſight of this edifice would have amply repaid a longer journey, even though leſs pleaſant, than that I had juſt experienced; and what enhanced the pleaſure of the proſpect, was the unexpected ſight of it at an hour when the ſun was ſetting, and every turret was gilded with the radiance of his deſcending beams. The buſy aſſemblage of ſpires, pinnacles, buttreſſes, and windows; their deep projecting ſhadows, the Siberian ſolitude of the place, and the venerable appearance of the friars, rendered this one of the moſt remarkable ſcenes I ever beheld.

For my introduction to the Prior of this convent, I am indebted to a letter obtained through the favour of Mr. Searle, a Britiſh Merchant at Oporto, a gentleman from whom I experienced every hoſpitality and civility during my abode in that city. As ſoon as I approached this worthy Prior, I could not help contraſting his appearance and manners with thoſe of the Prior of St. B——; his face was marked by ſtrong angular lines, but apparently more the effects of thought than of age, which might be about fifty. He was tall, thin, of a reverend deportment, with a countenance replete with ſerenity; and though he preſided as chief lord of the manſion, his pre-eminence was conſpicuous only in his ſuperior wiſdom and modeſty.

This

This monaſtery is ſituated in a ſmall village called *Batalha*, in the province of Eſtremadura, about ſixty miles North of Liſbon; it was founded by John the firſt, king of Portugal, at the cloſe of the fourteenth century, in conſequence of a ſignal victory obtained by him over the numerous forces of Caſtile, in the hard-fought battle of *Aljubarota*.

The architecture is of that ſtyle called Modern Norman Gothic, and may be juſtly conſidered one of the moſt perfect and beautiful ſpecimens of that ſtyle exiſting. The whole, conſidering its age, is in good preſervation, and has ſuffered very little from the uſual injuries of the elements, owing to the durability of the materials, and the ſerenity of the climate; ſome parts, however, have been damaged by the fatal earthquake of one thouſand ſeven hundred and fifty-five, which the fathers, on account of the poor revenue of the convent, have not been able to repair; but as far as their means extend, they are careful in cleaning and preſerving it from accidents.

In the conſtruction of the church, we obſerve none of thoſe trifling and ſuperfluous ſculptures, which but too often are ſeen to crowd other Gothic edifices; whatever ornaments are employed in it, are ſparingly, but judiciouſly diſpoſed; particularly in the inſide, which is remarkable for a chaſte and noble plainneſs: and the general

neral effect, which is grand and ſublime, is derived, not from any meretricious embelliſhments, but from the intrinſic merit of the deſign.

The forms of its mouldings and ornaments are alſo different from thoſe of any other Gothic building that I have ſeen. The difference chiefly conſiſts in their being turned very quick, cut ſharp and deep, with ſome other peculiarities which cannot be well explained in writing. Throughout the whole are ſeen a correctneſs and regularity, evidently the reſult of a well-conceived original deſign; it is equally evident, that this deſign has been immutably adhered to, and executed in regular progreſſion, without thoſe alterations and interruptions to which ſuch large buildings are commonly ſubject.

The extent of the building, from the Weſtern entrance to the Eaſtern extremity, is four hundred and ſixteen feet. From North to South, including the monaſtery, it meaſures five hundred and forty-one feet. The entire, except the inferior offices and dormitories, is built of marble originally, not very diſſimilar in colour to that of *Carrara*; but that colour is now changed internally to a modeſt grey; externally the ſtone has contracted a yellow ſcoria, highly picturesque to the eye of the artiſt.

*Principal*

*Principal Entrance.* (See Plate III.)

In every thing that constitutes the ornamental or the elegant, the principal Entrance certainly ſtands unrivalled by any other Gothic frontiſpiece in Europe. The Portal, which is twenty-eight feet wide by fifty-ſeven high, is embelliſhed with upwards of one hundred figures in *alto relievo*, repreſenting Moſes and the prophets, ſaints and angels, apoſtles, kings, popes, biſhops, and martyrs, with their reſpective inſignia. Each figure ſtands on an ornamented pedeſtal, beneath a canopy of delicate workmanſhip; they are ſeparated from each other by an aſſemblage of mouldings, terminating in pointed arches.

Below the vertex of the inferior arch is a triangular receſs, where there is ſeated on a throne, beneath a triple canopy, a figure with a celeſtial crown, his left-hand reſting upon a globe, the other is extended in the act of admonition. This figure repreſents our Saviour dictating to the four Evangeliſts who ſurround him, attended by their reſpective attributes.

The ſummit is crowned with an ornamental railing, at the height of about an hundred feet from the pavement of the church. The ſpace between that and the Portal is occupied by a large window of ſingular workmanſhip; it conſiſts of tablets of marble, formed into numerous compartments, whoſe interſtices are filled up with ſtained glaſs. In the evening, when the ſun is oppoſite to this window, its beams dart through the perforations, and cover the walls and pillars of the church with myriads of variegated tints. It is impoſſible to convey an adequate idea of the beauty of the effect, or the agreeable ſenſations they excite in the ſpectator.

*Chapter-Houſe.*

In point of conſtruction, the Chapter-Houſe might be conſidered a maſter-piece of architecture. Its plan forms a ſquare, each ſide of which meaſures ſixty-four feet, and is covered with a vault of hewn ſtone. The principal ribs ſpring from ſlender ſhafts, and branch out in different directions as they approach to the centre, where all the radiating nerves, in the form of a ſtar, encircle an ornamented patera.

It is recorded, that in building that magnificent arch, it fell twice in ſtriking the centres, with great injury to the workmen. But the king, deſirous at all events to have a room without the defect of a central ſupport, promiſed to reward the architect if he could accompliſh it; at this he was animated in ſuch a manner, that he began it again, as if confident of ſucceſs. The king, however, would not recommit the lives of his workmen in ſtriking the

the centres; therefore he ordered, from different prisons of the kingdom, such delinquents as were sentenced to capital punishment, in order that, if the like disaster happened a third time, none should suffer but those who had already forfeited their lives to the offended laws of their country.

## *Mausoleum of King Emanuel.*

At the rear of the church is an unfinished Mausoleum of a curious form, wherein the architect has exhibited no superficial knowledge of geometry, or the principles of sound and elegant design. In point of workmanship, neither the pen nor the pencil is adequate to express its real merits; for, though most objects when transferred to the canvass appear to advantage, this, on the contrary, though delineated by the most ingenious artist, upon examination, will appear more beautiful than any representation of it upon canvass or paper. And for these reasons, the marble is polished, the sculpture in many parts detached from the centre of the block, and so minutely carved, that to preserve all the expressive marks and touches of the chisel, it is not possible to condense them into a smaller compass: so that, to convey a true idea of the whole, the picture would require to be as large as the prototype. To give an instance; there is a figure at the entrance, representing one of the fathers of the church, not more than twelve

 inches

inches in height, yet the sculptor has expressed its worn tunic in a thread-bare state.

We may form some idea of the magnitude of the design, from the magnificence of the entrance; it is thirty-two feet wide at the splay; as it recedes, the breadth contracts, till it forms an aperture of fifteen feet wide by thirty-one feet high. De Sousa, the historian, calls this a moderate sized aperture; and, indeed, so it appears, for nothing is great or small but in a comparative relation.

Amongst the many thousands of ornaments with which this entrance abounds, we behold the following motto often repeated, *Tanyas erey*. The characters are Gothic, embossed, and encircled by rings knotted together. The writer whom we have just mentioned, has attempted to decypher this motto. The following extracts may give some idea of his manner of reasoning:

" As it is the duty of an Author to deliver his opinion
" on doubtful passages of history, it will not be deemed
" presumptuous in me to endeavour to untie or cut, with
" a short discourse, this, which is not a gordian knot,
" though it appertains only to Alexanders to touch those
" knots that are tied by kings.

" On consulting a person of great erudition about these
" words, we concluded that they were Greek: *tanyas*
" being

" being the accusative case of the Greek word *tanya*; and " *erey*, the imperative of the word *eréo*, which means " either *seek thou*, *inquire*, or *discover*. Words apparently " addressed from the Lord of the temple to King Emanuel; " saying, as it were, *go thou and explore* unknown regions. " Thus animating him not to desist from the enterprise " he had in contemplation at this time; namely, the dis- " covery of India."

In the Loggia contiguous to the above door we observe over a recess a shield, bearing the letters Ey between two armillary spheres. " One should suppose, (continues De " Sousa,) that the founder of the edifice intended to excite " the attention of the curious who came hither, and was " resolved that it should cost them more trouble to explain " his enigmas, than to decypher an Egyptian hierogly- " phick, or the Sibylline oracle. Indeed, it would be " easier to form a judgment of subjects of the latter kind; " because, with the assistance of words and allusive figures, " we may draw some satisfactory conclusion. But in the " former, the precise meaning of the Author is difficult " to be ascertained from a few insulated letters, subject to " receive, camelion-like, the colours we wish to give " them, or, like virgin-wax, susceptible of every volun- " tary impression.

" The first difficulty that occurs is to ascertain the lan- " guage to which these characters belong. I imagine they "are Greek, like those before mentioned: and as they "are guarded by spheres, and a cross of the order of "Christ *, there is unquestionably some mystery inveloped "in them.

"Indeed, the founder appears to have given us an em-"blem like that of the Temple of *Delphos* in Greece. At "the portal of which, as history informs us, there was "an inscription addressed to those who entered: Γνῶθι "σεαυτον; that is to say, *Know thyself*; and over the "door an emblem Ei, similar to ours, which signifies "THOU ART.

"That emblem so employed the thoughts of the an-"cient sages, that Plutarch composed a volume upon it, "wherein, after many arguments, he concludes, that by "the letter Ei is designated ONE ETERNAL GOD. His "words are as follow:

* The latter belonged to the arms of King Emanuel, as he was master of the order of Christ, an honour conferred on him when he was Duke of Beja, by his predecessor John the Second. He also added to the insignia of royalty an armillary sphere, pursuant to an advice given him by King John a short time before his death. Hence the King is supposed to have presaged the discoveries which ensued in the Eastern world. However that was, its prophetick appearance was very propitious to the Portuguese; for when Emanuel ascended the throne, he assembled his council to deliberate on the expediency of prosecuting the navigation to India; many of the counsellors endeavoured to dissuade him from the enterprize, yet the King, inspired by the happy omen of the sphere, persisted in his resolution, and accordingly dispatched Vasco de Gama in that glorious expedition in which he discovered India in the year 1498.

Vide *Osorio* and *De Sousa*.

"*Deus*

"*Deus enim eſt & eſt nulla ratione temporis, ſed æter-*
"*nitatis immobilis, tempore & inclinatione carnetis: in*
"*qua nihil prius eſt, nihil poſterius, nihil futuram, nihil*
"*præteritum: nihil antiqquius, nihil recentius: ſed unus*
"*cum ſit, unicus nunc ſempiternam implet durationem.*
"——*Non enim multa ſunt numina, ſed unum* *."

Our Author at length concludes, that the emblem Ey imports the anſwer of Emanuel to the before-mentioned motto, which deſires him to explore unknown regions;

* *Plutarch. lib. de Ei apud Delph.*—— The meaning of the above paſſage of Plutarch is nearly this: "That God hath no "dependence on time, but is a permanent "and immutable Eternity; an Eternity "without reference to time or change, "inſomuch that it contains nothing firſt "or laſt, paſt or future, nothing more "ancient or more modern. And ſince "He is but One, He alone fills perpe- "tual Eternity.—For there are not many "deities, but only one."—Father de Souſa obſerves, that "this is ſo conformable "to what we find in Holy Writ, that "one would think the Gentile Hiſtorian "took it from that part where we read, "*Ego ſum qui ſum, qui eſt, miſit me ad vos;* I "AM THAT I AM. I AM hath ſent me unto "you *." Dryden makes a ſimilar obſervation in his Life of Plutarch. It is not leſs improbable, however, that Plutarch, who was no ſtranger to the Mythology of the Egyptians, took the above idea of the Deity from the inſcription of the ſtatue of *Pallas* or *Iſis* at *Sais*; the meaning of which was this: *I am all that is, has been, and ſhall be; and no mortal has ever yet removed the veil that covers me.* Since we have mentioned the Egyptians, let us hear their notions of the Deity. "God is "neither the object of ſenſe nor ſubject to "paſſion; but inviſible, only intelligible †, "and ſupremely intelligent ‡. In his "body he is like the light, and in his "ſoul he reſembles truth §. He is the "univerſal ſpirit that pervades and diffuſes "itſelf over all nature. All beings re- "ceive their life from him ‖. There is "but one only God, who is not, as ſome "are apt to imagine, ſeated above the "world, beyond the orb of the univerſe; "but being himſelf all in all, he ſees "all the beings who fill his immenſity, "the only principle, the light of heaven, "the father of all. He produces every "thing; He orders and diſpoſes every "thing: He is the reaſon, the life, the "motion of all beings ¶."

*Chev. Ramſay's Theology of the Ancients.*

* Exodus, Chap iii v. 14. † Plut. Vita Numæ. ‡ Diog. Laert. lib. xii.
§ Vita Pyth. Porphyr. ‖ Lact. Inſt. lib. v. ¶ St. Joh. Sarm.



ſaying,

ſaying, "I know, O Lord, that nothing but Thee is "worthy to be ſought for. Thoſe ſeas and lands have "their limits and duration, but Thou alone art eternal, "immortal, infinite."

To return to the Mauſoleum; the architecture in ſome parts is Arabian, in others abſolute Gothic. The inſide preſents an octagon, the diameter of which, between the parallel ſides, is ſixty-five feet. This was to have been covered with a vault of hewn ſtone, as appears by the parts already commenced at the height of about ſeventy-one feet. The whole is carried up to the height of about ſeventy-five feet; and though it has been expoſed to the weather ſince the year one thouſand five hundred and nine, it ſcarcely exhibits any traces of decay.

Reſpecting the founder, there are different opinions: Some attribute it to King Emanuel, others to his ſiſter Queen Leanor, conſort of his predeceſſor John the Second, who intended it as a depoſitory for her huſband and the other royal perſonages interred in the convent without monuments ſuitable to their rank.

It appears, however, that if Emanuel was not the founder, it has been carried on under his auſpices, by his name being often repeated about the architraves of the windows. But at the death of his ſiſter, he drew all the artificers employed here to the convent of *Bellem* near

Lisbon, founded by him in testimony of his joy for the discovery of India; in consequence of which, this work has since remained in that neglected state.

The sides of the octagon, except the one at the entrance, are finished with arches leading to as many chapels, each distinguished by the devices of the princes for whom they were intended. The pious Leanor, in one of them destined for the sepulture of herself and the king her consort, has introduced her own maternal device; that is, the pelican in the act of piercing its breast.

Indeed, it is much to be regretted, that a fabrick which redounds so much to the honour of human ingenuity, should remain in such a state of neglect. If we may be allowed to judge from what is already done of it, had not the death of the above princess prevented its completion, the modern world would have to boast of a Mausoleum, in magnitude and construction not inferior to the celebrated Mausoleum of the ancients *; and the memory of Leanor would be transmitted down to posterity with as much applause as that of Artemisia.

The latter, although she lived but two years after the foundation of her Mausoleum, yet her survivors, out of respect and gratitude to the memory of so affec-

* See Pliny, b. xxxvi. c. 5 & 13. Fischer's Historical Arch. Tav. vi. See also my Designs of this Edifice in the Description of Batalha.

tionate a princeſs, who made a living ſepulchre of herſelf, by imbibing her huſband's aſhes, did not deſiſt till they finiſhed her deſign. Had the ſurvivors of the Chriſtian princeſs poſſeſſed ſo much gratitude or generoſity, Batalha, in point of architecture, would not be inferior to ancient Halicarnaſſus. And even in its preſent ſtate, were it not buried in an obſcure part of Portugal, it may be ſaid of it, as the Jews have recorded of the ſepulchre of Simon Maccabeus, that it was never without viſitors to admire it.

According to the account of thoſe who are ſuppoſed to have had their information from the records preſerved in the Royal Archives of Liſbon, the name of the architect of the church was Stephen Stephenſon, a native of England. But the Fathers *Cacegas* and *De Suiſa*, who have written the Hiſtory of Batalha with great accuracy, are ſilent on this head. They inform us, that the King, deſirous of building a monaſtery ſuperior to any in Europe, invited from diſtant countries the moſt celebrated architects that could be found. Now, as Gothic architecture at that time flouriſhed in England, it is not improbable that ſome of its artiſts might have embraced the invitation of ſo liberal a Prince, eſpecially as his conſort, Queen *Philippa*, a Princeſs endowed with many amiable qualities, was the eldeſt daughter of John of Gaunt, Duke of Lancaſter, ſon of Edward the Third.

The

The eſtabliſhment of the Monaſtery is as follows; *viz.* twenty-five maſs-friars of the Dominican order, four novices, two tonſures, and thirteen lay-brothers. They are governed by four prelates; to-wit, a prior or ſuperior, a maſter of novices, a vicar, and a chief confeſſor. The other dignitaries are as follow; *viz.* the three profeſſors, who are appointed to teach ſeculars, reading, writing, and grammar; the precentor, the ſacriſt, the inſpector of the corn ſtores, the ſuperintendant of the kitchen, the hoſtilarius, and the two treaſurers. There are fourteen ſervants, *viz.* a cook, who is paid four thouſand eight hundred *reis* * *per* year, with board and lodging; two carmen. at four moidores † *per* year without board; a ſhepherd and a hogherd, each at ſix hundred reis and four *alqueires* ‡ of Turkey corn *per* month; and two ſervants to attend the choir, theſe have no fixed ſalary. The others are the baker, ſhoemaker, laundreſs, and muleteers.

The annual revenue is computed at ten or twelve thouſand cruſades §, of which ſeven thouſand are expended on the maintenance of the friars; beſides, each is allowed four thouſand eight hundred *reis* a year for clothing. Of the remainder there are four hundred milrees || applied in cultivating their lands. The ſurplus, after paying ſer-

* Ten *reis* are equal to $\frac{27}{48}$ of a penny.

† A *moidore* is worth 1*l.* 7*s.*

‡ An *alqueire*, I believe, holds one peck three quarts and one pint. *Vieyra's Dict.*

§ A *cruſade* is worth 2*s.* 3*d.*

|| A *milree* is valued at 5*s.* 7½*d.*

vants

vants hire, is expended in repairs and other contingencies.

During a reſidence of thirteen weeks in this abode of peace and hoſpitality, I experienced every politeneſs and attention from the fathers, who, in every reſpect conſiſtently with the duties of their order, practiſe the virtuous precepts of their ſacred religion. In their mode of living there appears nothing to envy, but a great deal to admire and commend; they eat but twice in the four-and-twenty hours, dine at eleven o'clock, and ſup at eight. The daily allowance of each is two ſmall loaves, one pound and a quarter of meat, the ſame quantity of fiſh, beſides ſoup, rice, wine, and fruit: a great part of this is diſtributed among the poor. The rules of their order they obſerve with the moſt ſcrupulous rigidity; they are muſtered every morning in Winter at day-break, and in Summer at five o'clock, then each brings a vaſe full of water from the fountain, to waſh in, before he enters the choir. Their cleanlineſs, regularity, and exemption from the anxieties of the world, contribute to preſerve their health and faculties unimpaired to a very old age. And, notwithſtanding the bodily infirmities which phyſicians aſcribe to a ſtate of inactive life, every father in the convent exhibited a pleaſing exception to this maxim; for I could not diſcern one drooping with the weight of years, or who had loſt a tooth, or who had an eye dimmed with

with defluxion, though ſome of them had attained to the age of ninety and upwards. Such is the wiſe diſpenſation of Providence, that thoſe men who have voluntarily ſecluded themſelves from the mingled cares and enjoyments of the world, are compenſated, even on this ſide of the grave, by a long and ſerene evening of old age, free from the infirmities, diſappointments, and painful reflections, which embitter the expiring days of the libertine and inconſiderate.

On the nineteenth of March, a French pilgrim, who ſtiled himſelf Viſcount Clarârde, viſited the convent. The Prior received him with every mark of reſpect and civility due to the high rank he aſſumed: during three days he tarried with us, and greatly recommended himſelf by the agreeableneſs of his manners. His age might be about thirty; he was of a middle ſtature, had ſhort black hair, and a countenance which betrayed more of the levity of a rambler, than of the piety of a pilgrim. He was dreſſed in a long grey coat, a tawdry laced waiſtcoat, and a flouched hat, mounted with a ruſty cockade. A ſable ſcapulet of oil-cloth, ſtudded with variegated ſhells, adorned his ſhoulders. From his neck and girdle were ſuſpended roſaries of different ſizes, together with a tin caſe and a pouch.

A luſty fellow, juſt deſerted from the French ſervice, attended this pilgrim, and carried his baggage in a ſheep-

ſkin

ſkin wallet. He was now about to deſert from his maſter's ſervice, in conſequence of the ſeverity of his diſcipline; for as the Count conceived him to be a greater ſinner than himſelf, he oftener applied the knotty cordon of St. Francis to his ſhoulders than his own: the Prior, however, ſo far accommodated matters, that they departed in peace.

There are ſome particulars which, however trifling in themſelves, ſometimes make as laſting an impreſſion on the mind as objects of greater magnitude, at leaſt the few that I am about to offer have had that effect on me. The parental tenderneſs which poets and naturaliſts have aſcribed to the ſtork, I had the ſatisfaction of contemplating at this place: one of theſe birds, with its affectionate mate, has reſided for ages in a large neſt curiouſly formed on the calceolus foliage which crowns the ſpire of the church. As Solomon ſent the ſluggard to the ant to learn induſtry, ſo the diſobedient child would learn examples of filial piety from the numerous progeny of this connubial pair. The fathers and the people of the village would deem it little leſs than ſacrilege to moleſt them; and indeed their humane protection is amply repaid by the ſervices they render the country in deſtroying ſerpents, lizards, and other obnoxious reptiles.

In the village there lived a little male idiot, who came each day to the cloiſter to practiſe his favourite amuſe-

 ment,

ment, from which he could ſcarcely be drawn to ſatisfy hunger or thirſt. This amuſement conſiſted in an endleſs emulation between his toes for precedency; as he moved forward one foot, the other, as if jealous of being left behind, immediately advanced, and thus he moved on from morning till night.

This is the firſt place in which I had heard the warblings of the nightingale. The little ſongſter poured his plaintive ſtrains each night from a branch that ſhaded the window of my cell, and all Nature liſtened to the ſong, except the bittern *, whoſe loud and inceſſant ſcreams lull the mind into ſympathetic meditation.

Before we take leave of this Monaſtery, we muſt requeſt the reader's indulgence, while we attempt to give a brief account of ſome of the moſt remarkable characters who are interred therein. In the center of the Founder's chapel is an inſulated ſepulchre, with two cumbent effigies of white marble, the ſize of life. Theſe effigies repreſent the King and Queen; the former is dreſſed in a complete ſuit of armour, the latter in a long flowing robe, the graceful habit of the age; the head of each is dignified with a low open crown, beneath a triple canopy of curious workmanſhip, in the Gothic manner.

* The bittern is a ſpecies of bird that lives by ſuction in marſhy grounds.

The memorable tranſactions of thoſe royal perſonages are preſerved in Latin inſcriptions, finely ſculptured in black characters on the ſides of the monument, together with the mottos and emblems adopted by the King, expreſſive of his extraordinary atchievements.

*King John the Firſt.*

The reign of this Monarch is allowed by Hiſtorians to have formed a brilliant epoch in the Hiſtory of Portugal. He was the natural ſon of Don Pedro, ſurnamed the Juſt, by Dona Tereza Lorenza, a Galician lady. He was born at Liſbon in the year one thouſand three hundred and fifty-ſeven, and at the age of ſeven was preſented for the firſt time to the King his father, who knighted him, and made him Maſter of the Order of Avis, agreeably to his preceptor's requeſt. This honour was conferred on him in a convent of the ſame order, wherein he purſued his ſtudies, and, happy for the nation, received a moſt excellent education, which ſo improved his ſtrong natural talents, that he became one of the politeſt ſcholars, as well as the greateſt ſtateſman and monarch, of his age.

At the death of Ferdinand his brother, who ſucceeded his father on the throne, the King of Caſtile laid claim to the crown of Portugal in right of his wife. At this a general

general discontent spread throughout the kingdom, which was then governed by the Queen, a worthless intriguing woman. Don John also asserted his right to the succession; but on being rejected, he resolved to depart for England. This being rumoured throughout Lisbon, the populace surrounded him and pressed him to stay, to protect them against the threatened power of Castile. He consented with apparent reluctance. The nobility were summoned to meet at the Town-house, to take into consideration the expediency of electing him Protector. As soon as they assembled, a cooper rushed into the midst of them, and drawing his sword, threatened any who dared refuse his consent with death.

Thus was Don John proclaimed Protector by the multitude, though in opposition to the sense of the majority of the nobles. The prudent use, however, he made of power, soon gained him great reputation. Enabled by a liberal education, and a discerning mind, to discriminate the abilities of men; he made choice of his counsellors solely for their talents and virtues, regardless of every consideration of birth or title.

In order to increase his popularity, he caused the property of those who fled the kingdom, or declared in favour of Castile, to be confiscated, and distributed among his own adherents. And to conciliate those who had hitherto opposed his measures, he promulged a general pardon for all past offences, treason excepted; not conceiving, says Faria, that to support him, was the greatest of all treasons.

A few months after he was elected protector, the King of Castile with a numerous force entered Portugal. Almost every part at his approach surrendered, and acknowledged him as lawful sovereign. Having arrived before Lisbon, he invested it for the space of five months; but a plague which raged among his army, obliged him to raise the siege, and depart. Immediately after, the Protector was proclaimed King, in the twenty-eighth year of his age, and received in every part of the kingdom with demonstrations of joy.

The retreat of the Castilians, however, gave the new King but a short repose in the enjoyment of his crown; for they soon recruited their armies, and re-entered Portugal with all the forces of their kingdom.

Don John, understanding the approach of the enemy, drew together his troops from Coimbra, Oporto, &c. and marched out of Guimaraens to give him battle. On the morning of the fourteenth of August one thousand three hundred and eighty-five, he entered the plains of Aljubarrota, where he knighted several gentlemen. The Castilians

tilians at firſt intended to march directly to Liſbon, yet, after ſome conſultation, they reſolved to engage. The forces on both ſides were very unequal; the Caſtilians are reported to have been thirty-three thouſand ſtrong, and the Portugueſe but ſix thouſand five hundred; beſides, the latter had ſome local diſadvantages.

The Sun was ſetting when theſe two unequal armies engaged; the Caſtilians at the firſt charge broke the Portugueſe van-guard, but the King coming up, with his voice and example ſo animated his men, that in leſs than an hour the multitudinous enemy was put to the rout. The King of Caſtile, who headed his troops, being afflicted with an ague, was forced to ſave himſelf by flight *.

Moſt of the Portugueſe who ſided with Caſtile, and were in front of the army, were put to the ſword. The royal ſtandard of Caſtile was taken, but many pretending to the honour, it could not be decided by whom. Of the number of the ſlain no exact account is preſerved, but it is

* Don *Laurenzo*, Archbiſhop of Braga, who, according to *Caſtera*, (the French Commentator of the Luſiad,) fought at the above battle, gives the following account of the King of Caſtile's chagrin after his defeat, in a letter written in old Portugueſe, to the Abbot of Alcobaça:

" The Conſtable hath informed me, that " he ſaw the King of Caſtile at Santerem, " who behaved as a madman, curſing his " exiſtence and tearing his beard. And in " truth, my good friend, it is better he " ſhould do ſo to himſelf than to us; the " man who thus plucks his own beard, " would be much better pleaſed to do ſo " unto others."

is reported to have been very great on the part of the Caſtilians; three thouſand of their cavalry are ſuppoſed to have periſhed, among whom were many perſons of diſtinction.

This is the famous battle of *Aljubarrota*; ſo called becauſe it was fought near a village of that name: and in conſequence of which the Royal Monaſtery of Batalha was founded, agreeably to a vow made by the King, importing, that in gratitude to Heaven he would build a magnificent Convent, if Providence on that day crowned his arms with ſucceſs.

In conſequence of this important victory, Don John was fixed on his throne; yet he loſt no time in putting the kingdom in ſuch a ſtate of defence, that in future he ſhould have nothing to fear from the power of his rival.

Hitherto he only acted on the defenſive, but now he reſolved to aſſail the enemy in his own country; and the better to ſucceed in his enterpriſe, he prevailed on the Duke of Lancaſter to embrace this opportunity of enforcing his title to the crown of Caſtile, to which he pretended to have had a legal title, in virtue of Conſtance his lady. Accordingly the Duke landed at Gallicia, with two thouſand cavalry, and three thouſand archers. His two daughters, celebrated for their beauty and accompliſhments, accompanied him. The elder, named Philippa, was married to the King of Portugal, and Catherine, the younger, to the King of Caſtile's eldeſt ſon. In conſequence of which, hoſtilities ceaſed between all parties, and the Duke returned to England.

A period of ſix-and-twenty years had elapſed without hoſtility between the two rival Powers; during which time, the happineſs of his people, and the inſtruction of his children, ſolely occupied the attention of Don John. Convinced of the ſuperiority which he himſelf derived from a liberal education, he reſolved that his ſons ſhould inherit a ſimilar advantage, and hence he became their preceptor. Of the effects of his inſtruction, the annals not only of Portugal, but of all Europe, bear teſtimony. He had the felicity to live to ſee them attain the age of maturity, unrivalled in every manly accompliſhment. To one of them, named Henry, the world is indebted at this day for the ſource of all the modern diſcoveries in navigation. But of this hereafter.

The victorious King John at length overcome with age yielded to the ſtroke of Fate, in his ſeventy-ſixth year, and the forty-eighth of his reign. No prince was ever bleſſed with more domeſtic happineſs, or more beloved by his people. He was a deep politician, a bold commander, kind to his friends, and haughty to his enemies. It is true, he raiſed himſelf to the throne by many acts of cruelty, diſgraceful to human nature; acts which no virtuous

tuous man would perpetrate for an empire; yet when he obtained the object of his ambition, he supported his power, not by tyranny, but by the exercise of those virtues which constitute the happiness of a people. At times, however, he had recourse to severity *, when the assuaging and popular arts, in which he was eminently skilled, proved ineffectual. The free and affable manner in which he received all men, gained him many friends; for he pretended not to affect the pride of a monarch, though he never sunk below the dignity of one. The nobility dined every day at his table, and after his example cultivated and encouraged polite literature. To the poor he was a protector and benefactor; and true merit was never more liberally rewarded in Portugal, than during his reign.

Of his extraordinary prowess, all Historians bear testimony; and his effigy, which is over his tomb in the Convent of Batalha, said to have been sculptured after Nature, seems to corroborate the fact; for it represents him as a man of uncommon muscular strength. His helmet and battle-axe are also preserved here. I was not a little sur-

* Here is a striking instance of it: A gentleman of the bed-chamber, named Don *Ferdinand Alonzo*, though a favourite with the King, was apprehended for making too free with Dona *Beatrix*, one of the Queen's ladies. *Alonzo* made his escape from the officers, and took sanctuary in a church, affirming that he was privately married to her. But the King, whose ruling passion was jealousy, came in person, and dragged the unfortunate lover to the flames. The lady was banished to Castile, her native country.

prifed on examining the latter; perhaps there are but few men of this age could wield fuch a ponderous weapon *.

Indeed, he appears to have realized the ideas that Shakefpear and Agrippa entertained of the vigour of thofe children born out of wedlock; for, as we before obferved, he was the natural fon of Don Pedro by a Galician lady. "The "beds of adultereffes (fays Agrippa) have brought forth "the moft illuftrious heroes in the world; as Hercules, "Alexander, Ifhmael, Abimelech †, Solomon, Conftan-"tine, Clodoveus king of the Franks, Theodorick the "Goth, William the Conqueror, Raymond of Arra-"gon, &c."

As a further teftimony of this Prince's perfonal ftrength, take the following anecdote, which we give on the authority of a Portuguefe gentleman. Don John was fo fecure in the affections of his fubjects, that he frequently walked abroad without any attendants. In one of his morning perambulations, he chanced to obferve an old man, who was lame and blind, at the oppofite fide of a rivulet, waiting till fome one came to guide his fteps over a plank thrown acrofs it. As there was no one at hand but the King, he inftantly approached, threw him on his fhoulder, and carried him in that pofture to the next road. The poor

* Engravings of the above-mentioned battle-axe and helmet may be feen in the Author's defcription of Batalha.

† De Soufa, the Portuguefe Hiftorian, compares Don John to Abimelech.

man, ſurpriſed at the eaſe with which he was carried, exclaims, "I wiſh Don John had a legion of ſuch ſtout "fellows to humble the pride of the Caſtilians, who de"prived me of the uſe of my leg."

Here, at the requeſt of the King, he gave a ſhort account of the ſeveral actions in which he had been engaged. In the ſequel his Majeſty recollected that this was Fonſeca, the brave ſoldier, who had courageouſly fought by his ſide in the memorable battle of Aljubarrota, that fixed the crown on his head. Grieved to ſee him in ſuch a diſtreſſed ſtate, he deſired him to call next morning at the royal palace, to know how he came to be neglected by his ſervants in power. *Who ſhall I inquire for?* quoth the brave Beliſarius. "For your gallant companion at the "battle of Aljubarrota;" replied the King, departing.

A perſon who at a diſtance witneſſed the ſcene, ſhortly after accoſted Fonſeca, and informed him of what his Sovereign had done. "Ah!" ſaid he, (when he recovered from his ſurpriſe,) "I am now convinced of the truth of "what has often been aſſerted, the ſhoulders of monarchs "are certainly accuſtomed to bear great burthens. I re"joice in having devoted the prime of my life to the "ſervice of one who, like the Prince of Uz, is legs to the "lame, and eyes to the blind."

Contiguous to the tomb of the Founder are four mural ſepulchres of very elegant workmanſhip, in the Gothic manner, containing the remains of his ſons, *Pedro*, *Henry*, *John*, and *Eerdinand*. Firſt, of

*Prince Pedro.*

This Prince was Duke of Coimbra and *Monte Mor*, Knight of the order of the Garter, &c. During the minority of Don Alfonſo the Fifth, his nephew and ſon-in-law, the government of the kingdom devolved to him; and all the Hiſtorians of that country allow, that the law was never diſpenſed with more impartiality, or better tempered with mercy, than during his adminiſtration, which continued eleven years.

Nor was he leſs eminent as a ſtateſman, than as a general and a traveller. He diſtinguiſhed himſelf in various engagements in Africa, where he headed an army of Portugueſe againſt the Moors. He alſo ſignalized his valour in Germany againſt the Turks, under the ſtandards of the Emperor Sigiſmond.

On account both of his voyages and eloquence, he was called the Ulyſſes of his age. In the year one thouſand four hundred and twenty-four he ſet out from Portugal, and ſpent four years in travelling over a great part of

Europe, Asia, and Africa. Travels at that time being very rare, especially among persons of his rank, his adventures gave rise to many fabulous reports. Faria says, that he wrote several books, but does not mention their titles, nor could we obtain any intelligence on that head, so little are they known at present; if they contain matter of information, we trust they will no longer be with-held from the Public.

Don Pedro having furnished the annals of his country with the brightest examples of wisdom in the cabinet, and courage in the field, was put to death by the King his nephew, at the instigation of some of his favourites, whom he offended when he held the administration of public affairs. The rash, giddy King soon repented his having deprived the world of so great a man; but by inverting the order of justice, his repentance came too late: he first ordered him to be slain, then gave him a fair trial; and on being found innocent of the alleged offence, he endeavoured to expiate his own guilt, by publishing the innocence of Don Pedro to the world, and giving his remains an honourable interment in the Monastery of Batalha.

*Prince Henry*

Seems to have been born for the good of mankind; "born to free them from the fœodal syſtem, and to give to the whole world every advantage, every light that may poſſibly be diffuſed by the intercourſe of unlimitted commerce." With all the noble accompliſhments that elevate human life, he poſſeſſed the amiable talents that embelliſh it. His motto, *Talent de bien faire*, was verified in all his actions, which were invariably directed to the happineſs of his fellow-beings. The ſpirit of navigation, which had hitherto ſlumbered on the ocean, under his auſpices ſpread her wings, and ſought the remoteſt ſhores.

The King his father, having ſubdued his neighbouring enemies, prepared to crown the return of peace with grand feſtivals; in the courſe of which he purpoſed to confer the honour of Knighthood on his ſons. But as they juſtly conſidered that this diſtinction ought to be the reward of well-earned merit, they mutually agreed to repreſent to his Majeſty, that the treaſure he reſolved to expend on that ceremony, would be employed to greater advantage in the field of battle; wherein they would have an opportunity of evincing to the world, that they merited his intended diſtinction. The reſult of the prudent remonſtrance was the capture of Ceuta, where they were knighted by the King, amidſt the acclamations of the army.

The priſoners whom the fortune of war had thrown into his power on that event, experienced a bountiful maſter; and Henry had the good fortune to find among them ſome Arabians who had travelled over ſeveral parts of the Eaſt. Their information contributed to enlarge the ſphere of his knowledge in coſmography, his favourite ſtudy, to which he had now totally reſigned himſelf. And in order to avoid all interruption, he retired to a ſolitary village named Sagres, in the kingdom of Algarve. Here, like the great Newton, he lived in perpetual celibacy, cultivating all the noble ſciences. "And here, where the view of the ocean inſpired his hopes and endeavours, he erected his arſenals, and built and harboured his ſhips; leaving the temporary buſtle and cares of the ſtate to his father and brothers."

"Having received all the light which could be diſcovered in Africa, he continued unwearied in his mathematical and geographical ſtudies. The art of ſhip-building received very great improvement under his direction; and the truth of his ideas of the ſtructure of the terraqueous globe are now confirmed. He it was who firſt ſuggeſted the uſe of the compaſs, and of longitude and latitude in navigation, and how theſe might be aſcertained by by aſtronomical obſervations: ſuggeſtions and diſcoveries which would have held no ſecond place among the conjectures of a Bacon, or the improvements of a Newton."

Prince Henry for upwards of forty years proſecuted his diſcoveries along the coaſt of Africa. Puerto Santo and the Madeira Iſlands were the firſt fruits of his enterpriſe. The Azores and Cape Verd Iſlands were alſo diſcovered by him, and his commanders, after traverſing the coaſt from Cape Bojador to Siera Leona, a diſtance of three hundred and ſeventy leagues, paſſed the Equinoctial Line, and failed as far as the Iſland of Saint Matthew, which is in the ſecond degree of South latitude.

"The Prince, now in his ſixty-ſeventh year, yielded to the ſtroke of Fate, in the year of our Lord one thouſand four hundred and ſixty-three, gratified with the certain proſpect, that the rout to the Eaſtern world would one day crown the enterpriſes to which he had given birth. He had the happineſs to ſee the naval ſuperiority of his country over the Moors eſtabliſhed on the moſt ſolid baſis, its trade greatly upon the increaſe, and, what he eſteemed his greateſt happineſs, he flattered himſelf that he had given a mortal wound to Mahommediſm, and had opened the door to an univerſal propagation of Chriſtianity and the civilization of mankind. And to him, as to their primary author, are due all the ineſtimable advantages which ever have flowed, or will flow, from the diſcovery of the greateſt

greateſt part of Africa, of the Eaſt and Weſt Indies. Every improvement in the ſtate and manners of theſe countries, or whatever country may yet be diſcovered, is ſtrictly due to him; nor is the difference between the preſent ſtate of Europe, and the monkiſh age in which he was born, leſs the reſult of his genius and toils. What is an Alexander, crowned with trophies at the head his army, compared with a Henry contemplating the ocean from his window on the rock of Sagrez! The one ſuggeſts the idea of the evil dæmon, the other of a tutelary angel *."

The cumbent effigy of Prince Henry, which is ſeen on his tomb, is dignified with a royal crown; for, according to De Souſa, he was elected King of Cyprus; he was alſo Maſter of the order of Chriſt, Duke of Viſeu, and Knight of the Garter. This Pharo of navigation has been celebrated by the Hiſtorians and Poets of every nation in Europe. The Prince of the Portugueſe Bards has paid the following tribute of praiſe to his memory, in which his brother Don Pedro above mentioned is alſo included:

Illuſtrious, lo, two brother-heroes ſhine,
Their birth, their deeds, adorn the royal line;
To every king of princely Europe known,
In every court the gallant Pedro ſhone.

* See Mickle's Hiſtory of the Diſcovery of India. See alſo Father de Souſa's Deſcription of Batalha, Faria's Hiſtory of India, De Barros's Account of the Diſcovery of Madeira, &c. From theſe Authors we have extracted the above memoirs.

The

The glorious Henry——kindling at his name,
Behold my ſailor's eyes all ſparkle flame!
Henry the chief, who firſt, by Heaven inſpired,
To deeds unknown before, the ſailor fired;
The conſcious ſailor left the ſight of ſhore,
And dared new oceans, never ploughed before.
The various wealth of every diſtant land
He bade his fleets explore, his fleets command.
The ocean's great Diſcoverer he ſhines;
Nor leſs his honours in the martial lines:
The painted flag the cloud-wrapt ſiege diſplays;
There Ceuta's rocking wall its truſt betrays.
Black yawns the breach; the point of many a ſpear
Gleams through the ſmoke; loud ſhouts aſtound the ear.
Whoſe ſtep firſt trod the dreadful paſs? whoſe ſword
Hew'd its dark way, firſt with the foe begor'd?
'Twas thine, O glorious Henry! firſt to dare
The dreadful paſs, and thine to cloſe the war.
Taught by his might, and humbled in her gore,
The boaſtful pride of Afric tower'd no more.

*Luſiad*, book viii.

Our Britiſh Bard, in deſcribing the ſtate of Europe at the commencement of the fifteenth century, thus celebrates Prince Henry:

——For then, from ancient gloom emerg'd
The riſing world of trade: the Genius, then,
Of Navigation, that in hopeleſs ſloth
Had ſlumber'd on the vaſt Atlantic deep
For idle ages, ſtarting, heard at laſt
The LUSITANIAN PRINCE, who, Heaven-inſpir'd,
To love of uſeful glory rous'd mankind,
And in unbounded commerce mixt the world. *Thomſon.*

*Don John.*

Of this Prince there is nothing very remarkable on record; he was maſter of the order of St. James, and Lord High Conſtable of Portugal. On the pannel of his ſepulchre are repreſented branches bearing wild ſtrawberries, a pouch, and ſhells. The two latter appertained to his order, and De Souſa ſuppoſes he adopted the former, as an emblem to expreſs his devotion for the glorious Baptiſt, who lived on wild fruit, and on account of his name being John.

*Don Ferdinand,*

After gaining many victories in Africa, laid ſiege to Tangier, in company with his brother Henry, where the Moors ſurrounded them, and all the Portugueſe under their command, amounting to ſeven thouſand. The forces of the enemy are ſaid to have been ſix hundred thouſand. The Princes, in order to extricate themſelves and their men, offered to deliver up Ceuta, on condition that they ſhould be allowed to return home. The enemy gladly accepted the offer, and demanded one of the brothers as an hoſtage for the fulfilment of the terms, whereupon Ptince Ferdinand offered himſelf, and was accordingly detained.

When

When the account of this difafter reached Lifbon, the Government was much divided in opinion. The King was willing to comply with the terms, to redeem his brother, but the Court, feconded by the Pope, urged the neceffity of keeping Ceuta, as a check on the Infidels. In the mean time, large fums were propofed for the ranfom of the Prince, but in vain.

Don Edward, who had now afcended the throne, finding negociation fail, refolved to releafe his brother by force; but juft as he was about to embark with a formidable army, he was feized with a plague, and died; leaving orders with his Queen to deliver up Ceuta for the refcue of his brother. This, however, was never performed; fo that the unfortunate Prince ended his days in captivity.

The piety of his manners, and the magnanimity of his behaviour, made Don Ferdinand the object of univerfal regret; and this regret was heightened by the cruel treatment he received from the Infidels. His virtues and patient fufferings became a fine fubject for writers of romance, and they have not failed to draw the tear of compaffion in many a pathetic tale. Ferdinand is reputed a Saint in Portugal to this day. The friars of Batalha commemorate his anniverfary with great folemnity on the fifth of June.

 On

On the ſepulchres of the above Princes, and alſo that of the King their father, are ſculptured *in mezzo relievo* various devices, characteriſtic of their reſpective actions or diſpoſitions. They had likewiſe, for the ſame purpoſe, their reſpective mottos: they are written in the French language; becauſe, as De Souſa tells us, that language was much eſteemed in their time, and very current among Princes, on account of its courteſy and politeneſs. The mottos are as follow:

| | | |
|---|---|---|
| King John I., | - - | *Il me plait pour bien.* |
| Don Pedro, | - - | *Deſir.* |
| Don Henry, | - - | *Talent de bien faire.* |
| Don John, | - - | *Je ai bien raiſon.* |
| Don Ferdinand, | - - | *Le bien me plait.* |

## *King Edward.*

This Prince was the eldeſt ſon of John the Firſt, whom he ſucceeded on the throne. His effigy, with that of his conſort Leanor, are on a tomb at the foot of the great altar of the church. He reigned but five years and one month: in this ſhort period the kingdom experienced many diſaſters, both from the wars of Africa and the plague, which raged thoughout the country; to the latter he himſelf, with many of his ſubjects, fell a ſacrifice. In his adminiſtration he was juſt, and rendered the country confiderable fervice, by reducing the laws to a regular code, and commanding the nobility to look after their eftates. A fimilar ordinance would not, perhaps, be injurious to the health or fortune of the prefent nobility of Portugal.

According to the Portuguefe Hiftorians, Don Edward was one of the moft accomplifhed men of his time; he fpoke and wrote Latin elegantly, and was author of feveral books. We cannot fay much for their merit, for they are fcarcely known at prefent; his memory could not preferve them from finking into oblivion. The writings of Princes are fubject to the fame fate with thofe of the humbleft of their fubjects. Faria mentions one of thofe books, and but one, a treatife on horfemanfhip. Perhaps the author's kinfman, Prince Alfonfo, fon of John the Second, who is interred in the Chapter-houfe, never read that treatife, or he would not have loft his life by bad horfemanfhip.

### *King John the Second.*

In one of the chapels at the Eaft end of the church is depofited the remains of John the Second, without a monument, or even an infcription. But his actions will perpetuate his memory, when the proudeft monuments are funk into duft. His corpfe remains, from the time of its

its interment, in one thousand four hundred and ninety-five, to this day, uncorrupted, though it was not embalmed, nor prepared to withstand that dissolution which awaits on mortality: whether this proceeds from the nature of the disease of which he died, (an hæmorrhage, supposed to be brought on by drinking of the water of a poisoned spring near Evora,) or from any antiseptical properties of his coffin, or both, the naturalist can best determine. There are some, I am aware, more devout perhaps than philosophic, who attribute this phenomena to the Monarch's sanctity. I should be sorry to disturb so harmless an opinion.

If the characters of Princes are to be estimated by the services they render mankind, this Monarch has great claims on the gratitude of posterity. His court was considered as the Lyceum of Europe. The learned and ingenious men of the times flocked to it, and were encouraged in proportion to their talents, the only recommendation to his munificence.

Nor did religious opinions rise as a barrier between real worth and royal favour; in the circle of his statesmen, physicians, and missionaries, were to be found Jews of distinguished abilities; for, to do justice to the Israelites of Portugal, they have in general been remarkable for fidelity and attachment to their King and country, before the establish-

establiſhment of that inauſpicious tribunal that has thinned the nation of its inhabitants, and reared the baſiliſk of perſecution on the ruins of the temple of humanity.

His profound knowledge of mathematicks ſuggeſted to him, that a ſhorter and ſafer way of navigation than hitherto known was not impracticable. The learned men of his court took the problem into conſideration, and cultivated it with ſuch ſucceſs, that the world is indebted to them for the invention of the Aſtrolabium *, and the firſt tables of delineation for the uſe of pilots.

By theſe inventions he was enabled to enlarge the boundaries of his dominions. Various diſcoveries were now made under his auſpices, along the coaſt of Africa, whence his fleets returned laden with the moſt valuable products of thoſe countries; but what gave him the greateſt ſatiſfaction, was the opportunity theſe diſcoveries afforded him of propagating the light of the Goſpel. We may conceive what progreſs he made in converting the Africans, by the numbers that were baptiſed in the kingdom of Congo alone, which (if there be no miſtake in the calculation) amounted to an hundred thouſand.

* The *Aſtrolabium* is an inſtrument by which are aſcertained the altitude of the Sun, and diſtance of the Stars. It is ſaid to have been invented by Roderigo and Jozé, two Jew phyſicians at the court of John the Second. Martin of Bohemia, one of the moſt celebrated mathematicians of that age, is ſuppoſed by ſome to have aſſiſted them.

Anxious

Anxious to carry the peaceful banners of Chriſtianity ſtill farther, he diſpatched Bartholomew Dias on that expedition in which he made the firſt diſcovery of the Cape of Good Hope; a diſcovery which inſpired him with the livelieſt hopes of diſplaying his enſigns on the banks of the Ganges.

The better to ſucceed in his deſigns, he diſpatched *Pedro Covillam* and *Alonſo de Payva* over-land into India, for ſuch information as they could obtain of the ſtate of that country; hoping thereby to facilitate his intended expedition to the Eaſt. Having travelled together as far as Toro in Arabia, they parted, and took different routs. *Covillam*, after viſiting Cananor, Calicut, Goa, Sofala, Mozambique, Quiloa, Mombara, Melinda, &c. returned to Grand Cairo, where he heard of the death of his companion. Shortly after their departure from Liſbon, the King diſpatched a Jew, named *Rabbi Abraham*, a native of Baja in Portugal, upon the ſame errand; he met at Cairo with *Covillam*, who ſent him home with every intelligence that he had acquired in thoſe countries, and he himſelf proceeded to Abyſſinia for further information, but unfortunately was never heard of more.

The flattering accounts the King received from the Jew, ſtimulated his natural propenſities to diſcoveries; but, alas! he was obliged to ſuſpend his meritorious projects for

for his perſonal ſafety and the quiet of the kingdom. The Duke of Viſeu, at the head of a diſcontented party, conſpired againſt his life. His Majeſty having eſcaped the hand of the aſſaſſin three different times, ſent for the Duke and walked with him in a garden, where he converſed with him on the relative duty of the King and the ſubject, and at the end put this emphatic queſtion to him, "What wouldſt thou do unto the man who attempted to "take away thy life?" To which the Duke anſwered, "I would take his firſt, if I could." "Then verily," ſaid the King, "as Nathan ſaid to David, Thou art the man!" and immediately plunged a dagger into his breaſt.

This was the Prince to whom Pope Alexander the Sixth, out of the plenitude of his generoſity, preſented one half of the globe, to put an end to the diſpute between the Crowns of Portugal and Caſtile, relative to the ſovereignty of the Ocean. Here was the manner his Holineſs adjuſted the buſineſs: he meaſured one hundred leagues to the Weſtward of the Cape Verd Iſlands, from which point he ordered a line to be drawn from pole to pole: then taking his ſpiritual ſector, he divided this round O into two parts, and gave the Eaſtern hemiſphere, with all its lands and ſeas, to the King of Portugal; the other he preſented to the King of Caſtile; interdicting, at the ſame time, all but the ſubjects of the two Crowns to viſit thoſe parts, under pain of excommunication. But King John, not ſatisfied with his ſhare of the orb, inſiſted

 that

that his rival was entitled, not to a hemiſphere, but to a ſegment. The Miniſters of the two contending Powers at length met, and decided the buſineſs, by extending the line of ſeparation two hundred and ſeventy leagues farther to the Weſt, than his Holineſs had appointed.

*Leiria*,

One of the moſt ancient cities in Portugal, is ſituated on the banks of the river *Lis*, in the midſt of a fertile country, finely diverſified with hill and dale. The ſoil is ſo productive, that with little labour it yields abundance of corn, grapes, and olives; yet with all theſe advantages, both the plough and the loom are neglected; no wonder then that an air of ſadneſs and deſolation is viſible in every ſtreet.

The remains of a palace *, formerly the reſidence of King Diniz, ſurnamed the Huſbandman, ſtill makes a conſpicuous figure, on the brow of a precipice contiguous to the town. It is impoſſible to ſurvey thoſe veſtiges, without

* A great part of that palace is thought to have been built of the fragments of an ancient city called Callipo, which Hiſtory ſhews to have once flouriſhed near this place. I ſaw a gold coin that was lately found there among the rubbiſh, bearing a figure of a bull on the reverſe, finely executed. The name perhaps ſhould be written *Calliope*. As it was a Roman city; it might have been ſo called after the mother of Orpheus, and Muſe of Epic Poeſy.

without emotions of honour and veneration for the memory of a Monarch who ſtudied the intereſt of his country and of the human race, by his having wiſely converted the ſpear into the plough-ſhare.

When King Diniz had ſecured the tranquillity of his dominions, he turned his attention towards the cultivation of the ſoil: his firſt ſtep towards the accompliſhment of this great object was to reſtrain the feudal ſyſtem, under which the wretched peaſantry had long groaned; and the better to promote his favourite purſuit, he erected farm-houſes in every part of the kingdom, which he viſited in rotation, and diſtributed gratuitouſly all kinds of implements of agriculture among the huſbandmen, whom he conſidered as the pillars of the ſtate, and the peaceful companions of Nature.

Portugal, which now-a-days does not annually produce ſufficient corn for three months home conſumption, was conſidered in his reign as one of the firſt granaries in Europe. This ſcarcity, as ſome have erroneouſly ſuppoſed, is not to be attributed to any change in the ſoil, (for that is permanent, if any thing terreſtrial can be called permanent,) but to a great change in the ſentiments of the people. The modern Portugueſe, contrary to the maxims of their anceſtors, ſeek for wealth far from Luſitania, in the deep mines of the Braſils; whilſt they forget that more ſubſtantial wealth may be found in

 their

their native fields, and that within ſix inches of the ſurface. King Diniz was ſo well aſſured of the truth of this, from the knowledge he had of the productions of the country, that he never had occaſion to apply to his neighbours for the neceſſaries or luxuries of life; it even ſupplied him with gold and ſilver. He had a magnificent crown and ſceptre made of gold collected on the ſands of the Tagus.

But, alas! even the moſt exalted characters are taxed by humanity with ſome imperfection. He is charged, like our illuſtrious Henry the Second, with too great a paſſion for the fair ſex. He had not, however, the ſame apology for departing from his conjugal ties as the Britiſh hero; for his Queen poſſeſſed every virtue that can adorn her ſex. Far from viſiting the ſins of the father upon the children, ſhe took all his illegitimate offspring (who were not a few) under her protection, and had them educated with as much care and tenderneſs as her own. And thus, by her patient and meek behaviour, we are told that ſhe prevailed on him to abandon that vice at a good old age. This pious Queen was canonized in the reign of Philip the Fourth of Spain.

There is one noble inſtitution of Don Diniz ſtill extant, which will ever bear teſtimony of his wiſdom; that is, the celebrated Univerſity of Coimbra, which he founded in the year one thouſand two hundred and ninety-one. He alſo planted the foreſt at Marinha, which is one of the moſt extenſive in Europe. Portugal has, and ſtill continues to derive more advantage from theſe ſettlements, than from all the victories of King Emanuel. Camoens, ſenſible of the merits of ſo great a Prince, has paid the following tribute to his memory:

—— Now brave Diniz reigns, whoſe noble fire
Beſpoke the genuine lineage of his Sire *.
Now heavenly peace wide wav'd her olive bough,
Each vale diſplay'd the labours of the plough,
And ſmil'd with joy: the rocks on every ſhore
Reſound the daſhing of the merchant-oar.
Wiſe laws are form'd, and conſtitutions weigh'd,
And the deep-rooted baſe of Empire laid.
Not Ammon's ſon with larger heart beſtow'd †,
Nor ſuch the grace to him the Muſes ow'd.
From Helicon the Muſes wing their way;
Mondego's flow'ry banks invite their ſtay.
Now Coimbra ſhines, Minerva's proud abode;
And fir'd with joy, Parnaſſus' bloomy God
Beholds another dear-lov'd Athens riſe,
And ſpread her laurels in indulgent ſkies. *Luſiad*, book iii.

* King Diniz was the eldeſt ſon of Alfonſo the Third. He was born at Liſbon on the 9th of October 1261.

† The liberality of Diniz became proverbial. When he was appointed as arbitrator to compoſe the difference which ſubſiſted between the Kings of Caſtile and Arragon, he made the moſt valuable preſents ever known in his time to the royal families and nobility of Spain. A few days before he returned home, a Caſtilian gentleman obſerved, whilſt he was at dinner, that his Majeſty's munificence extended to every one except himſelf; upon which Diniz deſired him to take the only preſent he had left of what he had brought with him; that was, the ſilver table upon which he dined.

There

There is a confiderable fair held annually in the city of Leiria, on the twenty-fifth of March. It was much crowded with dealers, who expofed to fale various articles of Englifh manufacture, particularly woollen cloths of a fecond quality, and hard-ware of every kind. The principal articles furnifhed by the natives were plate, jewellery, linen cloths, and pottery; the quantity of the former was very great, but more to be valued for the weight than the workmanfhip.

In a confpicuous part of the market, two French *Charletans* erected their booths; one a doctor, the other a dentift. The latter ftood on a table, and performed feats of empiricifm that aftonifhed the gaping crowd; and in reality his dexterity in tooth-drawing was very remarkable, they feemed to fly from their rooted focket at the touch of his finger. He affured me, that he expected to earn a moidore a day during the fair, though he charged the poor but ten reis a tooth.

The doctor, who vended his *panacea* under an adjoining fhed, had not fo many patients as his companion, nor were his abilities fo apparent to the vulgar, though he bore all the external marks of a perfon of deep refearch; he was fhort-fighted, pale, meagre, and wrinkled as a rib-ftocking; yet thefe *fapient indices* were loft on the multitude. His long and fuccefsful practice, he faid, had enabled him to

condenfe

condenſe the whole *pharmacopœia* into one medicine, which (though in fact but a ſimple ſalve) he applied indiſcriminately to all complaints, whether chronical or acute; and

> "With this he cur'd both poor and rich,
> "Yet was himſelf all over itch."

A ſtranger has an opportunity of obſerving the perſonal ſtate of the inferior claſs of this diſtrict, from the number of peaſantry who flock annually to the fair. Their appearance in general indicates more happineſs than is promiſed by the uncultivated ſtate of the land. The men wear ſhort brown jackets, and boots of the ſame colour; each carries a ſtaff about ſeven feet long, which he wields in combat with great dexterity.

The women wear long clokes, of a red or pearl colour, fringed with ribands; their necks and wriſts are ornamented with gold chains.

The former ſex are remarkably low of ſtature and feeble, which ſome attribute to their eating too much oil: but if that operated as the cauſe, we ſhould expect to find the females affected by it in like manner: whereas it is juſt the reverſe; for they are ſtrong, well-proportioned, and though but of a moderate ſize, yet when ranged with the men they look like Amazons, and if they poſſeſſed their gallantry or warlike ſpirit, they might transfer the diſtaff

 to

to their husbands, and *lord* it over them like the women of Metelin.

In the Cathedral of this city I witnessed a spectacle very humiliating to our nature. It was on a Sunday, during divine service, when a woman, about the age of five-and-twenty, possessed of an evil spirit, as it was supposed, entered the church. The Sacristan conducted her before one of the lateral chapels, where she stood with her mouth open, making a hideous noise, which seemed to issue from the *venter*. The painful sensations her eyes and countenance expressed, excited the commiseration of all the congregation; but I could find none capable of giving any satisfactory reason respecting the cause or nature of her distemper.

*May* 28th. The season now arrived in which the people are entertained with bull-feasts. After an absence of some weeks I returned to Leiria to see the diversion, and was surprised to find the effect it had on the inhabitants, particularly the lower class, who, with every demonstration of joy, testified their attachment for that favourite amusement. The combat was exhibited in a quadrangular area, or square, formed by the houses in the middle of the city. The spectators were accommodated with seats gratuitously in the balconies of these houses, whence they had a complete view of what was passing in the arena.

About

About three o'clock the diverſion began, when one of the bulls ruſhed into the arena, ſmarting with the wounds he had received in the ſtable, which were juſt ſprinkled with pickle. The combatants were about ſixteen in number, each holding a ſpear or dagger in the right hand, and a cloak of red ſilk on the left arm. The enraged animal now ran at one of them, who, notwithſtanding the danger, ſtood firm and undaunted till the bull dropped his horns to gore him, then he moved on his left foot from behind the cloak, and plunged a dagger into his neck.

The greater part of the exhibition was but a repetition of ſuch attacks; as here they have none but pedeſtrian performers, of whom there were two who excelled the reſt in courage, execution, and activity; one was a Spaniard, the other an African. Each of them, in more than one inſtance, diſpatched a bull at the firſt onſet, by aiming his dagger in a tender part between the horns, in conſequence of which the animal inſtantly dropped, and was not ſeen afterwards to betray the leaſt ſymptoms of life.

The moſt hazardous part was executed by a perſon who, unarmed, attacked one of theſe bulls. He threw himſelf between the two horns, and graſped the animal about the neck; in this poſture he was carried about the arena, till diſengaged by the united aſſiſtance of all the combatants, who overthrew the bull, which, in this inſtance, agreeably to the rules of the feaſt, became their property.

M When

When they found a bull that was ſtronger and wilder than the reſt, they protracted his exiſtence longer than uſual, amidſt the moſt excruciating tortures that ingenious cruelty could deviſe. The body was pierced in various parts, and a number of broken ſpears ſtuck into the fleſh. Whilſt the poor animal was thus bleeding at every pore, ſeveral tubes, filled with ſquibs and rockets, were faſtened to darts and plunged into the body. As ſoon as theſe were ſet on fire he ſtood in the midſt of the arena, tearing up the ground and bellowing, whilſt clouds of ſmoke (which he inhaled in breathing) iſſued from his mouth and noſtrils.

Though there are many enlightened people in Portugal who do not approve of theſe barbarous entertainments, yet the common people are ſo attached to them, that it would be very difficult to aboliſh them immediately. By degrees, however, they might be put an end to, and ſome manly, generous diverſion introduced in their ſtead: civilization, it muſt allowed, would loſe nothing by the exchange, and humanity would rejoice at it.

We ſhall conclude this ſubject with a ſhort extract from a letter of Mr. Upton's, reſpecting Spenſer's *Fairie Queene*. "In the tenth book of Heliodorus you will find that "Theagenes both tamed and rode on the back of a wild "bull. We have at Oxford now, a very valuable monu- "ment of this ſtrange kind of ſport.—This was a ſport "to

" to inure the youths to warlike exercifes, ufual at Thef-
" faly, and by Cæfar brought to Rome. But as Dr. Pri-
" deaux has already treated of this fubject in his Dif-
" fertation upon the Arundel Marbles, I fhall only add,
" that the modern bull-feafts in Spain feem plainly to be
" derived from this ftrange exercife and fport; firft be-
" gun by the Centaurs, who, from their hunting and
" driving away the herds of their neighbours, had their
" original names; then a public paftime among the
" Theffalians, afterwards among the Romans, and at laft
" ending in Spanifh bull-feaft."

*Marinha Grande.*

Here I fpent the month of May, at the hofpitable feat of William Stephens Efquire, the proprietor of an extenfive glafs manufactory, which he eftablifhed at this place about thirty years ago. The kingdom and its colonies are fupplied from hence with every article of glafs-ware, bottles excepted. It is the only factory of the kind in Portugal; and the glafs imported is very trifling, as the duty laid on it amounts almoft to a prohibition. The greateft inconvenience attending this fabrick, is its diftance from Lifbon, which is about nineteen leagues. The ware is ſent thither by carriers, who occupy three days in the journey: but this inconvenience is compenſated by the local advantages Marinha Grande poſſeſſes in wood, ſand, and kelp.

There is a noble foreſt of pine-trees computed at thirty miles in circumference, at a ſhort diſtance from this place. This foreſt was planted by the good King Diniz, for the benefit of poſterity, and has ſince remained the property of the crown. Previous to the diſcovery of America, the Portugueſe drew all their ſhip-timber from hence; at preſent there is very little uſe made of it, except what Mr. Stephens uſes in his glaſs-houſe, who has the privilege of felling the decayed trees.

The land about *Marinha Grande* is very unproductive; the greater part of it is a waſte of marſh or ſand. Mr. Stephens has reclaimed about thirty acres, which were covered with ſand; and he aſſures me, that it now yields ſeven or eight abundant crops of lucern every year, though for ages paſt it did not yield a blade of graſs.

The

The following Paper, for which I am indebted to the gentleman above mentioned, may, perhaps, be uſeful to thoſe who are intereſted in the culture of Bees:

*An Account of the Manner of treating Bees in Portugal.*

"To form a colony of Bees, a ſpot of ground is choſen for the hives, expoſed towards the South or South Eaſt, well ſheltered from the Northern blaſts, and ſurrounded with ſhrubs and flowers; of the latter, the beſt is roſe-mary. The richer the neighbouring grounds are, the better; for Bees are ſaid to range for food to the diſtance of a league from their homes. The ſituation being choſen, lanes muſt be cut through the ſhrubby thickets of five or ſix feet wide. The fences between the lanes ſhould be about the ſame dimenſions, and formed at intervals into ſmall receſſes, like bowers or niches, to receive the hives.

"The figure of the hives uſed here in general are cylindrical; in height about twenty-ſeven inches by fourteen diameter. They are formed of the rind of the cork-tree, and covered with a pan of earthen-ware inverted, the edge of which projects over the hive like a cornice. The whole is faſtened with pegs made of ſome hard and durable wood, and the joints ſtopped with peat. In the front of the cylinder, at the height of about eight inches, there is a ſmall aperture where the Bees enter. The inſide is divided into three equal diviſions, which are ſeparated by croſs ſticks: here the Bees form their combs or cells.

"When the Bees ſwarm, which is uſually in the month of May or June, the hives are placed to receive them where they alight. If they deſcend on a tree, they are ſhaken off: the perſon who performs this operation muſt not be afraid of them, as they do not commonly ſting unleſs they are irritated; it will be ſafer, however, to cover the head with a wire-maſk, and the hands with gloves.

"Some Bees are ſo wild, that they fly away in attempting to collect them, but they may be caught again in this manner: a ſheet is placed by night on the ground contiguous to the ſwarm, and when they alight, the hive is placed over them, with the entrance ſtopped, then the whole is covered with a ſheet, in which they are carried home. But they ſhould not be placed near the hive whence they had originally departed.

"When the time arrives for taking out the honey-combs, which is generally in the month of June, when the flowers begin to decay, it ſhould be done in the heat of the day, as the greater part of the bees are then abroad, but not during a high wind, or at the commencement of a new or full moon. The hiver muſt have his face

and

and hands defended, as above mentioned, and accompanied by a perſon holding a chafing-diſh, with a coal-fire, covered with moiſt peat, to make the greater ſmoke: this ſmoke being infuſed among the Bees from the top of the cylinder, they fly away, or remain intoxicated at the bottom, then the hive is taken to pieces, by drawing out the pins. The combs are cut out without deſtroying the Bees, except two cells, which are left around the hive; and leſt the Bees ſhould feed on what remains, the inciſion is covered with pulverized clay; after this the hive is put together as before.

"The combs ſhould not be taken out but when they are full of honey; it is rarely good the firſt year the Bees aſſemble. In the months of March and Auguſt the wax is taken out, which is lodged in the firſt diviſion of the hive, after which the Bees form other combs, and generate a young colony.

"The hiver ſhould often viſit the ground, and repair any accidents that have happened. If ſnakes frequent the place, they ſhould not be killed, ſince they do not moleſt the Bees, but deſtroy the toads and lizards, which are obnoxious to them.

"When the hives are decayed, they are taken aſunder and fumigated; then the Bees forſake their habitations, and take ſhelter in an adjoining hive, previouſly prepared for

 that

that purpose. This should be performed in the Spring, when the flowers begin to open and afford them succour. The same method may be used in taking out the honey; but if repeatedly practised, it will extinguish the colony.

"As the Bees, in returning from their excursions, are loaded and fatigued, there should be nothing near the hives to obstruct their descent, which is not in a perpendicular course, but in an oblique one."

*Royal Monastery of Alcobaça.*

The Royal Monastery of Alcobaça is seated in a pretty village of the same name, about fifteen leagues North of Lisbon; it is well sheltered, particularly towards the West, by rising grounds, which gradually ascend to an immense elevation. Every part of the neighbouring country is well cultivated, and produces corn and fruit of various kinds.

In examining the origin of the religious structures of the twelfth century, we find the greater part of them have been founded in grateful remembrance of some divine favour in battle, or else with a view to expiate the sins of the founder; so that they may not be improperly called the temples of gratitude and repentance. This magnificent

ficent ſtructure is indebted for its origin to the former cauſe. It was founded in the year one thouſand one hundred and ſeventy, by Alphonſo the firſt King of Portugal, in conſequence of taking the fortreſs of Santerem from the Moors, the capture of which he previouſly vowed to commemorate by a Monaſtery.

Faria relates, that St. Barnard (who at this time reſided in Claravallis in France) being inſpired with the King's pious determination, ſent two Monks to begin the Monaſtery on the very day the vow was made. It is further obſerved, that the ſite originally intended for it, is not that on which it is built; as the lines were laid out to dig the foundation cloſe to the road, an Angel came in the night and carried them ſeveral feet back, to a more eligible ſituation. This remarkable circumſtance is repreſented in a large painting, to be ſeen at this day in the gallery of the Hoſpitium.

The ſame Angel would have done a laudable action, by extending a ſimilar act of kindneſs to the pariſh church, which is raiſed oppoſite to the Monaſtery, in the centre of the high-road; a ſituation better adapted for a triumphal arch than a houſe of worſhip.

Miracles of this ſort, though rarely known in our days, were not, it ſeems, uncommon in former times. We are aſſured by very grave Writers, that when Conſtantine the

N Great

Great intended to transfer the ſeat of empire to the Eaſt, he pitched on Chalcedon for the ſite of his Capital; as the workmen began to lay the foundation of it, certain eagles, the ancient meſſengers of Jove, carried away the lines, and let them fall over Bizantium; upon which the Emperor altered his reſolution, and built his city where it now ſtands.

It is much to be regretted, that theſe guardians of architecture do not pay a viſit to London; very few of the citizens would be ſorry to hear that St. Clement's church in the Strand was numbered among the above miracles.

But to return to our ſubject: This Monaſtery might be ſaid to commemorate three remarkable events; *viz.* the origin of the Portugueſe Monarchy, the commencement of the Bernardine order of Monks, and the introduction of a new ſpecies of architecture into that kingdom, which our antiquaries call *Modern Norman Gothic.* The Church is entirely built in this ſtyle, except the Weſt front, which is more modern than the reſt, and exhibits a ſelection of the defects of the Tuſcan and Gothic ſtyles.

On entering the Church at the Weſt front, one is ſtruck with the grandeur of that general effect peculiar to the inſide of Gothic Churches, but very few poſſeſs that property to a higher degree than this. The proſpect at the

East end is terminated by a magnificent Glory, placed over the altar, at the distance of three hundred feet from the entrance; but the apparent distance is considerably more, on account of the narrowness of the nave, and the regular succession of the pillars, which are twenty-six in number; that is, thirteen at each side. The longitudinal distance from the centre of one pillar to that of the other is but seventeen feet three inches: according to the rules observed in the best proportioned Gothic edifices, this distance is too little by one-third. The proportion of the pillars is likewise defective; their dimensions being greater than the impulse of the vaults require. Indeed, the architect appears not to have been acquainted with the *lex minimum* in construction, which experience or science taught his successors in this art. On the whole, there is very little difference between the architecture of this structure and that called Ancient Norman, or Saxon, except that the arches, instead of being semicircular, as in the latter, are pointed; in other respects we observe the defective proportions and rude sculpture of the Saxon churches in every part: the capitals, in particular, are almost plain blocks; the bases of the pillars have but few mouldings; the ribs of the vaults and architraves of the windows want that depth and sharpness which produce an air of lightness.

The East end, or choir, is of a semicircular form, after the manner of the ancient Churches, or Basilisks, and which the Abbé Fleury supposes to have been made in that manner by the Chriſtians, to imitate that part of the Jewiſh Temples where the Sanhedrim aſſembled.

The Gothic work which formerly decorated the choir, is now concealed by Grecian columns, with their appendages. This alteration was made about eighteen years ago by an Engliſh ſculptor, named William Elſden, at the requeſt of the Friars. Nothing can be more diſguſting to every admirer of antiquity, or indeed any man of the leaſt taſte, than this jumble of Grecian work, patched up in the moſt ſtriking part of a ſtructure, executed in the ſimple Gothic manner.

As the Church of Alcobaça is one of the earlieſt ſpecimens of the modern Norman Gothic in Europe, and perhaps the moſt magnificent of the early period in which it was founded, we ſhould be glad, were it not foreign to our ſubject, to give a more particular account of its architecture, and to illuſtrate the ſame by engravings. We ſhould then be enabled to make it appear, that the conjectures reſpecting the origin of the Gothic ſtyle are not warranted from this edifice, as we find nothing in it that has the moſt diſtant reſemblance to bowers or groves, to Mooriſh or Saracenic architecture, whence the pointed arch is ſuppoſed to be derived.

The Weſt front of the Monaſtery, including the church, which is in the centre, extends ſix hundred and twenty feet, the depth is about ſeven hundred and fifty feet. The incloſed ſpace is occupied by dormitories, galleries, cloiſters, &c. A Portugueſe Writer, in ſpeaking of the magnificence of this Monaſtery, obſerves, that its cloiſters are cities, its ſacriſty a church, and the church a baſiliſk.

The better to convey an idea of it, we ſhall give the dimenſions of ſome of the apartments. The kitchen, for example, is near an hundred feet long, by twenty-two broad, and ſixty-three feet high from the floor to the intrados of the vault. The fire-place is twenty-eight feet long by eleven broad, and is placed, not in the wall, but in the centre of the floor; ſo that there is acceſs to it at every ſide. The chimney forms a pyramid reſting upon eight columns of caſt iron. A ſubterranean ſtream of water paſſes through the centre of the floor, which is occaſionally made to overflow the pavement, in order to cleanſe it.

Notwithſtanding the magnitude of this apartment, there is not an inch of it unoccupied from morning till night; for all the induſtry of the Convent is concentred in it; the operations are carried on under the inſpection of one of the lay-brothers.

The refectory is ninety-two feet long by ſixty-eight broad; the breadth is divided into three porticos by two

ſeries

ſeries of ſtone columns. The tables are placed next the two ſide and end walls; at the extreme end, where the Prior takes his ſeat, are two large pictures; the one repreſenting the Laſt Supper, the other Chriſt and the two Diſciples at Emmaus.

We ſhould not omit to notice the cellar, as it is one of the moſt valuable apartments belonging to the Monaſtery; there are forty large caſks in it, which are ſuppoſed to contain near ſeven hundred pipes of wine.

It is very remarkable, that theſe people, avowedly aſſembled for the purpoſe of ſtudying as well as praying, have not a library in their convent, unleſs that deſerves the name of one which is not larger than a cloſet, and ſcarcely contains as many books as there are pipes of wine in the cellar.

The North Weſt wing of the Monaſtery is ſet apart for the reception of ſtrangers; hence it is called the *Hoſpitium*, the whole extent, which is two hundred and thirty feet, is diſtributed into ſtately and convenient apartments. In the anti-rooms are ſome good pictures, particularly one of the Judgment of Solomon, and ſeveral portraits of Popes and Cardinals, very well executed, by a Portugueſe artiſt named *Vaſques*; among the latter we find the portrait of St. Thomas of Canterbury.

The

The rooms of ſtate are furniſhed with the portraits of the Sovereigns of Portugal, from the commencement of the Monarchy to the preſent: they have been lately painted by an artiſt named *Antino Amarel.* I am ſorry that truth will not allow me to ſay that they are well done; the painter appears to have been an utter ſtranger to light and ſhade, and had but a very imperfect idea of drawing. There is one portrait here, painted by a Portugueſe lady named *Joſepha*, that is worth the whole collection.

The above ſeries of portraits are ranged in the following chronological ſucceſſion:

| | | | | | |
|---|---|---|---|---|---|
| 1. | ALFONSO I. the founder of this Monaſtery, and the firſt King of Portugal, *vixit anno* 77, *obit anno* | 1185. | 13. | JOHN II. - *obit anno* | 1495. |
| 2. | SANCHO I. - - | 1211. | 14. | EMANUEL I. - - | 1521. |
| 3. | ALPHONSO II. - - | 1223. | 15. | JOHN III. - - | 1557. |
| 4. | SANCHO II. - - | 1248. | 16. | SEBASTIAN I. - - | 1578. |
| 5. | ALFONSO III. - - | 1279. | 17. | HENRY I. - - | 1580. |
| 6. | DENIZ I. - - | 1325. | 18. | PHILIP II. of Caſtile, - | 1598. |
| 7. | ALFONSO IV. - - | 1357. | 19. | PHILIP III. - - | 1621. |
| 8. | PETER I. - - | 1367. | 20. | PHILIP IV. - - | 1665. |
| 9. | FERDINAND I. - - | 1383. | 21. | JOHN IV. - - | 1656. |
| 10. | JOHN I. - - | 1433. | 22. | ALFONSO VI. - - | 1683. |
| 11. | EDWARD I. - - | 1438. | 23. | PETER II. - - | 1706. |
| 12. | ALFONSO V. - - | 1481. | 24. | JOHN V. - - | 1750. |
| | | | 25. | JOSEPH I. - - | 1777. |
| | | | 26. | Queen MARIA I. born 17th December - - | 1734. |

In the apartment called the Hall of Kings, are ſeveral Statues of the Sovereigns of Portugal, made of Plaſter of Paris, ſome placed in niches, and others ſtanding on corbels at at the height of eight or nine feet. The name of the artiſt I do not remember; nor perhaps will it ever be found regiſtered in the catalogue of the imitators of nature.

The third day after my arrival here, I was conducted by two of the Fathers up ſeveral flights of ſtairs to the Novices apartment; on entering the gallery I found about a ſcore of them, between the age of fourteen and eighteen, drawn up in a line, like a ſquadron of ſoldiers; they ſtood in a reclined poſture, with their eyes fixed on the ground, whilſt their Superior, called the *Padre Meſtre*, ſtood oppoſite to them, with a book in his hand. I was not a little ſurpriſed to find that the preſence of a ſtranger did not induce any of them to raiſe his head.

The Novices chapel contains one of the fineſt collection of pictures in the kingdom. I had only time to examine a few of them attentively (without treſpaſſing too much on the patience of the Fathers); one was a ſmall figure of a Madona, ſuppoſed to be painted by Titian: it is certainly in his manner; the colouring is exquiſite, and though thinly laid on, the effect is grand and forcible, from the artful manner in which the different tints are contraſted. Strangers, I underſtand, are but ſeldom allowed to viſit the Novices apartments, otherwiſe I would have taken a catalogue of this valuable collection.

From

From thence I paſſed to the oppoſite ſide, through a corridore, at each ſide of which is a range of ſmall cells, belonging to the Novices, who had now retired into them; the dimenſions of each might be about fourteen feet by nine. I wiſhed to ſee the inſide, but was told the Superior had the keys. In one of the doors was a ſmall aperture, through which I obſerved a graceful youth, of a pale and macerated countenance, about the age of ſixteen; he was dreſſed in a long black robe, on his knees, in the act of prayer, with a roſary in his hand; his eyes fixed on a crucifix. The walls about him were without pictures, or any other ornament; and, leſt the view of external objects ſhould interrupt the courſe of his meditation, there was but one ſmall aperture in the cell to admit day, and that was placed next the cieling; the bottom and ſides of it were ſplayed ſomewhat like a loop-hole, ſo that the rays of the evening Sun, which now ſhone through it, fell on his tonſure, whilſt all about him appeared in ſhade. Had Raphael transferred the ſupplicatory object to the canvaſs, he could not have choſen light better adapted to produce a grand effect.

It is not my intention to interfere with the doctrine of the church, relative to the extinction or regulation of the paſſions; I ſhall only obſerve, that if obedience and ſolitude are foremoſt in the claſs of virtues, great muſt be the reward of theſe probations.

In order that the Fathers might want for nothing that contributes to the convenience or happiness of the monastic life; they are accommodated with a large garden at the rear of the church, which is planted with trees and shrubs, and distributed into pleasant walks. Here they recreate themselves every afternoon. At intervals there are arbours formed in the thickets, and furnished with benches, where the Friars retire from the heat of the Sun, to study or meditate. In the centre of the garden is a fine oval pond, of an hundred and thirty feet on the transverse diameter, with an obelisk in the centre of it.

There are various cypress trees at the farther end of the garden, the leaves of which are *ingeniously* formed by the shears into figures representing men; some in the act of shooting, and others praying; some with long cues, and others with perukes. This species of sculpture, though hitherto not classed among the branches of the fine arts, approaches the nearest to Nature, perhaps, of any other; for these Sylvan figures absolutely grow, and are daily fed, with the produce of the soil. They have their Winter and Summer, Spring and Autumn, their existence and dissolution, like other animated beings.

Contiguous to the above garden there is a rabbit-warren belonging to the Monastery, upon a construction different from any I had ever seen. It is two hundred feet long by an hundred and twenty-five broad, incloſed on every ſide by walls about ſixteen feet high. The floor is paved with large ſquare flags, and the joints filled with cement. There are little ſheds ranged along the foot of the wall, where oval earthen pots are placed, of eleven inches in depth by nine inches in height. The front of each has a round tube through which the rabbit enters; here they breed, and rear up their young ones. On the area of the warren are alſo ſeveral ranges of pots, apperently ſet apart for the male rabbits. The whole, which are ſaid to amount to five or ſix thouſand, are fed with plants brought from the neighbouring fields and gardens, together with the offals of the Convent.

The Fathers of this Convent, like thoſe we before mentioned at Oporto, are not allowed to appear on foot out of doors, except in the gardens belonging to their Monaſtery; ſuch as have occaſion to go abroad travel on mules, or in carriages; they have a number of theſe animals in their ſtables, which it ſeems they prefer to horſes, but for what reaſon I could not learn, perhaps from motives of humility; for Guevara tells us, that till his time, it was a mark of diſgrace in Spain for a gentleman to ride on a mule.

John the Second of Portugal, finding the breed of horſes nearly extinct, endeavoured to revive them in his dominions by prohibiting the uſe of mules. The clergy re-

 fuſed

fused to comply with the ordinance, and appealed to the Pope to justify them. But the King, not willing to fall out with this class of his subjects, on consideration, thought it prudent to revise the edict, and inserted a clause allowing all the clergy within his dominions to keep mules, but ordained at the same time that no one should shoe them, under pain of death. Thus he silenced their objection, and gained his point.

* The reader will easily conceive what a vast revenue it requires to keep up this institution, wherein there are about three hundred people, including servants, living in a splendid manner. But the royal founder took care to provide for all contingencies; for at the moment he vowed to build it, he endowed it with all the land and sea that can be seen from the summit of a neighbouring mountain, which commands a wide horizon. The revenue arising from this vast tract of country renders Alcobaça one of the richest and most magnificent institutions of the kind, not only in Portugal, but in Europe.

Of late years some of its privileges have been restrained; many people, however, are of opinion that it still possesses too many. They also think the revenue is too great, from an idea that wealth promotes feasting more than praying. But during a residence here of near three weeks I could perceive no just grounds for such remarks; on the contrary, I found the greatest temperance and decorum,

 blended

blended with hospitality and cheerfulness, prevail in every part.

Each Father holds his rank according to seniority or election. The junior Friars are very respectful and submissive to their superiors, and all are obedient to the Abbot-general, who presides as chief. This prelate has no spiritual superior in the kingdom, except the Cardinal; he holds the rank of a Bishop, is Almoner to the King, and Chief of all the Monasteries and Nunneries of the Bernardine Order in Portugal. The office is elective every three years. This is the second time the present worthy General has served in that capacity.

Every stranger who visits the convent is sure to meet with a polite and hospitable reception. Many youths of the district are maintained and educated by the Fathers. The superfluities of the refectory are distributed among the poor; besides, there are pittances purposely prepared for them twice a week; so that hundreds of indigent people are constantly fed at their gates; and their tenantry are apparently as comfortable as any in the kingdom. Those who declaim against their opulence, would do well to inquire, whether there be a nobleman or gentleman in Europe, possessed of a revenue equal to that of this Monastery, who diffuses so many blessings among his fellow-beings as the Fathers of Alcobaça.

In

In the archives of the Monastery is preserved, among several other sacred utensils, a gold chalice of exquisite workmanship, which has excited the curiosity of some learned and ingenious men. It is studded with many precious stones of divers colours, and ornamented with several groups of beautiful figures *in demi relief*, representing the Passion of Christ.

The Fathers can give no satisfactory account of it, neither do their records mention at what time it was made, nor by whom it was presented; according to some, it was bestowed by King Emanuel, others suppose it was purchased with the jewels of Dona Ignez de Castro, who is entered here; whilst others conjecture that it was bought with the treasure of diamonds and rings, which Alfonso the First bequeathed to the Monastery at his death. Without presuming to decide which of these opinions is right, I shall offer the following memorandums for the consideration of the curious.

On the cup, or upper part of the chalice, are twenty-seven embossed letters, distributed around the circumference in six divisions, thus:

NETO
VIRHP
ASBM
MIGLK
HOAM
VEDIK.

The

The foot of the chalice is about nine inches diameter, and contains an hundred and ten letters, which are distributed into twelve divisions about its circumference, in the following order *:

MDSXIB
QVEKIP: THSFCIE
MLDNE
RGATOI, VELTHBE
XIDKMT
RVSNEB. ILCAL
MFOKV
IHPTXV. ESTDMIN
ATVFOL
RHVEBSI. NOPALX
CVIHGI
RMLOEI. NTKVFE.

The Rev. Dr. Bluteau, in a work consisting of various academical pieces, intitled *Prosas Portuguezas*, has given a long dissertation on these letters, wherein he attempts, though evidently in vain, to ascertain their meaning. As he was looked upon as an Author of no inconsiderable merit in his time, perhaps his manner of treating the subject in question might apologize for the length of the following extracts, which we have endeavoured to translate as literally as possible:

"—— Upon my inquiring of the Fathers, if they knew the signification of these letters, they answered in the negative,

* As the letters on the neck of the chalice are placed in a hexagon, and those on the foot in a duodecagon, we are at liberty to begin at any side of the polygons; these have been copied from left to right.

gative, though many ingenious men had endeavoured to explain them. This roused my curiosity to copy the mysterious characters, not with a presumption to decypher them, but with a view to devote a few leisure hours in examining them in the tranquillity of retirement.

" Now, on the one hand, I figured to myself that all this metallic literature might be a mere artifice, to attract the curiosity of the ingenious; on the other, it appeared to me injustice to suppose, that such fine letters should have no meaning, and occupy so much gold to no purpose. But every time I consulted the curious about the interpretation of them, we became more entangled than the Argonaut in the Golden Fleece, which, according to some, was likewise an enigma of golden letters. In this perplexity, as I had not, like Jason, a Medea to conduct me through the maze, I conceived that the caballistic art alone would give a thread to guide my steps through this labyrinth.

" *Cabala*, or *Kabbala*, a Hebrew word, which signifies *reception*, is derived from *kibbel*, which means *delivered*, or *taught*. These two etymologies are verified by the application of the word *caballa*; for in ancient times *caballa* was the science of instructing without books or writings, and was communicated by successive tradition delivered *viva voce*.

" Between

" Between the Caballa of the modern and ancient Hebrews there is a wide difference: that of the latter was a noble myſterious doctrine, promulged by Moſes. In confirmation of this, *Celio Rhodiginio* ſays, that Moſes received two laws on the Mount; one literal, which he wrote by order of God, and preſented to the eyes of the people; the other ſpiritual, which he revealed to ſeventy of the Elders. And we know that theſe people had ſucceſſively, from one to the other, transferred the myſteries of their ſublime doctrine; whence they called it *Mercava*, that is to ſay, *the ſcience of tranſferring*. It had for its object all things appertaining to intellectual matters.

" By means of this ſecret communication the ſons were made heirs of their fathers' ineſtimable treaſures of divine ſcience, and not only the Hebrews, but alſo the Chaldeans, Pythagoreans, and Druids, (ancient Philoſophers of Gallia,) for the ſpace of many centuries, were initiated in an oocult manner into all ſpiritual matters, without books or writings. By the Greeks it was called *Agrapha*, now it is known by the original name *Caballa*. But as time perverts all things, the Hebrew Doctors inſenſibly loſt ſight of this occult ſcience, and by ill-placed curioſity, their Theologiſts degenerated into Hereſiarchs, their Aſtronomers into Judicial Aſtrologers, their Logicians into Sophiſts, their Natural Philoſophers into Alchymiſts, &c. and thus the ſpeculative purſuits of the Hebrew Doctors dwindled

dwindled into what they call Allegories; hence the name Allegorical Caballists, or Allegorists.

"These Caballists taught their followers, that the allegorical sense of writings is much superior to the literal, in as much as the latter is practical, whereas the other is speculative; the practical being embarrassed with circumstances of place and time, whereas the speculative exalts the soul to the knowledge of temporal, celestial, and eternal objects, which are the images of the Divine immutability.

"Finally, Allegorists ascertain Caballas by the observation of letters, in which, after a great deal of labour, they scarce produce any thing worthy of notice.

"The last Caballa is divided into *Gametria*, *Notarica*, and *Themura*. The first ascertaining the words by the transposition of the letters; the second supposes each letter to stand for a word, or explains one word by another which contains an equal number of letters. And the *Cabella Themura*, which is likewise called *Ziruph*, consists in interchanging the letters, and then supposing each of them to be equivalent to certain other letters.

"The two latter will not answer my purpose, because of the number of letters of the chalice, and because they are only

only uſed where there are but few letters, as may be inferred from the following inſtances:

" In the ſecond verſe of the third Pſalm, where we read *Multi inſurgunt adverſum me*, the *Caballa Notarica* decyphers the word *Multi*, and ſhews that in the Hebrew language it is written with R, B, I, M; which characters, after much ſpeculative inquiry, are ſuppoſed to be the initials of the names of the *Romans*, *Babylonians*, *Ionians*, and *Medes*. In a few letters this Caballa might be applied; the Romans made uſe of it in their epitaphs and other inſcriptions, as we find by the letters S, P, Q, R, which mean *Senatus Populuſque Romanus*.

" This Caballa has given riſe to ſome curious conjectures on the four letters of the name ADAM, which are interpreted to be the initials of the four quarters of the world; *viz*. *Anatoli*, which in the Greek ſignifies the Eaſt, *Dyſis* the Weſt, *Arctos* means the North, and *Meſembria* the South, or Mid-day. Thus, with a myſterious brevity, the name of the firſt Monarch is a cabaliſtical indication of the four parts of his empire.

" The Caballa Notarica draws ſignifications from letters according to the meaning they have in other alphabets, particularly in thoſe where every letter is an entire word; as in the Hebrew alphabet *Aleph*, *Beth*, *Daleth*, *Ghimel*,

 *&c.*

&c. and in the Greek *Alpha*, *Beta*, *Gamma*, *Delta*; and in many other idioms we may form lines with two or three letters of their alphabet, as in the Chaldean, for example, the letter A is called *Elpha*, in the Syrian, *Olaph*, or *Alyn*; in the Arabick, Turkiſh, and Perſian, it is called *Aliph*; in the Egyptian, *Athomus*; in the Ethiopian, *Alph*; in the Arminian, *Aip*; in the Sclavonian *Alemoxi*, and ſo of others.

" The word *Aluph*, or *Aleph*, which is the A of the Hebrews, means *Prince*; and for this reaſon it was placed at the head of their alphabet, as the Prince of their letters.

" The *Alpha* of the Greeks, in the language of the Syrians, means an ox. It is related, when Cadmus began to found a city in Bœotia, he chanced to meet an ox, and cauſed the name of it (*Alpha*) to be placed at the head of the alphabet, from the great utility of this animal, which the Syrians conſider as the Prince of the animals of the field.

" The ſecond *Caballa*, called *Themura*, or *Ziruph*, is as little to my purpoſe as the former. The third *Caballa*, called *Gametria* by the Hebrews, conſiſts in tranſpoſing of the letters in ſuch a manner as to produce ſignificant words; for example, the twenty-third chapter of Exodus, verſe the twentieth, is written in the Vulgate *Præcedetque te*

*Angelus*

*Angelus meus.* In the place of *Angelus* the Hebrew verſion ſays Malachi, and by the anagramatic tranſpoſition of the letters of this name, the Caballiſts ſhew that Malachi means Michael; hence they pretend that the Angel of whom the Scripture ſpeaks in the above place was Saint Michael."

Our Author next proceeds to ſhew the numerous interpretations to which the letters of the chalice are ſubject: "When, according to Father Malebranche's Treatiſe on Algebra, the combinations of the twenty-four letters of the alphabet amount to 1. 391. 721. 658. 311. 264. 960. 263. 919. 898. 102. 100. *"

Hence he concludes, that the languages uſed all over the world muſt be more numerous than is generally ſuppoſed. "According to Father Vaſconcellos the Jeſuit's account of the Brazils on the banks of the river Amazon, there are more than an hundred and fifty languages ſpoken, and theſe, we are aſſured by Father Vieira, are as different from one another as ours is from the Greek.

* According to *Tacquet*, the various combinations of the twenty-four letters of the alphabet (without repetition) amount to 620. 448. 401. 733. 239. 439. 360. 000. *Clavius* the Jeſuit has alſo calculated theſe combinations, and makes them infinitely ſhort of the other two. Here is his computation, 5. 852. 616. 738. 497. 664. 000. So much for the uncertainty of progreſſive arithmetic, when applied to ſubjects of this nature.

*Tranſlator's Note.*



"If

"If to these we add the several hundred languages which are used among the different nations of the world, we cannot help asking with admiration, What is the primary source of so many modes of speech? Whence so many flowers and figures of rhetoric? What repository supplied the Latin, Greek, and Hebrew idioms? To what source are the Italians indebted for their courteous and political expressions? What Nymph or Muse inspired the French with that sweetness of diction? What fierce and severe warrior gave the Germans their military terms and frightful vocality? What Prince, what Potentate enthroned in Portugal and Castile the words of a grave and majestic eloquence? Finally, What materials were used by the people of China, Japan, Arabia, Turkey, Margui, Armenia, Malabar, Bengal, Malacca, the Negroes of Africa, the Inhabitants of America, and all other nations, to invent significant terms of customs, negociations, commerce, trade, tactics, battles, arts, sciences, rites, ceremonies, religion, and sacrifices?

"This vast ocean of literature is still further supplied by numerous other vocabularies flowing into it, like rivers into the sea, from proper names and family appellations, from the various dialects, and the different modes of pronouncing the same language in different parts of a state; as in the Greek language, the Attic, Eolic, Corinthian, and common dialects: In the Italian language, the dialects of of Genoa, Bergamoſa, Venice, Naples, Sicily: In the French, the dialects of Picardy, Gaſcony, Normandy, &c.; and in the Portugueſe, the particular words peculiar to Beira, Minho, Alenteju, Algarve, &c. Theſe and the innumerable other dialects ariſing from the letters of the alphabet, with the divers words of the mother tongues, make altogether an ineffable variety of ſpeech."

Our Author, after wandering far from the queſtion, returns to the ſubject, and concludes, that the meaning of the letters of the chalice is this: *Hic eſt calix ſanguinis mei, novi & æterni teſtamenti, qui pro vobis & pro multis effundetur. Joakim Kludphik fudi, Bolduk. A. Dom. Mil.* C. LXXXVII. *

* Doctor Bluteau has made ſome miſtakes in copying the letters of the chalice; the following, for inſtance, NOPALX, which are on the foot of it, he attributes to the neck. An anonymous Writer has given a different interpretation of theſe letters in the before-mentioned work, (*Proſas Portuguezas,*) wherein he makes each letter the initial of a word. And, in order to make the ſenſe coincide with his meaning, he ſubſtitutes ideal letters for real ones, though perhaps it happened through miſtake. However that was, his interpretation of the enigma is, if poſſible, more improbable than that of Doctor Bluteau.

Among

Among the perſonages interred in this Monaſtery there are but two; namely, Don *Pedro* and Dona *Ignez de Caſtro*, of whom I could collect any thing remarkable. We ſhall attempt to give a ſketch of the hiſtory of this celebrated pair, and then take our leave of Alcobaça.

*Don Pedro and Dona Ignez de Caſtro.*

Contiguous to the tranſept of the church belonging to this Convent, there is a Gothic Mauſoleum of hewn ſtone, in the midſt of which are two magnificent ſepulchres of white marble, containing the remains of Don Pedro the Firſt, King of Portugal, and of Dona Ignez de Caſtro, his conſort.

A cumbent effigy of each, the ſize of life, is placed on their reſpective tombs; by which the former is repreſented with a long beard, a ſevere countenance, and in the act of drawing his ſword. The latter is repreſented with a beautiful innocent countenance; dreſſed in royal robes, and adorned with the diadem.

There are but few perſonages recorded in hiſtory, who have been oftener celebrated by dramatic writers than this Princeſs. There have been no leſs than five tragedies formed from

from her pitiful narrative; *viz.* two in Englifh, one, in French, one in Spanifh, and one in Portuguefe. The latter, perhaps, approaches the neareft to the truth of hiftory, and is not inferior in point of poetical merit. The Author, *Senhor Nicola Luis*, had no occafion to refort to fiction to heighten the paffions of an audience, as the fimple facts are fufficient to fill up all the fcenes of pity and terror, and to fhew to what lengths love and revenge are capable of tranfporting the human mind.

The fubject of this tragical piece is as follows: Don Pedro, fon of Alonfo the Fourth, King of Portugal, and heir apparent to the crown, having fallen in love with a lady of the court, named Dona Ignez de Caftro, thought he could not fhare the crown which awaited him with a more amiable perfon. She united to all the charms of beauty, the moft graceful and accomplifhed manners. The Prince, waving all confiderations of birth and fortune, was privately married to her by the Bifhop of *Guarda*.

Notwithftanding the nuptials were performed with all the fecrecy imaginable, yet they reached the King's ear, who had premeditated a confort for Don Pedro in the King of Caftile's daughter. He queftioned him as to the truth of the report; but knowing his father's arbitrary difpofition, he thought it prudent then to conceal the fact.

The Nobility alſo had intimation of the marriage, and the preference given to Ignez had awakened their jealouſy. Hence they took every opportunity of repreſenting her as a woman of the greateſt ambition, and pretended that very fatal conſequences were to be apprehended from ſuch an alliance; they alſo condemned the Prince as a raſh and diſobedient ſon.

The King, who was a man of weak underſtanding, gave ear to their calumny, and they worked upon his paſſions to that degree, that he reſolved to murder the unfortunate Princeſs. Accordingly, he ſet out to perpetrate the horrid deed, accompanied by three of his courtiers and a number of armed men.

Dona Ignez at this time reſided in Coimbra, in the palace of Santà Clara, where ſhe paſſed her time in the moſt private manner, educating her children, and attending to the duties of her domeſtic affairs.

The Prince, unfortunately, was abroad on a hunting party when the King arrived. The beautiful victim came out to meet him, with her two infant children, who clung about his knees, ſcreaming aloud for mercy. She proſtrates herſelf at his feet, bathes them with tears, and ſupplicates pity for her children, beſeeching him to baniſh her to ſome remote deſert, where ſhe would gladly wander an exile with her babes.

The feelings of Nature arrested his arm, just raised to plunge a dagger into her breast. But his counsellors urging the necessity of her death, and reproaching him for his disregard to the welfare of the nation, he relapsed into his former resolution, and commanded them to dispatch her; at which they rushed forward, regardless of the cries of innocence and beauty, and instantly struck off her head!

Soon after the above transaction the Prince arrived; but, alas! found those eyes that were wont to watch his return with impatience, closed in death. The sight of his beloved Ignez weltering in gore filled his mind with distraction, and kindled every spark of revenge within his soul. In all the agony of rage, he called aloud on the avenging hand of Heaven to punish those monsters who deprived him of all he held dear upon earth.

As soon as her remains were interred, he put himself at the head of an army, who sympathized with his distress; they carried fire and sword through the adjacent provinces, and laid waste the estates of the murderers. The royal troops could not oppose them; they fled at the appearance of the gallant avengers of innocence. But the King, wretched man! could not fly from himself; the cries of his grand-children still echoed in his ears, and the bleeding image of their unfortunate mother was constantly before his eyes. Death at length commiserated his situation, and he expired full of repentance for his accumulated crimes. He was an undutiful ſon, an unnatural brother, and a cruel father.

The Prince now aſcended the throne, in the thirty-ſeventh year of his age. He no ſooner obtained the power, than he meditated to revenge the death of his beloved Ignez. The three murderers; namely, Pedro Coello, Diogo Lopez Pacheo, and Alvaro Gonſalvez, had fled into Caſtile, previous to the death of the late King. The Prince ordered them to be tried on a charge of high treaſon, and being found guilty, their eſtates were confiſcated. Next, he contrived to ſeize their perſons, by agreeing with the King of Caſtile that both ſhould reciprocally deliver up the Portugueſe and Caſtilian fugitives, who ſought protection in their reſpective dominions. Gonſalvez and Coello were accordingly arreſted, and ſent in chains to Portugal; Pacheo eſcaped into France.

The King was at Santerem when the delinquents were brought to him; he inſtantly ordered them to be laid on pyre that was previouſly formed, contiguous to which he had a banquet prepared. Before the torch was kindled, and whilſt they agonized at every pore under the moſt lingering tortures, their hearts were cut out, one at his breaſt, the other at his back. Laſtly, the pyre was ſet on a blaze, in preſence of which he dined, whilſt they evaporated in flames.

Having

Having thus far appeaſed his inſatiable thirſt of revenge, he ordered his marriage with Dona Ignez to be publiſhed throughout the kingdom; then her body was taken out of the ſepulchre, covered with regal robes, and placed on a magnificent throne, around which his miniſters aſſembled, and did homage to their lawful Queen.

After this ceremony, her corpſe was tranſlated from Coimbra to Alcobaça, with a pomp hitherto unknown in the kingdom; though the diſtance between theſe two places is fifty-two miles, yet the road was lined on both ſides all the way, with people holding lighted tapers. The funeral was attended by all the Noblemen and Gentlemen in Portugal, dreſſed in long mourning cloaks; their Ladies alſo attended, dreſſed in white mourning veils.

The cloud which the above diſaſter caſt over the mind of Don Pedro was never totally diſperſed; and as he lived in a ſtate of celibacy the remainder of his life, agreeably to his vow, there was nothing to divert his attention from ruminating on the fate of his beloved ſpouſe. The impreſſion her death made on him was ſtrongly characteriſed, not only in the tortures he inflicted on her murderers, but alſo in all the acts of his adminiſtration, which, from their ſeverity, induced ſome to give him the appellation of Pedro the Cruel; by others he was called Pedro the Juſt: and, upon the whole, it appears that the laſt title moſt properly appertained to him.

It muſt be allowed, however, that he puniſhed ſome offences rather ſeverely, particularly in caſes of adultery. In all tranſgreſſions of this nature, his laws were more rigid than thoſe of Solon; as will appear by the following inſtances: He ordered a man to be hanged for having had communication with a woman previous to his marriage with her. Another, detected in the act of adultery, was, with his miſtreſs, committed to the flames. A Friar, who was diſcovered to be the father of a boy who ſtruck his nominal father, was put into a caſe formed of cork, and ſawed through the body.

Now, it is ſurpriſing that Don Pedro himſelf ſhould have been guilty of ſins ſimilar to thoſe for which he inflicted ſuch ignominious deaths on others. Yet ſuch is the fact: witneſs his amours with Dona Tereza Lorenza, by whom he had that illuſtrious character Don John, the founder of Batalha. (See page 50.)

Indeed, his manner of puniſhing other offences was leſs reprehenſible. To give an inſtance; a gentleman having borrowed ſome ſilver utenſils of a countryman, refuſed, after many ſolicitations, to return the ſame; upon which the lender, finding all other means ineffectual, appealed to the King, who made the gentleman not only return the goods to the owner, but alſo pay him nine

times

times their value, the penalty to which thieves were then subject; and further, made him responsible for the countryman's life.

The clergy, who hitherto could not be tried for alleged offences but by the ecclesiastical court, he rendered amenable to the common courts of justice, and punished them with death when their crimes were capital. When solicited once to revise the sentence of such criminals, and to refer it to a higher tribunal, (meaning that of the Pope,) he answered very calmly, "I shall most certainly send them "to the highest of all tribunals, *that of the Omnipotent* "*Being*."

To prevent all tedious litigations, and the baneful consequences attending them, he purged the nation of attornies, and limited the procedure of counsellors in such a manner, that a suit was determined in a few days. And when the Judge was found guilty of bribery, as was the case in one instance, he immediately ordered him to be hanged. In short, his inexorable justice, and indefatigable zeal to check the progress of vice, were such, that no consideration of rank, or fortune, or particular privileges, could screen the guilty from the sword of the law. The infinite service he rendered the country during the ten years he reigned, have left a lasting impression on the minds of the Portuguese. They have still a saying among them,

them, *that Providence either ſhould not have ſent Pedro, or elſe not have taken him away.*

It remains for us now to ſpeak a few words reſpecting the tragedies that have been formed from the Hiſtory of *Ignez de Caſtro.* Of the two we have in Engliſh, the one, named *Elvira,* was copied from the French of *M. de la Motte.* The other is named *Inez de Caſtro*; and was publiſhed in the year one thouſand ſix hundred and ninety-ſix. As the public are already well acquainted with the merits of theſe two, we ſhall notice only thoſe written in the Portugueſe, Spaniſh, and French languages. And as theſe are not, perhaps, generally known among us, we ſhall give a few parallel extracts from each; by which the reader, who is acquainted with theſe languages, may be enabled to form ſome idea of their reſpective merits, and of the ſtate of the drama in the above nations. The ſcene to which the following extracts allude, is that wherein *Ignez,* accompanied by her two children, is ſupplicating the King for mercy the moment before ſhe is murdered.

---

From

*From the* PORTUGUESE *of* NICOLA LUIS.

*Ignez.* Piedade, Senhor,
*Rei.* Como poſſo livrar-te do caſtigo,
Se todo hum Reino tens por inimigo.
*Ignez.* Oh mizera de mim! filhos amados,
Eſpelho em que os meus olhos ſe revião!
* * * * * * *
*Aff.* Se accazo não tem dó de minha mãi,
Entaõ naõ quero ſer já ſeu amigo.
*Rei.* Naõ ha remedio, os filhos lhe tirai.
*Alv. e Egas.* Vinde, infantes.
*Aff.* Deixai-me vós tambem,
Se naõ, hei de dizello a meu pai,
Que vos ha de matar com huma eſpada.
*Ignez.* Meu filhos me lavais: oh deſgraçada,
Naõ me mateis, Senhor, por tantas vezes,
Tornai eſſas reliquias aos meus braços.
Mas ai! que intenta a força da crueldade
Partir-me a coraçaõ em mil pedaços.
*Rei.* Jâ he muito eaforçar a tolerancia!
Opprimido, ai de mim de mortal ancia
Me ſinto em mal taõ forte.
Egas, Alvaro, oh Ceos! ficai com ella,
Que naõ me atrevo a vera ſua morte.
*Ignez.* Com eſtes inimigos deſhumanos
Me deixais! que rigor! ſoltai tirannos
Soltai os meus infantes: Luzes minhas,
A abraçar-me tornai, neſtes retiros.
Em voſſos lindos roſtos,
Recebei os meus ultimos ſuſpiros:
Mas já falta o valor, ós juſtos Ceos!

*Rei.* Vinde, meus Netos.

*pega nos meninos.*

*Aff.* Minha Mai, a Deos,
Que por força nos leva noſſo Avó.

*Ignez.* Ah! meus ternos amores minha glorias,
Quando ſoubereis ter mais ſentimentos,
Funeſtas vos ſeraõ minhas memórias.
E vós ingrato á propria humanidade,
Que a vida me tirais na flor da idade,
Vede que apello da mortal ſentença
Para aquelle Supremo Tribunal
Onde recto ſe julga o bem, e o mal:
Vade que - - - mas ai triſte! a luz do dia
Aos meus alhos ſe vai eſcurecendo.
Treme o pè mal ſeguro - - - e da agonia
Me vai já ſoffocando o horror tremendos
Filhos, Filhos, eu morro! Pedro, Eſpozo!
Onde eſtás, que em martirio taõ penozo,
Naõ vens a ſoccorrer me, ah homicida,
O furor eſcuzais, que eſtou ſem vida.

*From the* SPANISH *of* VELEZ DE GUEVARA.

*Ines.* A mis hijos me quitais?
Rey Don Alonſo, Senor;
Porque me quereis quitar
La vida de tantas vezes?
Advertid, Senor mirad,
Que el coraçon a pedaços
Dividio me arancais.

*Rey.* Levaldos, Alvar Gonçalez.

*Ines.* Hijos mios, donde vais?
Donde vais ſin vueſtra madre?

Falta

Falta en los hombres piedad
Adonde vais luzes mais?
Como, que aſſi me dexais
En el mayor deſconſuelo
En manos de la crueldad.

*Nino Alons.* Conſuelate madre mia,
Y a Dios de puedas quedar,
Que vamos con nueſtro abuelo,
Y no querrá hazernas mal.

*Ines.* Poſſible es, Senor, Rey mio,
Padre, que anſi me cerreis
La puerta para el perdon?
* * * * *
Como, Senor? vos os vais
Y a Alvar Gonçalez, y a Coello
Inhumanos me entregais?
Hijos, hijos de mi vida,
Dexad me los abraçar;
Alonſo, mi vida hijo,
Dionis, a mores, tornad,
Tornad a ver vueſtra madre:
Pedro mio, donde eſtas
Que anſi te olvidas de mi?
Poſſible es que en tanto mal
Me falta tu viſta, eſpoſo?
Quien te pudiera aviſar
Del peligro en que afligida
Dona Ines tu eſpoſa eſta.

From

*From the* FRENCH *of* M. DE LA MOTTE.

*Inés.* Eh bien, Seigneur, ſuivez vos barbares maximes;
On vous amene encor de nouvelles victimes.
Immolez ſans remords, & pour nous punir mieux,
Ces gages d'un himen ſi coupable à vos yeux.
Ils ignorent le ſang dont le Ciel les fit naitre:
Par l'arrêt de leur mort faites-les reconnoître:
Conſommez votre ouvrage; & que les mêmes coups
Rejoignent les enfans, & la femme & l'époux.
*Alphonſo.* Que vois-je! & quels diſcours! que d'horreurs j'enviſage!
*Inés.* Seigneur, du deſeſpoir, pardonnez le langage.
Tous deux à votre trône ont des droits ſolemnels.
Embraſſez, mez enfans, ces genoux paternels.
D'un œil compatiſſant, regardez l'un & l'autre;
N'y voiez point mon ſang, n'y voiez que le votre.
Pourriez-vous refuſer à leur pleurs, à leurs cris
La grace d'un héros, leur pere & votre fils?
Puiſque la loi trahie éxige une victime,
Mon ſang eſt prêt, Seigneur, pour expier mon crime.
Epuiſez ſur moi ſeule un ſévére couroux;
Mais cachez quelque tems mon ſort à mon époux;
Il mourroit de douleur; & je me flate encore,
De mériter de vous ce ſecret que j'implore.

The

The Reader will not be a little ſurpriſed on comparing the preceding paſſages, to find how inferior the French Writer is to the Portugueſe or the Spaniard. Both *Luis* and *Guevara* expreſs the natural feelings of the fair victim, and the poignant anguiſh which overwhelm her, from the apprehenſion of being deprived of her children, her lover, and her life. *De la Motte*, on the contrary, gives us the idea of a daring heroine, regardleſs of all theſe endearing conſiderations. The two former have very judiciouſly preſerved the ſpirit of the beautiful Epiſode of *Camoens*; on which Voltaire has the following remark: *Il y a peu d'endroits dans Virgile plus attendriſſants & mieux ecrits* ———. There are few parts in Virgil more tender, or better written. Connected, therefore, as that Epiſode is with our ſubject, we ſhall add the following extracts from it, as tranſlated by Mr. Mickle:

Dragg'd from her bower by murderous ruffian hands,
Before the frowning King fair Inez ſtands;
Her tears of artleſs innocence, her air
So mild, ſo lovely, and her face ſo fair,
Mov'd the ſtern Monarch; when with eager zeal
Her fierce deſtroyers urg'd the public weal;
Dread rage again the tyrant's ſoul poſſeſt,
And his dark brow his cruel thoughts confeſt;
O'er her fair face a ſudden paleneſs ſpread,
Her throbbing heart with generous anguiſh bled,
Her beauteous eyes in trembling tear-drops drown'd,
To heaven ſhe lifted, but her hands were bound;

Then on her infants turn'd the piteous glance,
The look of bleeding woe; the babes advance.

The lovely captive thus: —— O Monarch, hear,
If e'er to thee the name of man was dear,
If prowling tygers, or the wolf's wild brood,
Inſpir'd by Nature with the luſt of blood,
Have yet been mov'd the weeping babe to ſpare,
Nor left, but tended with a nurſe's care;
As Rome's great founders to the world were given;
Shalt thou, who wear'ſt the ſacred ſtamp of Heaven,
The human form divine, ſhalt thou deny
That aid, that pity, which e'en beaſts ſupply?
Oh, that thy heart were, as thy looks declare,
Of human mould, ſuperfluous were my prayer;
Thou could'ſt not then a helpleſs damſel ſlay,
Whoſe ſole offence in fond affection lay.
Ah, let my woes, unconſcious of a crime,
Procure mine exile to ſome barbarous clime:
Give me to wander o'er the burning plains
Of Lybia's deſarts, or the wild domains
Of Scythia's ſnow-clad rocks and frozen ſhore;
There let me, hopeleſs of return, deplore
Where ghaſtly horror fills the dreary vale,
Where ſhrieks and howlings die on every gale,
The lions roaring, and the tygers yell,
There with mine infant race conſign'd to dwell;
There let me try that piety to find,
In vain by me implor'd from human kind:
There in ſome dreary cavern's rocky womb,
Amid the horrors of ſepulchral gloom,
For him whoſe love I mourn, my love ſhall glow
The ſigh ſhall murmur and the tear ſhall flow.

In tears ſhe utter'd—as the frozen ſnow
Touch'd by the Spring's mild ray, begins to flow;
So juſt began to melt his ſtubborn ſoul,
As mild-ray'd Pity o'er the tyrant ſtole;
But Deſtiny forbade: with eager zeal,
Again pretended for the public weal,
Her fierce accuſers urged her ſpeedy doom;
Again dark rage diffuſed its horrid gloom
O'er ſtern Alonzo's brow: ſwift at the ſign,
Their ſwords unſheath'd around her brandiſh'd ſhine;
O foul diſgrace, of knighthood laſting ſtain,
By men of arms an helpleſs lady ſlain!

—— Inez, while her eyes to Heaven appeal,
Reſigns her boſom to the murdering ſteel:
That ſnowy neck, whoſe matchleſs form ſuſtain'd
The lovelieſt face, where all the Graces reign'd,
That ſnowy neck was ſtain'd with ſpouting gore,
Another ſword her lovely boſom tore.
The flowers that gliſten'd with her tears bedew'd,
Now ſhrunk and languiſh'd, with her blood imbrew'd,
As when a roſe erewhile of bloom ſo gay,
Thrown from the careleſs virgin's breaſt away,
Lies faded on the plain, the living red,
The ſnowy white, and all its fragrance fled;
So from her cheeks the roſes dy'd away,
And pale in death the beauteous Inez lay:
With dreadful ſmiles, and crimſon'd with her blood,
Round the wan victim the ſtern murderers ſtood.

O Sun, couldſt thou ſo foul a crime behold,
Nor veil thine head in darkneſs, as of old,
A ſudden night unwonted horror caſt
O'er that dire banquet, where the ſires repaſt

The

The son's torn limbs supplied! — yet you, ye vales!
Ye distant forests, and ye flowery dales!
When pale and sinking to the dreadful fall,
You heard her quivering lips on Pedro call;
Your faithful echoes caught the parting sound,
And Pedro! Pedro! mournful, sigh'd around.

*Lusiad*, book iii.

---

On the twenty-second of June I set out for Lisbon, accompanied by a muleteer. The evening before my departure I was visited by the Reverend Abbot-general and several of the Superiors of the Convent; the former sent me a present of sweet-meats and scented soap, curiously made up in boxes by Nuns of the Bernardine order.

Nothing occurred on our journey the first day worthy of noting; the country was tolerable, the soil rich and pretty well cultivated, but the accommodations at the inns were as indifferent as usual; yet the masters of these miserable hovels think them palaces, in comparison to the inns in the other parts of the country.

*January* 23. We met a number of peasants employed in making roads, the margins of which were planted with olive trees, whose produce are to be applied to the keeping of the roads in repair. Spheric sun-dials and cisterns are

are erected at ſtated intervals for the accommodation of travellers.

The manners and opulence of the capital had a viſible effect on the inhabitants in proportion as we advanced. About one o'clock we arrived at Villa Franca, quite exhauſted from the ſcorching rays of the ſun, to which we had been expoſed ſince five o'clock in the morning. It was with difficulty we could get any refreſhment, as all the inhabitants of the village were gone to ſleep.

At five o'clock we embarked in a large paſſage-boat, and ſailed down the Tagus towards Liſbon. There were about fifty paſſengers on board, divided into two claſſes; the common people occupied the hold, the reſt took their ſeats at the ſtern. About ſeven o'clock one of the boatmen gave the compline ſignal, and all returned thanks to the Lord in a ſhort prayer.

Among thoſe who ſat at the ſtern of the boat was a man, who had apparently miſtaken his rank, if one may judge by his dreſs; he was barefoot, wore a long beard, and a pilgrim's ſcapulet over the remains of a Perſian habit: he was about thirty-ſix years of age, of a middling ſtature, well proportioned, of a ſwarthy complexion. I found by his language that he was a Spaniard. There was ſomething in his manners that intereſted me very much; his countenance was placid, and

 beſpoke

beſpoke a firmneſs of mind, ſuch as we admire in a virtuous man ſtruggling with misfortune. I muſt confeſs that he excited at once my pity and eſteem; and if Fate had not placed my lot ſo much on a level with his own, he ſhould not want a cloak to cover him, nor a cruſade in his pouch.

When we arrived at Liſbon, I requeſted he would permit me to pay his paſſage; he thanked me, ſaying, "I "have change ſufficient for that purpoſe; it is true, my "apparel beſpeaks poverty, (looking at his bare feet,) "therefore you may be ſurpriſed that I had the preſumption to take my ſeat in your company; but the true "Caſtilian thinks himſelf degraded or honoured, not by "his garb but his actions."

## LISBON.

Notwithſtanding the city of Liſbon is the conſtant reſort of merchants and travellers from every part of the globe, yet it ſeems extraordinary that hitherto we have not been favoured with any ſatisfactory account of its arts, antiquity, police, or public buildings. I ſhall not attempt to ſupply theſe points; the utmoſt I can promiſe are a few curſory remarks on ſuch objects as came within the narrow ſphere of my obſervation, during a reſidence of ten months in that city.

Liſbon, the capital of Portugal, is ſeated upon the delightful banks of the Tagus, in the fruitful province of Eſtremadura; latitude 38° 48′. Its diſtance from the bar, where the Atlantic Ocean and the river form a junction, is about ſeven miles. The harbour is very deep and capacious, preſenting, to a mind devoted to commerce, one of the fineſt proſpects imaginable, as it is conſtantly crowded with ſhips of various nations.

As we approach the capital, the churches, convents, caſtles, villas, and gardens on the North-weſt ſide, have a grand and beautiful appearance; but the ideas of magnificence they excite at a diſtance, are greatly diminiſhed upon a cloſer inſpection. The country on the South-eaſt

 ſide

ſide is alſo highly pictureſque, from its lofty mountains and high impending cliffs.

The attention is ſoon drawn from theſe ſcenes by the appearance of the city, which gradually aſcends from the verge of the river in all the magnificence of wealth and grandeur. The ſite is the moſt eligible imaginable for a Metropolis; towards the North-weſt it is ſheltered by a ridge of mountains, and opened towards the South-eaſt. The buildings are raiſed on ſeven hills, with their intermediate vallies; the greater part of which command a proſpect of the river, and of the country on the oppoſite ſide, called Alenteju; any diſadvantage, therefore, attending the inequality of the ground is compenſated by the beautiful proſpects its elevation afford, and its vicinity to the ſea renders it at once delightful and healthy. The narroweſt part of the river Tagus, oppoſite to the city, is computed at two miles Engliſh, and at the broadeſt part it is not leſs than nine. When we reflect on the advantages Portugal enjoys in point of commerce, from ſuch a magnificent river and commodious harbour, ſo happily ſituated for trading with the Eaſtern and Weſtern hemiſpheres, we cannot but wonder that Liſbon is not ſuperior in riches, magnitude, and population to any capital in Europe. Here follows an account of the ſhips of various nations which entered the port of Liſbon in the year one thouſand ſeven hundred and eighty-nine.

3 from

| Portugueſe Ships. | Names of Places. |
| --- | --- |
| 3 | from BENGAL. |
| 6 | —— MACAO. |
| 1 | —— GOA. |
| 2 | —— other ports of ASIA. |
| 12 | from all ASIA. |
| 23 | —— BAHIA. |
| 26 | —— MARANHAON. |
| 13 | —— PARA. |
| 2 | —— PARAIBA. |
| 1 | —— PENAIBA. |
| 33 | —— PERNAMBUCO. |
| 16 | —— RIO JANEIRO. |
| 1 | —— SANTOS. |
| 2 | —— CAPE VERD. |
| 117 | —— various ports of EUROPE. |
| 6 | Men of War. |
| 252 | Total number of PORTUGUESE Ships. |

| Foreign Ships. | |
| --- | --- |
| 75 | from AMERICA. |
| 4 | —— BERMUDE. |
| 24 | —— DENMARK. |
| 1 | —— GENEVA. |
| 81 | —— FRANCE. |
| 10 | —— HAMBURGH. |
| 22 | —— SPAIN. |
| 64 | —— HOLLAND, including ſix Men of War. |
| 6 | —— TRIEST and OSTEND. |
| 5 | —— LUBEC. |

Carried over 292

| Foreign Ships. | | Names of Places. |
|---|---|---|
| Brought over 292 | | |
| 7 | from | the KING of PRUSSIA's Dominions. |
| 1 | —— | RUSSIA. |
| 7 | —— | RAGUSA. |
| 2 | —— | SWEDEN. |
| 12 | —— | VENICE, |
| 319 | —— | GREAT BRITAIN and IRELAND, including 29 Packets and 4 Men of War. |
| 640 | | Total number of Foreign Ships. |

## *Origin and Progreſs of Liſbon.*

The origin of Liſbon, like that of many other cities, is involved in obſcurity, though many Writers have attempted to develope it, among whom are not a few who do not, perhaps, deſerve to be called Antiquaries; for the true Antiquary, like the Mathematician, will not proceed farther in his inveſtigation than he is authorized by the light of connecting facts and concluſive reaſoning. Some of the above Writers, however, have had the courage to proceed in the dark as far as the deluge; but, unfortunately, the more they travel, the farther they appear to leave the truth behind.

The opinion that moſt generally obtains is, that Liſbon was founded by Ulyſſes after the deſtruction of Troy, and received

received his name *. However that was, there is no doubt but a ſiuation ſo inviting muſt have been peopled very early. Its firſt inhabitants, according to Pliny, were the ancient Turtuleans, from whom originated the modern Turtuleans of Andaluſia, a brave and politic people, as the Celtic and Phœnician tribes experienced in all their conteſts againſt them in Spain. Among the other nations that ſubdued Luſitania, the Romans are ſuppoſed to have peopled Liſbon ſhortly after they conquered the Carthaginians. It appears that Julius Cæſar made himſelf maſter of it, and diſtinguiſhed it by the title of *Felicitas Juliana*, as may be collected from various inſcriptions found in that city, which are publiſhed in *Cunha*'s Eccleſiaſtical Hiſtory of Liſbon.

* Luſus, the loved companion of the God,
In Spain's fair boſom fixt his laſt abode,
Our kingdom founded, and illuſtrious reign'd,
In thoſe fair lawns, the bleſt Elyſium feign'd,
Where winding oft the Guadiana roves,
And Douro murmurs through the flowery groves.
Here with his bones he left his deathleſs fame,
And Luſitania's clime ſhall ever bear his name.
That other chief th' embroider'd ſilk diſplays,
Toſt o'er the deep whole years of weary days,
On Tago's banks at laſt his vows he paid:
To Wiſdom's Godlike power, the Jove-born maid,
Who fired his lips with eloquence divine,
On Tago's banks he reared the hallowed ſhrine:
*Ulyſſes* he, though fated to deſtroy
On Aſian ground the Heaven-built towers of Troy,
On Europe's ſtrand, more grateful to the ſkies,
He bade th' eternal walls of Liſboa riſe. *Luſiad*, book viii.

About

About the year of our Lord four hundred and nine, the dominion of the Romans in Lusitania yielded to the invasion of the Alans, Suevi, and Vandals; and these again, in their turn, in the year seven hundred and sixteen, submitted to the superior power of the Arabians who inhabited Spain. The latter changed the name of the capital, which till then was called *Ulisipo*, or *Lispo*, to *Lisiboa*; because, says Castro, that in the Moorish alphabet the letter P is not used. Hence comes the word *Lisboa*, which we translate Lisbon.

The first check given to the Arabian power in Portugal was by Don Alfonso the Chaste, King of Galicia and Asturia; who, with the assistance of Charlemain, in the year seven hundred and ninety-eight, invaded Portugal and invested Lisbon. The besieged, after a resolute resistance, were compelled to yield to the arms of the Christian powers. During a period of near three hundred years, the Christians and Moors alternately retained a transitory possession of it, till at length the latter became tributary to Alfonso the Sixth of Castile, in the year one thousand and ninety-three.

In this state of subjection they continued under Count Henry, the source of the Portuguese monarchy, but revolted again under his successor Alfonso Henrique, the first Christian King of Portugal. This Prince made many attempts to reduce Lisbon, but in vain. Being one day on the

the mountain of Centra he diſcovered a fleet, conſiſting, of near two hundred ſail of Engliſh, French, and Flemings, under the command of *William Long Eſpe*, making towards the Tagus. They were deſtined for the Holy Land, but had touched here to water, and to repair the damages they received at ſea. The King made propoſals to them to aid him in capturing the city; to which they acceded; and the troops on board, amounting to fourteen thouſand, were drawn up with the Portugueſe forces before the city. During five months the ſiege continued with great ſlaughter on both ſides, when the confederate troops, on St. Urſala's Day, made a deſperate aſſault, and carried the city ſword in hand. According to Farria, the number of Infidels ſlain on this day amounted to two hundred thouſand.

The moſt authentic account of that ſiege which, perhaps, has yet appeared, is contained in a letter written in the Latin tongue, in one thouſand one hundred and forty-ſeven, by a perſon of diſtinction named Arnulfo, who was on board the combined fleet, to the Biſhop of Terona in France. It was diſcovered among the manuſcripts in the library of the Aquitenian Abbots in France, and is publiſhed in the collection of Martene and Durand, *tom.* i. *Veterum Monumentorum*, printed at Paris in the year one thouſand ſeven hundred and twenty-four. As that letter, perhaps, has not been hitherto publiſhed in our language, we ſhall attempt to give a tranſlation of it, with the addition

dition of Notes, for the satisfaction of the curious in the mode of attack and defence practised in ancient times.

—— "On the Monday after Whitsuntide we entered the bar of the river Douro, and anchored opposite to Oporto. The Bishop of this city, as if anticipating the orders of his King, was rejoiced at our arrival. Here we stayed eleven days, waiting for the arrival of *Count Arnoldo de Ardescot*, and *Christian* the *Constable*, who had been separated from us in a storm; during this time we were plentifully supplied with provision and delicacies of all kinds through the munificence of the Prince.

"As soon as the Count and the Constable arrived, we proceeded on our voyage; in two days we reached the Tagus, on the vigils of the Apostles St. Peter and St. Paul, and anchored before Lisbon. This city, which, according to the tradition handed down to us by the Saracenic Historians, was built by Ulysses after the destruction of Troy, is surrounded with walls of admirable construction, and has several towers upon a mountain impregnable to any human force.

"The moment we landed we began to erect our tents, and, with the Divine assistance, took the suburbs of the city on the first of July. After various assaults against the walls, not without great loss on both sides, we were occupied until the first of August in preparing machines.

" Towards the river we erected two formidable towers; one at the East, in which the Flemings were posted; the other at the West, of which the English took possession. We likewise formed four bridges of our ships; so that we had six different posts to attack the enemy.

" On the day of the invention of the Protomartyr St. Stephen we began to advance and batter with our engines and ships; but being repulsed, not only with adverse winds, but also with the *Magnellis* * of the enemy, we retreated with some loss. Whilst our men were actively engaged with the Saracens, the English, with less circumspection, guarded their tower, which unfortunately was set on fire, and they were not able to extinguish the flames.

" Shortly after this we began to batter the walls with our machines, which the Moors no sooner beheld, than they poured forth oleagenous fire †, which almost destroyed

* *Magnellis.*——Perhaps these were engines similar to those which Du Cange calls *Mangonellus:*—*Mangonellus diminutivum, a mangana hoc est, minor machina jaculatoria. De Mezeray*, in his Treatise upon ancient Sieges, supposes the *Mangonellus*, or *Mangonas*, to be a general term for any engines used in throwing stones and darts; of which there were different kinds; as the *matafunda, petrary, turbuchet, warwalf*, and *mangana*, all constructed upon a principle somewhat similar to that of the *balista*.

† *Oleagenous fire.*——Of the artificial fire used in ancient sieges we have many accounts transmitted to us, but the manner in which it was prepared is not clearly expressed. The *Malleoli* mentioned by Vitruvius, book x. c. 13. are supposed to have been instruments filled with artificial fire, similar to that which was afterwards called the Greek wildfire. The Turks made

ſtroyed them. They likewiſe made conſiderable havoc among us with their arrows and *magnellis*. Our people were much diſheartened from the wreck of the apparatus * and the fall of their companions; yet, truſting to the mercy of God, they reſumed their courage, and ſet about repairing the engines.

"In the mean time the beſieged were greatly diſtreſſed for proviſions; not but ſome had abundance, yet they withheld it from the poorer claſs of the citizens in ſuch a manner, that numbers of them died of hunger. Some, to preſerve their lives, were conſtrained to eat cats and dogs; a great part threw themſelves on the mercy of the Chriſtians, and received the ſacrament of baptiſm, whilſt others were ſent to the walls, with their hands cut off, and ſtoned to death by their companions. Many other direful and ſucceſsful ſcenes incident to war were witneſſed by us here, which, to avoid prolixity, we ſhall not detail.

made uſe of this fire in their wars with the cruſadors, which they emitted from a machine called *Petrary*. It is reported to have burnt ſo intenſely, that it conſumed even flint and iron, and could not be extinguiſhed but by a mixture of vinegar, ſand, and urine. Father Daniel ſays, that Philip Auguſtus, King of France, brought a quantity of this fire ready prepared from Acre, which he uſed at the ſiege of Dieppe, for burning the Engliſh veſſels then in the harbour.

* *Wreck of the apparatus.*——The ancients, in order to guard the *teſtudines* uſed in filling ditches, covered the planks laid over the beams with ſlender green twigs, cloſely interwoven; and over theſe they laid doubled raw hides, ſewed together, and ſtuffed either with ſea-weeds, or elſe with ſtraw macerated in vinegar, by which means they reſiſted the attacks of the baliſtæ and fire-brands.

*Vide Vitr.* book x. c. 20.

"On

" On the day of the Nativity of the bleſſed Virgin Mary, an Italian of great ingenuity, a native of Piſa, began to conſtruct a lofty tower of wood, in the place where the former one was deſtroyed, in which the Engliſh had been poſted. This important work was completed about the middle of October, through the bounty of the King and the exertions of the armies. With equal exertions another engineer, aſſiſted by many hands, were occupied in making excavations, in order to undermine the wall of the fortreſs. The Moors, apprehenſive of theſe operations, ſallied out privately, and gave us battle over the mine, from three o'clock in the morning until the afternoon on the Feſtival of St. Michael.

" During this time we were warmly engaged with the Infidels, whilſt our archers ſo obſtructed their retreat, that few or none of them eſcaped without being wounded. Afterwards our people worked by day and night in the mines, which were finiſhed and propped with wood at the appointed day on which the tower was to have been brought up, wherein the King in perſon, with the Engliſh troops, were to attack the walls. On the night of the Abbot St. Gallo the mine was ſet on fire, and when the wood-work was conſumed *, the wall gave way, and made an opening of about two hundred feet in length.

" The

* *When the wood-work was conſumed.*— The props and planks uſed in mines of this ſort for ſupporting the incumbent earth, were generally prepared with combuſtible matter, ſuch as pitch, tar, oil, and alſo dry faggots thrown looſely about; ſo that as

"The alarm excited by the crash roused our people, they fled to arms, and with shouts rushed forward to the breach, expecting that the guards, who were posted on the walls, would have fled: But the enemy advanced in crowds to defend that part which was difficult to force, as being on the declivity of a mountain. The contest continued from midnight till nine o'clock the next day, when our men, fatigued and wounded, withdrew for a while, till the tower was brought to bear; now the enemy was distracted.

"The tower, manned with valiant troops, being drawn up close to the wall, the signal was made; our people, with astonishing resolution, charged the enemy in every part at the same time. The Lorenese fought in the breach. Those who were engaged in company with the King in the tower, harassed with the *magnellis* of the Saracens, were less successful; the moors sallied out, and would certainly have destroyed the tower, had not some of our men come up and repulsed them.

"As soon as we had intimation of their perilous situation, some of our best battalions hastened to the defence of the tower, that our hopes might not be frustrated. But

* as soon as the fire was applied, the whole apparatus was instantly in a blaze. The centres being thus consumed, the earth fell in, and likewise such parts of the wall as were immediately over it. We may readily conceive, that these mines must have been pretty broad, or else the superstructure would stand independent of the centres.

when

when the Saracens beheld the Lorenese and Flemings furiously mounting the rampart of the tower, they became so terrified, that they threw down their arms, and offered to shake hands, as a signal of peace, which they now besought.

"In consequence of this, the Alcaide, or Prince of the town, surrendered, and agreed that our army should take possession of the stores, together with all the gold and silver which he possessed; and that the city, with its inhabitants, and all the land which appertained to it, should be delivered up to Alfonso. Thus concluded this memorable siege, not human, but divine, on the Festival of the Eleven Thousand Virgins, with the loss of two hundred thousand and five hundred Moors *."

* "The conquest of Lisbon was of the utmost importance to the infant monarchy. It is one of the finest ports in the world, and before the invention of cannon was of great strength. The old Moorish wall was flanked by seventy-seven towers, was about six miles in length and fourteen in circumference. When besieged by Don Alonzo, according to some, it was garrisoned by an army of 200,000 men. This, not to say impossible, is highly incredible. That it was strong, however, and well garrisoned is certain. It is also certain that Alonzo owed the conquest of it to a fleet of adventurers, who were going to the Holy Land, the greatest part of whom were English. One *Udal ap Rhys*, in his Tour through Portugal, says, that Alonzo gave them *Almada*, on the side of the Tagus opposite to Lisbon, and that *Villa Franca* was peopled by them, which they called *Cornualla*, either in honour of their native country, or from the rich meadows in its neighbourhood, where immense herds of cattle are kept, as in the English Cornwall." *Lusiad*, p. 104. in Note.

The

The above victory is thus celebrated by Camoens:

——— famed Lisboa, whose embattled wall
Rose by the hand that wrought proud Ilion's fall;
Thou queen of cities whom the seas obey,
Thy dreaded ramparts own'd the hero's sway.
Far from the North a warlike navy bore,
From Elbe, from Rhine, and Albion's misty shore,
To rescue Salem's long polluted shrine;
Their force to great Alonzo's force they join:
Before Ulysses' walls the navy rides,
The joyful Tagus laves their pitchy sides.
Five times the moon her empty horns conceal'd,
Five times her broad effulgence shone reveal'd,
When, wrapt in clouds of dust, her mural pride
Falls thundering,—black the smoking breach yawns wide.
*    *    *    *    *

Thus fell the city, whose unconquer'd towers *
Defy'd of old the banded Gothic powers,
Whose harden'd nerves in rigorous climates train'd,
The savage courage of their souls sustain'd;
Before whose sword the sons of Ebro fled,
And Tagus trembled in his oozy bed. *Lusiad*, book iii.

* *Unconquer'd towers.*—"This assertion of Camoen's is not without foundation, for it was by treachery that Herminetic, the Goth, got possession of Lisbon."

*On the present State of Lisbon.*

Of the population of this city no exact account has been recently published, and the rapid increase of its inhabitants of late years must render any calculation of that nature very uncertain. In the year one thousand seven hundred and eighty, the forty parishes into which Lisbon is divided, were found to contain thirty-three thousand seven hundred and sixty-four houses; and in the year one thousand seven hundred and ninety, they amounted to thirty-eight thousand one hundred and two. Hence it appears to have increased four thousand three hundred and thirty-eight houses in the course of those ten years. Now, if we estimate each house, on an average, at six persons, which, perhaps, is within the truth, the population in the year one thousand seven hundred and ninety was two hundred and twenty-eight thousand six hundred and twelve. To these are to be added the religious of both sexes, with their attendants, who dwell in convents and monasteries, the soldiery, the professors and students of seminaries of education, and such of the Galician labourers as have no fixed dwelling; their aggregate amount, if my information be correct, is not very short of twelve thousand. Then, according to this statement, the population of Liſbon exceeds two hundred and forty thouſand.

From the magnitude of the city we ſhould be induced to ſuppoſe that its population was conſiderably more than above ſtated; for it is computed to be four miles long by one and a half broad, as may be inferred from the plan, Plate IV. But many of the houſes are accompanied with large gardens, and ſuch as have not theſe conveniencies are, in general, laid out upon a large ſcale, on account of the heat of the climate.

The fatal effects of the earthquake of one thouſand ſeven hundred and fifty-five are ſtill viſible in many parts of the city, and never fail to impreſs every ſpectator with an awful remembrance of that melancholy diſaſter; according to the moſt accurate accounts, there were not leſs than twenty-four thouſand fell victims to it. The old inhabitants are conſtantly relating the dreadful ſcenes with which it was attended; it is the epoch whence they date all modern events; and they ſtartle at every ſhock that has the moſt diſtant reſemblance to it. They are ſenſible, however, of the advantages the city now derives from the deſtruction of the ancient contracted lanes and unhealthy habitations. The ſevereſt viſitations of Divine Providence are often attended with manifold bleſſings, as they call forth the exertion of men, and impel them to ſeek reſources which otherwiſe would not be thought of. The Portugueſe have availed themſelves of this alternative, and, like the Engliſh, after the deſtructive fire of one thouſand ſix hundred and ſixty-ſix, they have turned the temporary evil into a permanent good.

All the new ſtreets erected in Liſbon, in the place of the old, are capacious, regular, and well paved, with convenient path-ways for foot-paſſengers, as in the ſtreets of London. The houſes are lofty, uniform, and ſtrong. (See plate V.) The manner of building them is rather ſingular: the carpenter is the firſt employed; when he has raiſed the ſkeleton of frame-work, the maſon is then employed to fill up the interſtices with rubble-ſtone and brick. The reaſon they aſſign for building in this manner is, that the concatenation of the walls with the wood-work contributes to reſiſt the ſlight concuſſions of earthquakes with which this city is conſtantly viſited.

The firſt ſtory of each dwelling-houſe, when not converted into a ſhop, is a magazine for merchandize of one kind or other. The merchants uſually keep their coaches in the halls, and ſometimes they anſwer for both coach-houſe and ſtable.

Notwithſtanding the excellent building-materials with which the diſtrict abounds, the rearing of a houſe here coſts more than one of the ſame dimenſions in London.

 This,

This, in a great meaſure, is owing to the want of proper machines for tranſporting the materials, and of convenient tools to facilitate the work; and yet it is extraordinary with what dexterity the people ſupply the want of theſe apparatus.

Of a houſe four ſtories high the attic is the pleaſanteſt floor; it is often furniſhed with a balcony, elegantly ornamented with rails of iron gilt, and furniſhed with an awning of ſilk or linen, under which the ladies ſit on cuſhions during the hot weather, employing their time in reading, ſewing, or caſting love-ſignals in the ſilent language of the fingers; a method of conveying their ideas, which they have reduced to an alphabetic ſyſtem.

The principal apartments of many of the nobility and merchants are furniſhed in a magnificent manner. The manufactures of India and of China are more common in their houſes than thoſe of Europe. In the diſtribution of the apartments, coolneſs and ventilation are conſulted, in preference to warmth. Here grates and chimney-pieces are almoſt unknown; in Winter, a warm cloak is the common ſubſtitute for a fire. The hall-doors are generally left open, and bells ſupply the place of knockers.

In point of cleanlineſs, Liſbon is no longer a ſubject of animadverſion for ſtrangers; but all is not yet done; it ſtill wants common ſewers, pipe-water, and *chambres des aiſances.*

There is no court-end of the town here, nor a houſe that will let to advantage merely on account of its ſituation. One of the principal modern ſtreets is chiefly inhabited by copper-ſmiths and tin-men.

The merchants and wealthy ſhop-keepers chiefly dwell in the neighbourhood of the Royal Exchange, near their warehouſes. The *Ribeira Velha* is the principal mart of traffic: here are ſome warehouſes belonging to the Hamburgh merchants, that have a very formidable appearance; the firſt I ſaw of theſe I took for a military magazine; but, on a cloſer inſpection, I found that the balls which were piled up in heaps were not cannon-balls, but ſimple cheeſes; each was about the ſize of a thirty-two-pounder, and very nearly as hard. They are ſaid to import annually into Liſbon ſixty thouſand of theſe bullets.

### *Praça do Comercio.*

The new *Square*, or *Praça do Comercio*, is ſix hundred and fifteen feet long, by five hundred and fifty feet broad, bounded on three ſides by buildings, and on one ſide by the Tagus. The North wing is occupied by the Royal Exchange and Cuſtom-houſe; whereof we here preſent a view, a view, (Plate VI.) as taken from on board a veſſel on the Tagus. A continued arcade extends the whole length of the wing, which affords communication with the ſeveral offices and ſtores. In the diſtribution of theſe apartments, both externally and internally, convenience and ſtrength are all the architect appears to have had in view, and indeed very little more is neceſſary for any Cuſtom-houſe. Here are no palaces for commiſſioners to dwell in, nor dark cells for clerks to write in, nor cellars floating with water to hold dry goods; whoever wiſhes for theſe *improvements*, will find them, and a great deal more, in the new Cuſtom-houſe of Dublin.

## *Equeſtrian Statue of Joſeph* I.

In the centre of the above ſquare is an Equeſtrian Statue, of bronze, of Joſeph the Firſt; a work of no inconſiderable merit, and the only one of the kind that was ever erected to any of the Sovereigns of Portugal. The Marquis de Pombal was the promoter of this work; intending thereby to honour his Royal Maſter, and at the ſame time to add a ſprig of laurel to his own brow. The portrait of this miniſter, executed in bronze, was placed on the ſide of the pedeſtal, but it continued there no longer than he maintained his power; it was torn down immediately when he loſt his maſter and his place, by thoſe who a few days before paid homage to the original. We cannot but admire the indifference he evinced when informed

formed of this circumſtance: *I am glad of it*, ſaid he, *for it was not like me*.

When we conſider the humble ſtate of the arts in Portugal, and the difficulty of executing ſuch a magnificent Statue, we muſt allow that great praiſe is due to thoſe who had the conducting of it. The model was made by a ſculptor named Joaquim Machado de Caſtro, who alſo deſigned and executed the emblematic groups at the ſides of the pedeſtal. It is from the latter every artiſt and amateur will judge of the merits of this ſculptor, particularly the group at the North ſide, which muſt be allowed to poſſeſs great taſte, delicacy, and ſpirit.

The figure and the horſe are alſo very noble productions; but in caſts of this kind we muſt not look for excellence in the detail, as the delicate touches of the chiſel are always loſt in the foundry; if the general form and the maſſes will bear the teſt of criticiſm, we can expect no more, and in this reſpect De Caſtro has acquitted himſelf in a maſterly manner.

Nor has *Bartholomew de Coſta*, the founder of this Statue, been deficient of abilities, as far as related to his part; he caſt the whole in one piece, without failing even in a ſingle member; a circumſtance which, one excepted, has not, perhaps, occurred in any other work of the kind of equal magnitude, ſince the reſtoration of the art of caſting

caſting Equeſtrian Statues in bronze *. And yet I am not certain if this be not larger than the exception we allude to; namely, the Equeſtrian Statue of Louis the Fourteenth, in the *Place de Vendome* at Paris; which, if it ſtill exiſt, is twenty-one French feet in height, and was caſt in one piece by Balthazar Keller, a native of Zurich. But De Coſta not only caſt the above Statue, but alſo conveyed it from the foundry, and raiſed it on the lofty pedeſtal on which it ſtands.

The ſculptor and founder are both natives of Portugal; the latter has been honoured and rewarded for his ingenuity, by being promoted to the rank and pay of brigadier in the ſervice; and it is allowed by all who know him, that his talents do honour to that high rank. But Mechado de Caſtro, the ſculptor, who has an undoubted claim to the principal merit of the work, as the deſigner and modeller of it, is neglected and forgotten: indeed, there is not one Portugueſe in a thouſand who knows that he was the author of it; and though his talents entitle him to be ranked with the firſt artiſts of the age, he is ſcarcely known in his native country. It is true, that his Majeſty created him a Knight on that occaſion; but ſince then, he has been left to pine in obſcurity in an attic cell. A ſhort time before I left Liſbon, I was aſſured, from reſpectable

* *M. Boffrand*, if he were not the firſt who reſtored the art of caſting Equeſtrian Statues in one piece, contributed at leaſt very eſſentially, by his memoirs, towards the perfecting of that art.

authority,

authority, that he petitioned a gentleman high in office to have the floor of his wretched apartment repaired.

Portugal, like Ireland, is become celebrated for the manner in which at all times ſhe has treated her native ſons of diſtinguiſhed merit. We find in the annals of both nations men, whoſe works have enlightened ſucceeding generations, perſecuted, deſpiſed, and the rays of ſcience given to illumine mankind, expiring in a priſon or an hoſpital, like an exhauſted lamp. The great Prince Henry was reviled and ſcorned by thoſe who conſidered themſelves as the great men of his country, as Galileo was by the Italians, and looked upon as an Aquatic Knight Errant, whilſt (to ſpeak in the language of allegory) he was enlarging the boundaries of the univerſe. Admiral Pacheo, who aſtoniſhed the Eaſtern world with the greatneſs of his actions, and at his return to Liſbon received honours adequate to a triumph, was ſoon after caſt into priſon, loaded with chains; and though he was found innocent of the alleged miſdemeanors, he was left to ſubſiſt the remainder of his days upon charity. The fate of Magellen, Vernei, and Vieira are well known, and alſo that of Camoens, the Virgil of Portugal, who ended his days in an alms-houſe; and whilſt he was giving the laſt hand to his immortal numbers, lived on the pittance begged for him by his black ſervant in the ſtreets of Liſbon. We wiſh, for the honour of Portugal, that Machado de Caſtro may cloſe its catalogue of neglected talents.

*Cannon of Dio.*

The Cannon of Dio, ſo called on account of its being taken from the King of Cambaya, at the ſiege of Dio in India, was ſent to Portugal, with other trophies of victory, by Nuno de Cuna, about the year one thouſand five hundred and thirty-nine, and depoſited in the caſtle of St. Julian, at the entrance of the port of Liſbon. Here it remained till the above equeſtrian ſtatue was about to be caſt, when it was brought, with other pieces of braſs, to be melted for that purpoſe. There happened to reſide at this time at the court of Liſbon an Ambaſſador from Tunis, who, in examining this Cannon, chanced to caſt his eye on an Arabic inſcription on the breech of it; he immediately explained it to the Portugueſe interpreter, the Reverend Father de Souza; in conſequence of which, the Cannon was reſcued from the furnace, and depoſited in the foundry or armory at Liſbon. It is twenty-eight palmos long; that is, upwards of twenty feet Engliſh meaſure, and of a proportionable caliber. Annexed is a copy of the inſcription (A, Plate VII.), which, together with the Portugueſe interpretation of the ſame, I am indebted for to the friendſhip of the above Father; I ſhall give both exactly as he wrote them for me.

*Inſcripçaõ Arabe, que eſtá em huã Peça chamada de Dio; aqual ſe acha na Fundiçaõ: Com a traduçaõ da dita em Portuguez.*

*Portuguez. Lida, e traduzida, pelo Padre Fr. João de' Souza, Religiozo da 3ª Ordem da Penitencia da Provincia de Portugal.*

*Do Nosso Soberano Mahêy; Rei dos Reis do Seculo, Filho, da Nobre Senhora Rahân; Defensor da Lei Mahometica; Vencedor dos Táneos;* * *Expugnador, e destruîdor dos Ebaditas,* † *no memoravel dia da peléja, antes do Rei Sálib. Herdeiro do Rei Sulîman; Confidente em Deos; Pai da Patria, e das Sciencias; Rei de Madárchah.*

*Foi fundida a 5 do mêz de Zil Kâde, anno de 939 da Hegîra; que corresponde a 16 Janeiro de 1526.*

*Translation.*

A copy of an Arabic inscription, which is upon a Cannon brought from Dio, to be seen at the foundry at Lisbon, with a translation of the same in the Portuguese language; copied and translated by Father John de Souza, a Friar of the third Order of Penitentiaries of the Provincialship of Portugal.

From our Sovereign Mahêy; King of the Kings of the age, son of the noble Lady Rahân, Defender of the Ma-

* *Os Taneos, são huns Povos, que vivem junto a Ethcopia.*

† *Os Ebadítas, são certos Povos descendentes de Ismael; os quaes occupavão a Mesopotamia, e as margens do Rio Eufrate.*

 hommetan

hommetan Law, Conqueror of the Táneos *, Exterminator and Vanquisher of the Ebadîtas †, (on the day of the memorable battle with King Salib,) Heir to King Suliman, Confident of God, Father of his Country and of the Sciences, King of Madárchah.——This Cannon was cast on the 5th day of the month of Zil'Kâde, in the year 939 of the Hegîra, which corresponds with the 16th of January, A. D. 1526.

A copy of the inscription B, (Plate VII.) was also given to me, without a translation, by Father de Souza. The original, he informs me, is upon an ancient fountain near the castle of the town of Moura.

### *Roscio.*

The next square of any note in Lisbon is the *Roscio*; most of the houses are occupied by shop-keepers. Here the celebrated Inquisition is situated; a large empty building, now as silent as the Temple of Janus. Over the pediment, in the centre of the elevation, is a group of figures, representing Religion trampling on a prostrate heretic.

* The *Táneos* are a people who dwell near Ethiopia.

† The *Ebadîtas* are descendants of Ishmael; they dwell in Mesopotamia on the banks of the Euphrates.

In

In the month of March, one thouſand ſeven hundred and ninety, I was preſent here when three criminals, found guilty of burglary or aſſaſſination, were led to the ſquare to be executed, eſcorted by five battalions of infantry. The people, unaccuſtomed to ſcenes of this kind of late years, flocked in numbers to ſee the execution, but many of them had to repent their curioſity. One of the ſoldiers on guard happened to quarrel with a ſailor in the crowd; the guards on the oppoſite ſide, thinking it was an attempt to reſcue the criminals, attacked the mob with fixed bayonets, and in a few minutes the former remained maſters of the ſcene of action. Several people were dangerouſly wounded, and others, in the precipitancy of retreat, left ſome fragments of their apparel behind.

## *Public Walks and Amuſements.*

Contiguous to the Roſcio are the public Walks eſtabliſhed by the Marquis de Pombal, who was a great friend to the fair ſex, and as ſuch, endeavoured to aboliſh the reſtraint under which they have long been unjuſtly kept; for this purpoſe he planned theſe promenades, with a view to introduce a more general intercourſe between both ſexes. The walks are elegant, bordered with eſpaliers, and the intervals planted with trees and ſhrubberies. Yet the inſtitution does not appear to have produced that ſocial intercourſe to the extent the Marquis had in view. The inhabitants think, however, that the females enjoy more ſociety at preſent than at any former period, and that the jealouſy of the men, and the cauſes or ſuſpicions which gave riſe to it are diminiſhing every day.

There are two Theatres here for dramatic performances; on Sundays they are much crowded. I could perceive but few ladies among the audience, and theſe, with few exceptions, ſat, not promiſcuouſly in the company of the men, as in other theatres, but apart. The muſic was excellent, the dreſſes and ſcenery tolerable, the acting indifferent, or rather bad. Of late years no females are allowed to perform on the ſtage; hence, the men are obliged to aſſume the female garb. How provoking it was to ſee the tender, the beautiful Ignez de Caſtro repreſented by one of theſe brawny artificial wenches, eſpecially in that affecting ſcene where ſhe appears, with her two infant children, at the King's feet ſupplicating for mercy. The ſimple recital of this affecting paſſage, as written by Luis, is ſufficient to melt an audience into tears, yet the man-*mid*-wife who delivered it brought forth no tears, but the tears of the Poet, for the abortion of his piece. Inſtead of the delicate faltering accents of the fair victim, he roared,

—— like the ocean when the winds
Fight with the waves —— ——
—— dying accents fell, as wrecking ſhips
After the dreadful yell, ſink murmuring down,
And bubble up a noiſe. *Lee's Oedip.*

The

The other actors, particularly thoſe who repreſented King Alfonſo and Don Pedro, were not deficient in ſentiment or action. They poſſeſſed a good deal of that graceful unconſtrained manner we admire in the French actors.

The Circus for the bull-feaſts is but a ſhort diſtance from the above Theatres. This amuſement is declining very faſt in the capital. The performances I witneſſed here were inferior to what I ſaw at Leiria, but not quite ſo cruel. And after all, perhaps the manner of tearing the bulls with maſtiffs, as in England and other parts of Europe, is not leſs barbarous than the manner of tormenting them in Spain and Portugal; but we are apt to ſee defects in our neighbours, whilſt we are blind to our own, like the Lamian Witches, who, according to the facetious Rabelais, in foreign places had the penetration of a Lynx, but at home they took out their eyes and laid them up in wooden ſlippers.

As we have already given an account of a bull-feaſt at Leiria, it is unneceſſary to add that of Liſbon, which is almoſt ſimilar. A ſcene of a more novel nature invites our attention; that is, the manner of catching black cattle in Brazil.

I was preſent at the Circus when this curious ſpectacle was exhibited, the firſt of the kind, as I was told, ever represented in Lisbon. It conveyed a good idea of the manner in which the inhabitants of that fertile region catch their cattle. They kill the animals for the sake of the hides, which are brought to Portugal to be manufactured. Of the flesh I understand the Brazilians make but little account; they barely take as much as is sufficient for present exigence, and leave the rest a prey to the birds and beasts of the forests.

The Circus was very crowded on this occasion: about five in the afternoon a native of Pernambuca entered the arena mounted upon a spirited horse of the Arabian breed. The rider was of a copper colour, of a strong and active figure, his hair black, and his head uncovered. He wore a loose mantle, somewhat like the paludamentum of the ancient Romans. The skin of a wild beast was thrown loosely over the horse instead of a saddle, from which were suspended two cords for stirrups. The whole appeared quite in character.

As soon as the cavalier had paid his obeisance to the audience, a bull, whose natural ferocity was heightened in the stall, rushed in, and had nearly overturned him in the first onset; the fleetness of his horse, and the dexterity with which he managed the reins, only could have saved his life. The furious animal pursued him several times round the arena till he became tired, after which he stood panting in the middle of the ring.

The horſeman ſtill continued his circular courſe at an eaſy pace, holding a long cord in his hand, with a ſlip-knot at the end of it: having watched a proper opportunity, he caſt it over the horns of the bull, and rode twice round him; then ordering the gate to be thrown open, he made off in full ſpeed till he came to the full length of the cord; upon which he received a check that drew him on his back, and made the horſe caper on his hind feet; nevertheleſs he clung to him by his knees, and in this reclined poſture, held the cord in both hands and the bridle in his mouth. The bull at this time was entangled by the rope, with his head drawn in between his fore-feet, and incapable of motion. The Brazilian diſmounted, approached, and drew from beneath his mantle a ſhort hunting ſpear, which, with an apparent ſlight force, he darted into the head of the animal, in conſequence of which he inſtantly fell down and expired.

## *The Patriarchal Church*

Is ſituated at the North-eaſt ſide of the town, upon an eminence that commands a proſpect at once extenſive and beautiful. It would require a volume to deſcribe the treaſures of ſacred relics, gold, ſilver, precious ſtones, and coſtly furniture of this venerable edifice. The objects that moſtly attract the attention of travellers, are the nine great candelabri, and the croſs belonging to the King's chapel;

 the

the latter, which is of ſilver and gilt, is upwards of twelve feet high, and of exquiſite workmanſhip. Nor is the workmanſhip of the candelabri leſs deſerving of notice; they exhibit a variety of groupes in demi-relief, repreſenting the myſteries of Chriſt and of the Virgin Mary; in other parts of them we behold emblems characteriſtic of the kingdom, and of its former conqueſts and diſcoveries. Theſe are alſo formed of ſilver, gilt, and adorned with feſtoons: the ſpaces between the groupes are inlaid with lapis lazuli, and ſpangled with diamonds and other precious ſtones.

Antonio Arrighi (an Italian) was the deſigner of the above croſs and candelabri; they were executed partly at Rome and partly at Florence, in the year one thouſand ſeven hundred and thirty-two, and were greatly admired by the *amateurs* of the fine arts in both thoſe cities. The value of the whole is very great, as may be readily conceived, when the workmanſhip alone is ſaid to have coſt the ſum of three hundred thouſand *cruſados*, or thirty-three thouſand ſeven hundred and fifty pounds ſterling.

The greater part of the charge of the above, and the other embelliſhments of this Church, was defrayed out of the ſurplus of the revenue after paying the ordinary expences of the eſtabliſhment; which revenue, in the year one thouſand ſeven hundred and forty-ſeven, ſtood as follows, according to Father de Caſtro.

*An*

*An Account of the established Annual Revenue of the Patriarchal Church.*

| | Reis. |
|---|---|
| Ancient endowment - - - | 30,005,560 |
| Tributes of Bishoprics and benefices - - | 94,982,512 |
| Rents of churches, houses and reclaimed lands | 31,474,717 |
| Forfeitures and purchases - - - | 250,843,880 |
| Total | 407,306,669 |

*An Account of the ordinary Annual Disbursements of the Patriarchal Church.*

| | Reis. |
|---|---|
| 5 Principal Dignitaries - - - | 23,766,000 |
| 1 Dean - - - - - | 4,853,200 |
| 18 Secondary Dignitaries - - - | 83,757,600 |
| 72 Prelates - - - - | 115,200,000 |
| 20 Canons - - - - | 20,000,000 |
| 12 Beneficaries - - - - | 8,400,000 |
| 32 Second Beneficaries - - - | 16,000,000 |
| 32 Inferior Beneficaries - - - | 8,000,000 |
| 5 Masters of Ceremonies - - - | 520,000 |
| 7 Acolothists - - - - | 350,000 |
| 29 Chaplains - - - - | 4,560,000 |
| 2 Treasurers - - - - | 180,000 |
| 2 Depositories of the Sacristy - - - | 220,000 |
| 1 Depository of the wax store - - | 140,000 |
| 20 Sacrists - - - - | 1,488,000 |
| Carried over | 287,434,800 |

| | | Reis. |
|---|---|---|
| | Brought forward | 287,434,800 |
| 17 | Chaplains who celebrate mafs in the ancient Royal Chapels | 769,040 |
| 71 | Italian and Portuguefe Chorifters | 30,672,800 |
| 4 | Organifts | 520,000 |
| 1 | Italian Compofer | 180,000 |
| 1 | Door-keeper | 120,000 |
| 6 | Wardens | 320,000 |
| 12 | Provedores | 360,000 |
| 4 | Meffengers | 80,000 |
| 6 | Sweepers | 267,840 |
| 2 | Torch-bearers | 148,800 |
| 1 | Goldfmith | 640,000 |
| 2 | Upholfterers | 412,800 |
| 1 | Hair-dreffer | 9,480 |
| 2 | Bell-ringers with their affiftants | 400,000 |
| 1 | Modulator of the organs | 20,000 |
| | A Writer, an Illuminator, and an Engraver | 600,000 |
| 12 | Confeffors | 600,000 |
| 4 | Preachers | 94,000 |
| | Wax | 6,200,000 |
| | For painting the wax | 210,800 |
| | Proceffions, feats, and cleaning the Church | 2,000,000 |
| | Cleaning and repairing the filver utenfils | 250,000 |
| | Wafhing and making up the furniture | 392,000 |
| | Repairing the linen | 120,000 |
| | Oil for forty-five lamps | 500,000 |
| | Wine ufed in the celebration of the maffes | 150,000 |
| | Hofts | 24,000 |
| | Incenfe | 24,000 |
| | Charcoal | 20,000 |
| | Palm | 600,000 |
| | Calendars | 48,000 |
| | Carried over | 334,188,360 |

| | | Reis. |
|---|---|---|
| | Brought forward | 334,188,360 |
| St. Antony's offerings | - - - | 70,000 |
| Green and red cloths | - - - | 60,000 |
| Hanging the Church on feſtival days | - | 236,000 |
| School | - - - - - - | 1,800,000 |
| Contingencies | - - - - | 800,000 |
| | Total | 337,154,360 |

The aggregate of the above ſums when reduced to pounds ſterling will ſtand thus:

| | Reis. | | £. s. d. |
|---|---|---|---|
| Total Annual Revenue | 407,306,669 | = | 114,554 : 18 : 6 |
| Total Annual Diſburſements | 337,154,360 | = | 94,824 : 11 : 6 |
| | 70,152,309 | = | £. 19,730 : 7 : 0 |

Hence there appears a balance of nineteen thouſand ſeven hundred and thirty pounds and ſeven ſhillings remaining in the funds for repairs, furniture, utenſils, and other contingencies.

We do not include in the above eſtimates the eſtabliſhment of the Patriarch, which is very conſiderable on account of his great dignity. His Eminence takes precedence of all the Biſhops and Archbiſhops of the kingdom, is Firſt Chaplain to the King, and a Cardinal of the Conſiſtory at Rome. The principal revenue of his ſacred office ariſes from the tribute of the general mines; he has alſo a large endowment in church lands, and five thouſand ſix hundred and twenty-five pounds ſterling a-year out of the Royal Treaſury. At the loweſt computation we may ſtate the whole at thirty thouſand pounds *per annum*. Then the total amount of the eſtabliſhment of the Patriarchal Church will be 144,554*l*. 18*s*. 6*d*.

### *Loretto.*

The Loretto Church, built by the Pope's Nuncio a few years ago, is held in high eſtimation for its architecture; but its admirers muſt ſee excellencies in it that I could not perceive; and I am inclined to ſuſpect that any reputation it has obtained in that reſpect is owing, not to its intrinſic merit, but from its being deſigned in Italy. In the days of Palladio this would have been a ſtrong recommendation; we cannot, however, allow that privilege to the Italians of the preſent age, whoſe taſte in architecture is ſunk as low as that of moſt other nations of Europe, by the Borromini, the Bibiena, and their diſciples, the modern Vandals of that degenerated nation.

> *Nerveleſs in ſloth*, enfeebling *arts thy boaſt*,
> *Oh! Italy, how fallen, how low, how loſt!* Camoens.

There are ſeveral labourers employed in ſinking the mountain juſt by this Church, for the purpoſe of building dwelling-houſes; and it is curious to obſerve, that as far as they have hitherto ſunk, which in ſome parts is about thirty

thirty feet, they found nothing but a reddiſh clay, or ſand, mixed with ſtrata of petrified ſhells, chiefly of the cruſtaceous kind. Several hundred cart-loads of theſe ſhells have been cleared away from this ſpot; the height of which above the ſea apparently is not leſs than three hundred and fifty feet.

As we are in the neighbourhood of the Franciſcan Church, we cannot help noticing the inſcriptional ſtone placed in the North-eaſt angle of it. There is another, of a ſimilar nature, in the front of the *Carmo* Church. We ſhall not annex their ſublime contents; for the honour of our holy religion we wiſh they were taken down; or if that be contrary to the preſcriptions or laws of theſe Churches, perhaps there is no law in force againſt turning them inſide out.

## *Church of St. Roque.*

This Church formerly belonged to the Jeſuits. There is nothing in the architecture very remarkable for excellence of deſign or execution, though indeed it may be juſtly conſidered a very neat Church. The walls and ceiling exhibit ſome good pictures in freſco. But what is moſt deſerving of attention is a ſmall Chapel dedicated to St. John the Baptiſt, the moſt valuable of its ſize, perhaps, in Europe. Among the materials with which it is decorated, we obſerve lapis lazuli, Oriental granite, porphyry, amethyſt, alabaſter, verde antique, corallino, ſciena and carara marbles.

There are alſo three beautiful pictures in it, executed in moſaick in a maſterly manner; one is placed in a deuxtyle over the altar, repreſenting the Baptiſm of our Saviour; the other two, namely, the Annunciation and the Deſcent of the Holy Ghoſt, are placed one at each ſide of the altar. The floor is likewiſe of moſaick, embelliſhed with borders of *treillage*, and an armillary ſphere in the centre. The columns and dado of the altar are of lapis lazuli; the table of the latter is ſupported at the angles by cherubs of ſilver, and accompanied by two lofty candelabri of the ſame metal. The ſhafts of the columns are formed into ſtriæ by fillets of gold.

According to thoſe who rate the expence of theſe precious appendages at the loweſt, they coſt two millions of *cruſados*, or two hundred and twenty-five thouſand pounds ſterling. They were executed at Rome by the moſt eminent artiſts of that city, at the deſire of King John the Fifth, who preſented them to the Jeſuits of St. Roque, in the year one thouſand ſeven hundred and fifty-one. Every admirer of the fine arts muſt regret to find ſuch admirable productions ſqueezed into an obſcure chapel or cell, not more than ſeventeen feet long by twelve broad, at the ſide of the church.

New

*New Church.*

The New Church, built by her present Majesty, is the largest and most magnificent edifice raised in Lisbon since the fatal earthquake. It is said to have cost five millions of *crusados*; that is, five hundred and sixty-two thousand five hundred pounds sterling. The plan is in the form of a cross, and runs nearly East and West: indeed the Portuguese, in founding their Churches, are not very particular in this respect. They generally adapt the aspect to the situation, a custom worthy of our imitation; as that great Being, in honour of whom they are raised, is equally present at the North and the South, at the East and the West.

The centre is crowned with a magnificent dome of hewn stone rising over the quadrangle at the intersection of the nave and transept, which is gradually formed into a circle by pendentives springing from the angles of the piers. In point of execution this dome has great merit; and no wonder; for where shall we meet with such excellent stone-cutters as in Portugal? Perhaps not in Europe. Truth will not allow us, however, to say as much for its architects.

In the whole Church, indeed, as far as relates to these artisans, there is nothing to censure, and but very little to praiſe that relates to the architect. We ſhall take no notice of the towers, nor of the ball that crowns the cupola; a little knowledge of optics or perſpective might have remedied what is amiſs in both: but in the diſtribution of the compoſite tetraſtyle, the arcade and the logia of the Eaſt front, nothing more was required to make them as they ought to be, than a moderate knowledge of the rules of architecture. The columns of the former, inſtead of ſupporting the ſuperſtructure, ſuſtain but a diminiſhed entablature, and even this is intermitted; hence, the columns are of no real or apparent uſe whatever. An Athenian would imagine they were expoſed there for ſale; and the Italian who, not long ſince, prompted by an itch for paſquinading, poſted the following couplet on one of the columns of a great manſion in the neighbourhood of Saint James's in London, might apply it, with equal propriety, to the above columns:

*Care Colonne, che fatte lá?*
*Non lo ſappiamo in verità!*

Tell me, dear Columns, why do you ſtand ſo?
Indeed, Mr. Paſquin, we really don't know!

## *Cemetery of the Britiſh Factory.*

The Cemetery, or Burying-ground, belonging to the Britiſh Factory, is ſituated at the North-weſt ſide of the city, and is the only expoſed Burying-ground in Liſbon.

The

The natives, and all others of the Catholic communion, who die here, are interred in the cryptical tombs of the churches. When the corpse is reposited, it is strewed with lime, to dissolve it the more speedily, and to prevent any unpleasant smell.

The diseased, according to law, must not remain disinterred more than four-and-twenty hours; a very salutary regulation, called for by the heat of the climate; for, admitting it were possible that one in a thousand might be brought to life by continuing unburied, as with us, for the space of five or six days, it is more than probable, that thousands would fall a sacrifice to the experiment.

This Burying-ground was assigned to the English about the year one thousand six hundred and fifty-five, agreeably to the fourteenth article of the Treaty of Alliance concluded between England and Portugal in the time of Oliver Cromwell. The same article also includes the restrictions to which the English are subject with regard to the exercise of their religion. Here is a copy of it:

"And forasmuch as the rights of peace and commerce "would be null and useless, if the people of the Republic "of England should be disturbed for conscience-sake, "when they pass to and from the kingdoms and domi-"nions of the said King of Portugal, or reside there for "the sake of exchanging their merchandize. That com-

"merce may, therefore, be free and fecure both by land "and fea, the faid King of Portugal fhall take effectual "care, and provide, that they be not molefted by any "perfon, court, or tribunal, upon account of the faid "confcience, or for having with them, or ufing, any "Englifh Bibles or other books; and that it fhall be free "for the people of the Republic to obferve and profefs "their own religion in private houfes, together with their "families, within any of the dominions of the faid King "of Portugal whatfoever; and the fame to exercife on "board their fhips and veffels as they fhall think fit, "without any trouble or hindrance; and finally, that a "place be affigned for the burial of their dead. But "withal, the Englifh are cautioned not to exceed what is "written in this article."

Among the remains of the Britifh fubjects interred in the above Cemetery, are thofe of the celebrated Henry Fielding; but, I regret to fay, without a monument, or any other obfequious mark of diftinction, fuitable to his great talents and virtues.

In the year one thoufand feven hundred and eighty-fix, the Chev. de St. Mark de Meyrionet, the French Conful, who then refided at Lifbon, had a fmall monument made for that purpofe at his own expence, which remains to this day in the cloifter of the Francifcan convent. Why it has not been admitted into the Burying-ground I could not

not learn; but those who have excluded it were certainly justified for more reasons than one. In the first place, as a monument, it is a very contemptible design. Secondly, the epitaph is unappropriate and unpoetical. And, thirdly, it appears to be made rather from vanity than gratitude; rather with a view to confer honour on himself and his country, than to perpetuate the memory of Henry Fielding. This appears evident from the last line of the epitaph; of which we here annex a copy.

*Erigé en 1786, á Henry Fielding mort em 1754.*

Sous ces cyprès charniers, parmi ces os muets,
Tu cherches de Fielding les restes mémorables;
De la mort et du temps déplore les effets,
Ou déteste plutôt l'oubli de ses semblables.
Ils élèvent par-tout des marbres fastueux,
Un bloc reconnoissant ici manque à tes voeux,
Et ton pas incertain craint de fouler la cendre,
Sur laquelle tes pleurs cherchent à se répandre.

Vieillard, qui détruis tout dans un profond silence,
Ne dissous point ce marbre à Fielding consacré!
Qu'aux siècles à venir il arrive sacré,
Pour l'honneur de mon nom et celui de la France!

The

The following lines were written by way of Epitaph to Henry Fielding, by Mr. Smart.

The master of the Greek and Roman page,
The lively scorner of a venal age,
Who made the public laugh at public vice,
Or drew from sparkling eyes the pearl of price;
Student of Nature, reader of mankind,
In whom the poet and the patron join'd.
As free to give applauses as assert,
And skilful in the practice of desert.
Hence power consign'd the laws to thy command,
And put the scales of justice in thine hand,
To stand protector of the orphan race,
And find the female penitent a place.
From toils like these, too great for eye to bear,
From pain, from sickness, and a world of care,
From children and a widow in her bloom,
From shores remote, and from a foreign tomb;
Call'd by the WORD OF LIFE, thou shalt appear
To please and profit in a higher sphere,
Where endless hope, unperishable gain,
Are what the Scriptures teach and entertain.

*Royal Monastery of Belem.*

On the banks of the Tagus, about five miles South-west of Lisbon, is situated the magnificent Church and Monastery of Belem, founded by King Emanuel, in the year one thousand four hundred and ninety-nine, and completed

 by

by his ſon and ſucceſſor, John the Third, for the Friars of the Order of *St. Jeronymo.* Over the portal of the Monaſtery we obſerve the following inſcription, or diſtich, ſaid to have been written by the celebrated *André de Reſende*:

VASTA MOLE SACRUM DIVINÆ IN LITORE MATRI
REX POSUIT REGUM MAXIMUS EMMANUEL.
AUXIT OPUS HÆRES REGINI, ET PIETATIS UTERQUE
STRUCTURA CERTANT, RELIGIONE PARES.

Providence fortunately ſaved this beautiful ſtructure from the deſtructive effects of the memorable earthquake of one thouſand ſeven hundred and fifty-five, except the great arch of the tranſept, which received a ſhock in that diſaſter; in conſequence of which it fell the enſuing year. The Chevalier Frezier makes reſpectful mention of the vaulting of this church, than whom, I know but very few writers more competent to judge of theſe matters.

*On peut remarquer dans les anciennes Egliſes & Cloitres Gothiques, une varieté admirable de compartimens; ce que j'ai vû de plus beau & de mieux exécuté dans ce genre, eſt au Monaſtere de Bethlehem, auprès de Liſbonne en Portugal, tant à l'Egliſe qu'au Cloitre, où la plûpart des nervures ſont de Marbre.*

We may obſerve in the ancient Gothic churches and cloiſters an admirable variety of compartments; the moſt beautiful

'beautiful and best executed of the kind that I have seen, are in the Monastery of Belem, near Lisbon in Portugal, as well with regard to the church as the cloister, where most of the ribs are of marble.

*Traité de Stereotomic, tom.* iii. p. 28.

Here are interred many of the Royal families of Portugal, and other personages of distinction, as may be collected from the inscriptions of their monuments. The whole is executed in a species of architecture compounded of the Norman-Gothic, and Arabian styles. The cloister adjoining to the church exhibits some excellent specimens of Arabesque ornaments; they are designed with a good deal of taste and fancy, and executed with care.

The founder of this noble fabric, erected in the river opposite to the church a strong tower, with two batteries and several pieces of cannon, to defend both the Monastery and the entrance to the capital. Joseph the First also built an excellent quay with wharfs near the same place.

### *Bom-successo.*

This Monastery was founded in the year one thousand six hundred and twenty-six, for the Nuns of the Order of St. Jeronymo; but, through the munificence of Queen Louiza de Gusman, it was afterwards set apart for females, natives of Ireland, who entered into holy orders. It is dedicated

dedicated to St. Dominick, and under the controul of the Abbot-general of that Order, or his depute, the Rector of the Irish Dominican Convent at Lisbon. It maintains two Chaplains, who are also of the same Order, and natives of Ireland.

## *The Irish Convent.*

The Irish Convent, or College of the Dominican Order, was founded in the year one thousand six hundred and fifty-nine, by Queen Luiza de Gusman, who instituted the Irish nunnery above mentioned. That Convent was entirely destroyed by the earthquake of one thousand seven hundred and fifty-five. It is recorded that one of the Fathers, animated by a pious zeal to preserve the sacred pax, rushed into the midst of the ruins during the violence of the earthquake, brought it forth, and walked with it in procession to the church of St. Isabel, attended by a vast concourse of people, imploring the Divine mercy.

After several years had elapsed, the Fathers were enabled to rebuild their little seminary and church, through the munificence of the humane. Some respectable Catholic families in Ireland gave donations for that purpose; but the greater part of the expence was defrayed by the benevolent people of Portugal.

 The

The Inhabitants of the Convent, at present, are about eighteen, exclusive of servants; they live chiefly on voluntary contributions. The students are remarkably docile and sober; even the Portuguese, whose career from youth to age is rarely chequered with sallies of intemperance, hold them as models of imitation to the probationers of their monasteries. King Joseph the First had a particular esteem for these Fathers, though he once made a witty remark on them. One evening he observed, from the balcony of his palace, four or five of them crossing the Tagus in a ferry-boat, in which there were some females. "Your Ma-"jesty's Irish Friars," said one of the Lords in waiting, "are fond of mixing with the Ladies." *I am not afraid of their making love to them*, replied the King, *I would sooner trust them with my wife than the key of my cellar*.

Perhaps there is not in the code of Irish proscriptions a law that more clearly manifests the wretched policy of that country, than that which relates to the exclusion of Roman Catholic seminaries of education. You accuse their pastors with illiterature, whilst you adopt the most cruel means of making them ignorant; and their peasantry with untractableness, whilst you deprive them of the means of civilization. But that is not all; you have deprived them at once of their religion, their liberty, their oak, and their harp, and left them to deplore their fate, not in the strains of their ancestors, but in the sighs of oppression.

oppreſſion. I would wiſh to draw a veil over theſe grievances, which, thank God, are diminiſhing every day, as the beams of more enlightened legiſlature begins to dawn on that long-neglected iſle.

*Liſbon Aqueduct.*

This Aqueduct may be juſtly conſidered one of the moſt magnificent monuments of modern conſtruction in Europe; and in point of magnitude, is not inferior, perhaps, to any Aqueduct the ancients have left us. That part of it which is ſituated in the valley of Alcantara, about a mile from Liſbon, is an admirable ſtructure; conſiſting of thirty-five arches, by which the water is conveyed over a deep vale, formed by two oppoſite mountains. The dimenſions of it, in the moſt depreſſed part of the vale, are as follow:

| | Feet. | Inches. |
|---|---|---|
| Height of the arch from the ground to the intrados - | 230 | 10 |
| From the vertex of the arch to the extrados, excluſive of the parapet - - - - | 9 | 8 |
| From the extrados to the top of the ventilator - | 23 | 4 |
| Total height from the ground to the ſummit of the ventilator - - - | 263 | 10 |
| Breadth of the principal arch - - | 107 | 8 |
| Breadth of the piers of the principal arch - - | 28 | 0 |
| Thickneſs of the piers in general - - - | 23 | 8 |

The arches on each ſide of the principal one diminiſh in breadth, as the piers whereon they reſt decreaſe in height.

height with the declivity of the hills. In examining the refpective dimenfions of the feveral arches, I find they do not reciprocally diminifh in geometrical progreffion; indeed it is obvious to the eye, a very great obftruction to the beauty of the perfpective. The reader who is not acquainted with that ufeful problem, will find it fufficiently illuftrated in *Traité de Stereotomie*, by the *Chev. Frezier*, *tom.* ii. p. 120. pl. xxxv.

It would alfo contribute to the beauty of the ftructure, if all the arches were curves of the fame fpecies; inftead of which there are fourteen of them Gothic, or pointed arches in a range; the reft are femicircular. The architect feems to have been apprehenfive that the principal arches, if made femicircular, would become very expenfive, on account of their requiring a higher extrados than pointed arches to keep them in equilibrium; fince there is no arch, except the catenaria, that will fupport itfelf without an incumbent weight proportionable to the fubtenfe.

In the reft of the Aqueduct there is much judgment difplayed. No part of it has failed, or appears to have received the leaft injury from the great earthquake; a proof of the excellence of the contignation.

Over the arches there runs a vaulted corridor, nine feet fix inches high, by five feet broad, internally. A continued paffage runs through the centre of it, for the people who conſtantly attend to keep it in order, and a ſemicircular channel, or conduit, of thirteen inches diameter at each ſide through which the water is conveyed. It is worthy of remark, that theſe channels are laid, not in an inclined direction, as in other Aqueducts, but horizontally; to compenſate for this, a ſmall depreſſion is made at certain intervals, by which the water is impelled along the horizontal line; a manner ſuppoſed to require leſs declenſion in conveying water than a continued inclined line. There are two thoroughfares for foot-paſſengers along the Aqueduct; that is, one at each ſide of the corridor, which is five feet wide, and defended by a ſtone parapet.

From the remains of ſome ancient walls which were found here, it is ſuppoſed that the Romans who inhabited Luſitania attempted to build an Aqueduct in the place where the preſent one is raiſed.

King Emanuel had a ſimilar work in contemplation, by which he propoſed conveying the water to the *Praça do Roſcio*, and there to erect a magnificent fountain. The deſign was made agreeably to his orders by Franciſco do Olhando; it conſiſted of a figure repreſenting Liſbon ſtanding on a column, guarded by four elephants, from whoſe trunks the water was to have iſſued. But Emanuel had many more important deſigns to execute, and therefore left this unfiniſhed.

The Infanta *Don Luiz*, in the reign of John the Third, resumed the idea of the Aqueduct, but failed likewise in the execution of it. *Luis Marinho* says, the senate of Lisbon made a collection for that purpose, amounting to six hundred thousand *crusados*, which was lavished in public rejoicings at the entry of Philip the Third of Spain.

The honour of executing this noble structure was reserved for John the Fifth. This munificent Prince laid the foundation of it in the year one thousand seven hundred and thirteen, and in nineteen years after, the whole was completed. The city of Lisbon, in testimony of their gratitude, raised an arch to his memory, wherein, among other inscriptions, we observe the following:

JOANNES . V.
LUSITANORUM . REX.
JUSTUS . PIUS . AUG. FELIX . P. P.
LUSITANIA . IN . PACE . STABILITA.
VIRIBUS . GLORIA . OPIBUS . FIRMATA.
PROFLIGATIS . DIFFICULTATIBUS.
IMO . PROPE . VICTA . NATURA
PERENNES . AQUAS . IN . URBEM . INVEXIT.
ET.
BREVI . UNDEVIGENTI . ANNORUM . SPATIO.
MINIMO . PUBLICO.
IMMENSUM . OPUS . CONFECIT.
GRATITUDINIS . ERGO.
OPTIMO . PRINCIPI.
ET.
PUBLICÆ . UTILITATIS . AUCTORI.
HOC . MONUMENTUM . POS . S. P. Q. O.
ANNO . D. M.D CCXXXVIII.

*Manoel da Maya* was the name of the architect who designed and superintended the execution of the above Aqueduct. The expence of it was partly defrayed by a tax of one *Rei* upon every pound of meat sold in the capital. Of the produce of that tax we may form some idea from the following statement.

*Quantity of Butchers Meat sold at the Shambles of Lisbon in the Year* 1789.

| | | | Weight in Arrobas. |
|---|---|---|---|
| 27985 | Oxen | - - - | 324895$\frac{1}{4}$ |
| 1279 | Calves | - - - | 6033 |
| 27562 | Sheep | - - - | 18730$\frac{1}{4}$ |
| 11927 | Hogs | - - - | 31971$\frac{1}{2}$ |
| | | | 381630 |
| | | An Arroba is | 32 lb. |
| | | Total weight in lbs. | 12212160 |

The consumption of flesh meat is greatly reduced here by the quantity of fresh and salt fish, with which the markets are constantly supplied. The poor in general on days of abstinence use salt fish, imported by English ships from Newfoundland; they call it *Bacalhao*. In the year one thousand seven hundred and eighty-nine, there arrived at Lisbon sixty ships partly laden with this fish, which, according to the entries at the custom-house, weighed fifty-nine thousand and seventy-three quintals.

There

There are many other public buildings besides dwelling-houses in Lisbon well deserving of notice; to describe them all, would exceed the limits of this work: but there are few or no ancient remains of architecture to be found there, which is very extraordinary of a city that boasts such remote antiquity. An ancient inscriptional stone is now and then discovered in digging for foundations, but very little more. I have given in plate VIII. copies of such fragments of this kind as came within my observation. The inscription A was found in a subterranean cave in *Rua Bella da Rainha*, in the year one thousand seven hundred and seventy. The other four, *viz.* B, C, D, E, were discovered in a similar manner; the originals from whence these were copied, may be seen in the wall of a house at the corner of Magdalen Street.

## *Charitable Institutions.*

Public charities have always been considered as a leading feature in the character of every nation. When the rich share part of their superfluities with the indigent, when the healthy by their labour contribute to succour the feeble and distressed, then humanity performs the best offices of society. Portugal is not deficient in this respect; for the people, though not compelled by law, contribute voluntarily to the support of different charitable institutions.

Here

Here is a foundling hoſpital, properly named the *Miſericordia*; on the outſide of it is a cradle where the infant is laid, of which notice is given by the ringing of a bell. Theſe foundlings, as they advance in years, are carefully inſtructed in the principles of religion and morality; at a proper age male children are apprenticed to reſpectable tradeſmen, and the girls put to ſervice. In the year one thouſand ſeven hundred and eighty-nine the number of children received into this Hoſpital amounted to one thouſand two hundred and ſeventy-nine.

| | |
|---|---|
| Of theſe there died - - - | 405 |
| Claimed by their fathers - - - | 4 |
| Given out to nurſe - - - | 853 |
| Reared in the Hoſpital - - - | 17 |

The Royal Hoſpital of St. Joſeph receives the infirm of both ſexes of every nation; it is very well attended by phyſicians and nurſes; the patients are comfortably lodged, and in every reſpect well treated. In the year one thouſand ſeven hundred and eighty-nine, the number of patients received into this Hoſpital amounted to 11,020

| | |
|---|---|
| Remained in it ſince the foregoing year - | 778 |
| Total | 11,798 |

| | |
|---|---|
| Of the above number there died in the ſame year | 1,308 |
| Diſcharged as cured - - - - | 9,688 |
| Remained under cure - - - - | 802 |

 Beſides

Besides the above charitable institutions, there are societies here called the Brotherhood of the *Misericordia* who are constantly performing acts of charity. These venerable societies protect and comfort the distressed of every religion, sect, or country, within the limits of their observation. They are not content to await the solicitation of the afflicted, but seek them out in their wretched habitations, and administer to their wants. They take orphans and poor children of indigent parents under their protection, and rear them till they arrive at a proper age to be sent as apprentices; then they put them under the care of respectable tradesmen, and do not withdraw their guardianship till they are established in their respective trades, unless they forfeit it by ill behaviour. The females who are reared by them in a similar manner must be very circumspect in their conduct; when their characters are irreproachable, industrious tradesmen make choice of them for their wives, as well for the sake of the dowry to which they are entitled, as to gain the patronage of the brotherhood.

These humane societies visit the gaols and hospitals, and send provisions to the different prisoners who have neither money nor friends to support them, and such of them as are detained for the gaoler's fees, after being acquitted, are liberated through their humane bounty. When a delinquent is condemned to die, they visit him constantly, they console him and accompany him to the place of execution, exhorting

exhorting him to repentance. Their humanity does not reſt here; it extends to the grave, and even beyond the grave; for the remains of the victim are interred with decency, and a number of maſſes offered up for his ſoul. They perform ſimilar offices for every perſon who dies in indigent circumſtances. Indeed it would be almoſt impoſſible to enumerate all the beneficent acts of the venerable Brotherhood of the *Miſericordia*, acts founded on the pureſt principles of humanity and religion, without the leaſt alloy of oſtentation or hypocriſy. Oh merciful friends of the human ſpecies, how great the reward that awaits you when ſummoned before the great Tribunal of Mercy! Nor is Liſbon the only place where theſe pious inſtitutions are eſtabliſhed; they extend to every city and town in the kingdom, and every part ſubject to the crown of Portugal. We ſincerely wiſh they extended every where, and were limited only by the limits of the globe.

## *Obſervations on the Laws of Portugal.*

The King in perſon is ſuppoſed to preſide in all criminal courts of judicature, and the Judges, who derive their authority immediately from him, may pronounce ſentence of death on delinquents tried and found guilty; but execution is expreſsly forbidden till the expiration of twenty days after ſaid ſentence, in order that the criminal may have an opportunity of reviewing his trial, and proteſting againſt ſuch points in it as do not exactly bear upon the

 offence.

offence. This law was first promulged by Alfonso the Second at Coimbra, in the year one thousand two hundred and eleven.

Several prisoners, pursuant to this decree, have protracted their lives for many years. A striking instance of this appeared during the administration of the Marquis de Pombal; this Minister ordered a return to be made of all the prisoners in the kingdom, with the nature of their alleged crimes, and duration of confinement. The abuses practised by the officers of the prisons gave rise to the inquiry, for it was customary with the gaolers to liberate the prisoners on their parole on receiving a proportionate gratuity.

Among the number thus enlarged, there happened one on whom sentence of death had been passed seven years anterior to the above order; during which interval he lived in the country, and earned his bread very honestly. The gaoler now summoned him to appear, he instantly obeyed, re-entered the condemned cell, and was ordered for execution; but on a representation of his conduct being made to the King, he was pardoned in consideration of his punctual regard to his promise, and the blameless character he maintained in the neighbourhood wherein he worked.

There is one great defect in the administration of the criminal law, which calls loudly for redress. Prisoners committed

committed on alleged crimes, are ſuffered to remain many years in priſon before they are brought to trial. If in the interval an innocent man ſhould die, he ſinks into the grave with all the accumulated infamy of a delinquent.

During the reign of John the Second and of his ſucceſſor Emanuel, criminals, inſtead of being put to death, were employed in the Portugueſe fleets that viſited Africa or Aſia, and ſent upon hazardous expeditions in the newly diſcovered countries. If they ſucceeded in the object of their enterpriſe, their crimes were expiated for the ſervice they rendered to the ſtate; and it was not unuſual to find men of this deſcription, after a few years, reformed in mind and manners, and become uſeful members of ſociety. The puniſhment of tranſporting criminals to foreign ſettlements alſo originated with the Portugueſe, a mode of puniſhment, perhaps of all others, attended with the moſt ſalutary conſequences to the criminal and the community.

The Clergy, I am informed, are not confined for offences in the common priſons, there is one called the Aljube ſet apart for them; this priſon is ſituate near the patriarchal church, and under the juriſdiction of the Patriarch. Formerly the Clergy could only be arraigned by the canon law; but this privilege has been lately ſet aſide; they are now amenable to the civil law, an ordinance which gives great ſatisfaction to the kingdom at large.

There is a priſon at the South end of the city, on the verge of the Tagus, which at preſent is unoccupied. During the adminiſtration of the potent miniſter it was much crowded, particularly when the edict was firſt iſſued for the expulſion of the Jeſuits.

This priſon may be conſidered as the Baſtile of Portugal; the ſtrength of its walls, gratings and cells, ſtrike the ſpectator with horror; and what renders it ſtill more terrific, is a contiguous rope-walk, in which many an unhappy priſoner imagined he ſaw his deſtiny ſpun.

Impriſonment for debt was aboliſhed by an edict in one thouſand ſeven hundred and ſeventy-four; in its ſtead the law has preſcribed a more equitable mode to ſatisfy the reaſonable demands of the creditor.

The Engliſh ſubjects who reſide here are exempted, in ſome degree, from the eſtabliſhed laws of the country, as ſpecified in the following articles of the Treaty of one thouſand ſix hundred and fifty-four:

Acticle VII.—" For the judging of all cauſes relating " to the people of this Republic, a Judge Conſervator " ſhall be deputed, from whom no manner of appeal ſhall " be granted, except to the Senate of *Rellaçaon*, where the " law-ſuits commenced, and appealed to that court ſhall " be determined within the ſpace of four months."

ARTICLE VIII. "That if any of the people of this "Republic ſhall die within the kingdoms and dominions of "the moſt Serene King of Portugal, the books, accounts, "goods, and aſſets belonging to them, or to others of the "people of this Repulic, ſhall not be ſeized nor poſſeſſed "by the judges of the orphans and perſons abſent, or by "their miniſters and officers; nor ſhall they be liable to "their juriſdiction; but the ſame goods, merchandize, "and accounts ſhall be delivered to the Engliſh factors or "procurators reſiding in that place, who are nominated "or deputed by the deceaſed: but if the defunct, whilſt "living, did not nominate any, then the ſaid goods, mer- "chandize, and accounts ſhall, by the authority of the "Judge Conſervator, be delivered to two or more Engliſh "merchants reſiding in the place, and approved of by "the Engliſh Conſul, after having given ſecurity, by un- "exceptionable bondſmen, (who ſhall alſo be approved "by the ſame Engliſh Conſul,) for reſtoring the ſaid goods, "merchandize, and accounts to the right owners, or to "their true creditors; and the goods which ſhall appear "to have been the deceaſed's, ſhall be delivered to his "heirs, executors, or creditors."

ARTICLE XIII. "That none who are commonly "called Alcaydes, (*i. e.* Bailiffs,) or any other officers of "his Royal Majeſty, ſhall ſeize or arreſt any of the people "of this Republic, of what rank or condition ſoever,

"except

"except in a criminal cauſe, being detected in any fla-
"grant fact, unleſs he be firſt impowered in writing by
"the Judge Conſervator; and that the aforeſaid people,
"in all other reſpects, as to their perſons, domeſtics, and
"dwellings, books of accounts, intereſts, merchandize,
"and all other goods belonging to them, ſhall enjoy
"equal and the ſame immunity within the dominions of
"the moſt Serene King of Portugal, from impriſonment,
"arreſts, and other moleſtations whatſoever, as already is,
"or ſhall hereafter be granted to any other Prince or people
"whatſoever in alliance with the King of Portugal; nor
"ſhall they be hindered by any permit or protection, to
"be granted by the ſaid King to his ſubjects, or others
"frequenting his dominions, from recovering their debts;
"but they ſhall have a right to ſue any man to juſtice for
"the recovery of any juſt debt, although he be ſheltered
"under the patronage or protection of any perſon what-
"ſoever, or ſecured by any *Alvara*, or written law, or
"whether he be a farmer of the revenues, or inveſted with
"any other privilege."

Whether ſome clauſes of the above articles have not been modified during the adminiſtration of the Marquis de Pombal, I am not very certain; but the greateſt part, if not the whole of them, ſtill continue in force.

*Methuen Treaty.*

The laſt Treaty of Commerce concluded between Portugal and England was in the reign of Queen Anne. This is commonly called the *Methuen* Treaty, on account of its being ratified on the part of Great Britain by John Methuen Eſquire. As it is very ſhort, we ſhall give a copy of it.

*A Treaty of Commerce betwixt the moſt Serene Lady Anne, Queen of Great Britain, and the moſt Serene Lord Don Peter, King of Portugal and of the Algarves,* &c. *agreed upon and concluded in Liſbon, the 27th of December* 1703.

ARTICLE I. "His Sacred Royal Majeſty of Portugal "promiſes, both in his own name and that of his ſuc-"ceſſors, to admit for ever hereafter into Portugal the "woollen cloths, and the reſt of the woollen manufac-"tures of the Britons, as was accuſtomed till they were "prohibited by the laws. Nevertheleſs, upon this con-"dition; that is to ſay,

ARTICLE II. "That her Sacred Royal Majeſty of "Great Britain ſhall, in her own name and that of her "ſucceſſors, be obliged for ever hereafter to admit the "wines of the growth of Portugal into Britain; ſo that "at no time, whether there ſhall be peace or war between "the kingdoms of Britain and France, any thing more "ſhall be demanded for theſe wines by the name of cuſ-"tom or duty, or by any other title whatſoever, directly "or indirectly, (whether they ſhall be imported into Great "Britain in pipes or hogſheads, or other caſks) than what "ſhall be demanded for the like quantity or meaſure "of French wine, deducting or abating one half of the "cuſtom or duty. But if at any time this deduction or "abatement of cuſtoms, which is to be made as afore-"ſaid, ſhall in any manner be attempted and prejudiced, "it ſhall be juſt and lawful for his Sacred Royal Majeſty "of Portugal again to prohibit the woollen cloths, and "the reſt of the Britiſh woollen manufactures.

"Given at Liſbon, the 27th of the month of "December 1703.

"*John Methuen*, L. S."

As the trade of England with Portugal is well known, we ſhall not recapitulate it here: but as that of Ireland with Portugal is not generally known, ſome account of the ſame may not be unintereſting. A gentleman reſiding in Liſbon, who has good information in theſe matters, ſavoured me with the following paper, which I believe has not been hitherto publiſhed:

*Trade*

*Trade of Portugal with Ireland, from March 1781 till March 1782.*

| Exports. | Value. £. | s. | d. |
|---|---|---|---|
| Cork | 2,458 | 1 | 10½ |
| Drugs | 4,197 | 7 | 10 |
| Dying Stuff | 2,152 | 5 | 2 |
| Almonds | 599 | 12 | 11½ |
| Figs | 650 | 14 | 10 |
| Raisins | 1,997 | 10 | 2 |
| Succeces Liquoritia | 325 | 16 | 8 |
| Oranges and Lemons | 2,893 | 18 | 9 |
| Oil | 3,490 | 19 | 2 |
| Pot Ashes * | 5,687 | 10 | 0 |
| Salt | 23,656 | 5 | 4 |
| Raw Silk | 621 | 6 | 8 |
| Thrown Silk, undyed | 792 | 10 | 0 |
| Brandy | 4,605 | 18 | 0 |
| Vinegar | 459 | 3 | 9 |
| Wine | 43,821 | 10 | 0 |
| Small Articles | 1,146 | 11 | 0 |
| | £. 99,557 | 2 | 2 |

* What is here called Pot Ashes, is in reality Barilla from Spain; probably they gave it that name on account of the war. The wine also is partly Spanish.

 Imports.

| Imports. | Value. £. | s. | d. |
|---|---|---|---|
| Beef - - - | 19,118 | 0 | 0 |
| Butter - - - | 105,846 | 11 | 3 |
| Candles - - - | 729 | 4 | 2 |
| Cheese - - - | 1,501 | 7 | 6 |
| Fish - - - | 1,118 | 10 | 0 |
| Tanned Hides * - - | 4,550 | 0 | 0 |
| Linen Cloth - - - | 5,850 | 14 | 1½ |
| Pork - - - | 7,374 | 0 | 0 |
| Small Articles - - | 299 | 19 | 3½ |
| | £. 146,388 | 6 | 4 |

## *Observations on the Manners and Customs of Portugal.*

The Inhabitants of Lisbon may be ranked under four classes; *viz.* the Nobility, the Clergy, the Traders, and the Labouring People. The observations I am about to offer on each class contain very little more than may be collected by every one in the streets or the roads, in markets or cottages. To proceed in the most natural order, we should begin with the pedestals of the state; but for once, we shall reverse the order of the structure, and commence with what is called "the Corinthian "Capitals of polished Society."

* Part of the above articles were for Spain, but not mentioned on account of the war with Great Britain. The tanned hides, particularly, could not be for the use of Portugal, as the importation of them is prohibited in that country.

The

The Nobility may be conſidered as a body entirely diſtinct from the other three; the principal affairs of the ſtate are committed to their truſt; they reſide in the capital, or its environs, and ſeldom viſit their eſtates in the provinces. They eſteem it an honour to be born in the capital, and alſo to dwell there. They are educated likewiſe at Liſbon, in a college founded for that purpoſe by King Joſeph. Hence it is called the *Collegio dos Nobres*, the College of Nobles. Prior to the eſtabliſhment of this college they were educated at Coimbra, a place apparently much better adapted for that purpoſe; as it poſſeſſes many advantages not to be found in a commercial city. The fragrance of the air, the ſtillneſs of the country, and the delightful proſpects with which Coimbra abounds, are great incitements to ſtudy; beſides, it is enriched with immenſe literary treaſures, the accumulation of ages; and its buildings are very magnificent. Now, the ſeminary at Liſbon is deficient in all theſe points. It appears, therefore, that the Nobility have made a bad exchange. There is a wide difference between a College of Nobles and a noble College.

The Nobility, comparatively ſpeaking, are not very rich; for though their patrimonies are large, their rents are ſmall. I doubt if any of them has ever ſeen a map of his eſtate, or exactly knows its boundaries. If ever they deign to turn their attention towards the conſtructing of roads and canals, and not conſider agriculture a purſuit unworthy of Gentlemen, they will become the richeſt Nobility in Europe, on account of the vaſt extent of their landed poſſeſſions.

In the diſtribution of their fortunes they ſhew great prudence without the appearance of parſimony. A country wherein there are no race-horſes, licenſed gambling houſes, or expenſive miſtreſſes, a Gentleman may live ſplendidly upon a moderate income; fortunately theſe allurements to diſſipation are unknown to them. Nor do they excite the envy of the poor by midnight orgies or gilded chariots. Their time is ſpent between their duty at court, and the ſocial enjoyments of private parties.

The fine arts, which to the ſuperior claſſes of every nation of Europe are ſources of the moſt refined pleaſure, are almoſt entirely neglected by the Nobility of this country; neither do they appear to take much pleaſure in the cultivation of the ſciences, though they poſſeſs moſt excellent capacity for both. Their lives are an even tenor of domeſtic felicities, not remarkable for brilliant actions, and but rarely ſtained by vice. The fame of their illuſtrious anceſtors juſtly entitle them to every honour and reſpect; but whilſt they glory in the remembrance of their achievements, they ſeem to forget their maxims. It muſt be allowed, however, that they poſſeſs many amiable qualities. They are religious, temperate, and generous, faithful to their friends, charitable to the diſtreſſed, and warmly attached

attached to their Sovereign; whoſe approbation, and a peaceful retirement, conſtitute the greateſt happineſs of their lives.

With reſpect to the Clergy, I was not furniſhed with information ſufficient to form an accurate eſtimate of their true character, and I ſhall not preſume to ſpeak from report of ſo reſpectable a body. Among thoſe with whom I had the honour to be acquainted, I found ſome poſſeſſed of great liberality and talents; in proof of this I need only mention his Grace the Biſhop of Beja, whoſe piety and learning would do honour to the Apoſtolic or Auguſtan ages. I might alſo inſtance the Abbé Corrêa chaplain to his Grace the Duke de Alafoens, and Father de Souza author of ſeveral pieces on the Arabic language.

There are ſeveral other men of eminent talents among the Clergy, but concealed in gloomy cells; and what is extraordinary, the greater are their talents the more careful are they in ſecluding themſelves from all communication with the world. It may be aſked then, why they do not oblige the world with ſome of their acquirements? The reaſon is very obvious; the Portugueſe language is ſo little known, that there is little or no ſale for books written in that language out of the country, and in it, reading is very far from being general; very few books therefore will defray the expence of printing and paper, eſpecially if they treat on ſcientific ſubjects. Thus

are

are men of letters deterred from making themſelves known through this laudable channel, and the world is deprived of their experience and wiſdom.

It is true, that in all the learned profeſſions, men will be found who would render more ſervice to the community in an humbler ſphere, and among the Clergy there are, I am ſorry to add, but too many of this deſcription; who are better calculated by nature and education to ſollow the tail of the plough, than to diſcharge the important ties of that ſacred profeſſion.

The Merchants are remarkably attentive to buſineſs, and, as far as I could learn, juſt and punctual in their dealings: they live on a friendly footing with the foreign traders who reſide here, particularly the Engliſh. Bankruptcies are ſeldom known among them, and they are careful in avoiding litigations; for it is a well known fact, that the Gentlemen of the long robe in Portugal are not to be ſurpaſſed even by their brethren of the Engliſh Court of Chancery, in the art of protracting a ſuit.

A Liſbon merchant paſſes his hours in the following manner: he goes to prayers at eight o'clock, to 'Change at eleven, dines at one, ſleeps till three, eats fruit at four, and ſups at nine: the intermediate hours are employed in the counting-houſe, in paying viſits, or playing at cards.

To

To visit any one above the rank of a tradesman, it is necessary to wear a sword and *chapeau*; if the family you visit be in mourning, you must also wear black; the servants would not consider a visitant as a gentleman unless he came in a coach; to visit in boots would be an unpardonable offence, unless you wear spurs at the same time. The master of the house precedes the visitant on his going out, the contrary order takes place in coming in.

The common people of Lisbon and its environs are a laborious and hardy race; many of them by frugal living lay up a decent competence for old age; it is painful to behold the trouble they are obliged to take for want of proper implements to carry on their work. Their cars have the rude appearance of the earliest ages; these vehicles are slowly drawn by two stout oxen. The corn is shelled by the treading of the same animals as in the days of the Israelites; hence probably the scripture proverb, "thou "shalt not muzzle the ox that treadeth the corn." They have many other customs which to us appear very singular; for example, women sit with the left side towards the horse's head when they ride. A postilion rides on the left horse. Footmen play at cards whilst they are waiting for their masters. A taylor sits at his work like a shoemaker. A hair-dresser appears on Sundays with a sword, a cockade, and two watches, or at least two watch-chains. A tavern is known by a vine bush. A house to be let, by a piece

 of

of blank paper. An accoucheuſe door, by a white croſs. And a Jew is known by his extra catholic devotion.

The lower claſs of both ſexes are very fond of gaudy apparel; we obſerve even the fiſh-women with trinkets and bracelets of gold about the neck and wriſt. The fruit-women are diſtinguiſhed by a particular dreſs. In plate IX. figure A, we have given the repreſentation of one of them, with the aſs by which the fruit is conveyed to the market. The cuſtom of wearing boots and black conical caps is peculiar to theſe women; but for what reaſon, if any there be, I could not learn. Figure B, in the ſame plate, is a repreſentation of a woman of Beira in the uſual dreſs of the females of that province. And figure C is a ſketch of a female peaſant of the province of Alenteju.

All the drudgery is performed by Gallicians, who may be called the hewers of wood and drawers of water of this metropolis; they are patient, induſtrious, and faithful to a proverb. One of the principal employments, in which they are daily engaged, is ſupplying the citizens with water, which they carry on their ſhoulders in ſmall wooden barrels from the different fountains.

Every Gallician in this ſervitude is obliged, by the police of the city, to carry one of theſe veſſels filled with water to his lodgings every night, and in caſe of fire, to

haſten

haſten with it to aſſiſt in extinguiſhing the flames at the firſt ſound of the fire bell; any neglect in this reſpect is ſeverely puniſhed; on the contrary, they are ſure to be rewarded in proportion to their vigilance. But the people are ſeldom viſited by that dreadful ſcourge: during my reſidence here, there was not an inſtance of any accident by fire.

In the houſes of foreign merchants, the Gallicians are the only ſervants employed, and many of the Portugueſe prefer them to the natives in that capacity; they cook the victuals, clean the rooms, and make the beds. If there be any female ſervants in the houſe under the age of five and thirty, they are inviſible except to the miſtreſs and her daughters; after this age they are left to their own diſcretion, as their charms are then ſuppoſed to be ſufficiently faded to render them ſecure from the invaſions of gallantry.

The Ladies ſeldom breathe the pure air, except in their ſhort excurſions to the next chapel, which they viſit at leaſt once a day. The figures hereunto annexed (plate X.) are repreſentations of a Merchant with his wife and maid-ſervant going to church. Their reſpective dreſs may be inferred from thence. They walk exactly in the order in which they are here repreſented, that is to ſay, one after the other; hence we thought it reaſonable to ſacrifice to truth the rules of pictureſque grouping.

The Portuguese Ladies possess many amiable qualities; they are chaste, modest, and extremely affectionate to their kindred. No woman goes out of doors without the permission of her husband or parents. To avoid all suspicion, men, even though relations, are not allowed to visit their apartments, or to sit beside them in public places. Hence their lovers are seldom gratified with a sight of them except in the churches; here they make sighs and signals:

> Address and compliment by vision,
> Make love and court by intuition. *Hudibras.*

Notwithstanding the watchful eye of the Duenna, the lovers contrive to exchange *billet-doux*, and that in so subtle a manner, that none can perceive it whose breast glows not with a similar flame. The little boys who attend at the altar, are often the messengers on these occasions. When one of these wingless cupids receives the letter, he makes his way through the audience till he approaches the fair one, then he throws himself on his knees, repeating his *Ave Maris stella*, and beating his breast; after finishing his ejaculations and crossing his forehead, he falls on his face and hands, and fervently kisses the ground; in the mean time he conveys the letter under the Lady's drapery and brings back another.

At other times when the lovers are coming out of the church, their hands meet as it were by chance in the holy water font; by this means they exchange billets, and enjoy the delectable pleaſure of preſſing each other's fingers.

Various are the contrivances to which they are compelled to reſort, in order to elude ſuſpicion; and in no part of their lives do they evince more prudence than during their courtſhip. Their natural diſpoſition to ſecrecy is the means of their continuing for years under the impreſſion of the tender paſſion; and they muſt have fallen victims to it, were it not that refined, that virtuous love which Guevara deſcribes.

*Arde y no quema; alumbra y no danna; quema y no conſume, reſplende y no laſtima, purifica y no abraſa; y aun calienta y no congoxa.*

It glows, but ſcorches not; it enlightens, but hurts not; it conſumes not, though it burns; it dazzles not, though it glitters; it refines without deſtroying; and though it be hot, yet it is not painful.

Marriage-feaſts are attended with vaſt expence; the reſources of the lower claſs are often exhauſted in the preparations made on theſe occaſions. The nuptial bedchamber is ornamented in the moſt coſtly manner, with ſilks, brocades, and flowers; even the wedding-ſheets are trimmed with the fineſt lace.

In

In their chriſtenings and funerals alſo they are very extravagant; but in other reſpects very frugal and temperate, particularly the females, who ſeldom drink any thing but water; if they drink wine, it gives riſe to ſuſpicion of their chaſtity, and ſuſpicion is often held tantamount to a crime. The Empreſs Dona Leanor, daughter of Edward King of Portugal, endeavoured to introduce the like cuſtom among the German Ladies; but neither her Majeſty's example or perſuaſion could induce them to exchange the "milk of Venus" for the limpid rill.

The abſtemiouſneſs of the Portugueſe Ladies is conſpicuous in their countenance, which is pale, tranquil, and modeſt; thoſe who accuſtom themſelves to exerciſe have, nevertheleſs, a beautiful carnation. Their eyes are black and expreſſive; their teeth extremely white and regular. In converſation they are polite and agreeable; in manners aſſuaſive and unaffected. The form of their dreſs does not undergo a change, perhaps, once in an age; milliners, perfumers, and fancy-dreſs-makers are profeſſions as unknown in Liſbon as in ancient Lacedemon.

Widows are allowed to marry, but they do not avail themſelves of that privilege as often as in other countries. There are many Portugueſe, particularly thoſe of the good old ſtock, who look upon it as a ſpecies of adultery ſanctioned by the law.

Women

Women do not aſſume the family-names of their huſbands, as with us. In all the viciſſitudes of matrimony they retain their maiden names.

The men are generally addreſſed by their Chriſtian names, as *Senhor Pedro.* *Supernomes* are alſo very common here, which are derived from particular trades, remarkable incidents, places of reſidence, or ſtriking perſonal blemiſhes or accompliſhments.

Strangers' ſurnames are frequently tranſlated, eſpecially if they bear any alluſion to ſubſtantives or qualities. For example, Mr. Wolf, they call *Senhor Lobo*; Mr. Whitehead, *Senhor Cabeça Branca*. To the Chriſtian names of men and women are often ſuperadded thoſe of their parents, for diſtinction ſake. This cuſtom obtained very much among the ancient Iriſh, and is not unuſual at this day in the Southern provinces of that country.

With reſpect to the middling claſs, in their ideas and manners they differ from thoſe of the reſt of Europe; the unfrequency of travel, except to their own colonies, excludes them from modern notions and modern cuſtoms; hence they retain much of the ancient ſimplicity of their anceſtors, and are more converſant in the tranſactions of Aſia or America than of Europe.

Whether

Whether it proceeds from a fondness for ease, or want of curiosity, they appear to have an aversion for travelling, even in their own country. A Portuguese can steer a ship to Brazil with less difficulty than he can guide his horse from Lisbon to Oporto.

People, thus estranged from the neighbouring nations, are naturally averse from the influx of mere theoretical doctrines, which tend to disturb the tranquillity of established opinions. They exclude at once the sources of modern luxuries and refinements, modern vices and improvements.

Hence their wants, comparatively speaking, are but few, and these are easily satisfied; their love of ease exempts them from many passions to which other nations are subject; gross offences are rarely known among them, but when once offended they are not easily appeased; passions that are seldom roused act with the greater violence when agitated; under this impression individuals have sometimes been hurried to violent acts of revenge; but now, the vigilance of the magistrates, and the growth of civilization have blunted the point of the dagger.

The temperance of the people, and their exemption from hard labour; the fragrance of the air, and the number of mineral springs with which the country abounds,

are

are circumſtances ſo favourable to the human conſtitution, that we ſhould naturally expect to find the Portugueſe live to a great age, yet there are not many remarkable inſtances of longevity among them; but there are fewer cut off by natural cauſes before the age of threeſcore, than among an equal number, perhaps, in any other part of Europe. One rarely meets a Portugueſe, however aged, crippled with the gout, or bowed with infirmity.

The handſomeſt perſons of both ſexes are found in the province of Eſtremadura; that ſcourge of beauty, the ſmall pox, does not rage here with the ſame violence as in cold climates. The inhabitants neglect one thing, which, in a country like this, would tend to expand the human frame to its full perfection, I mean bathing; neither do they take exerciſe enough for the preſervation of health.

The lower claſs are endowed with many excellent qualities; they are religious, honeſt, and ſober, affectionate to their parents, and reſpectful to their ſuperiors. We muſt not, however, expect to find them poſſeſſed of theſe qualities on the verge of ſea-port towns, as their manners are there corrupted by mingling with refugee adventurers from various nations. Strangers, therefore, are often miſled, who form the character of the people through this adulterated medium. It is in the country only they can be found, uninfluenced by foreign manners or foreign cuſtoms, in their true national ſtate; and there we behold them honeſt, obliging, affable, and mannerly. A Portugueſe peaſant will not walk with a ſuperior, an aged perſon, or a ſtranger, without giving him the right-hand ſide, as a mark of reſpect. He never paſſes by a human being without taking off his hat, and ſaluting him in theſe words, *the Lord preſerve you for many years.* In ſpeaking of an abſent friend, he ſays, *morro com ſaudades de o ver:* I die with impatience to ſee him. Of a morning, when he meets the companions of his toil in the field, he ſalutes them in a complaiſant manner, and inquires after their little families. His day's work is computed from the riſing of the Sun to its ſetting; out of which he is allowed half an hour for breakfaſt and two hours for dinner, in order to refreſh himſelf with a nap during the meridian heat. If he labour in the vineyard, he is allowed a good portion of wine. When his day's work is over he ſings veſpers, and on Sunday he attunes his guitar, or joins in a fandango dance, as repreſented in Plate XI. His male children are educated in the neighbouring convent, whence he alſo receives ſuſtenance for himſelf and family, if diſtreſſed or unable to work. They all imagine their country is the bleſſed Elyſium, and that Liſbon is the greateſt city in the world. In their proverbial language they ſay, "he who has not ſeen Liſbon has ſeen nothing." Indeed they have proverbs for almoſt every thing, which, being founded on long experience, are generally true,

though

though the above is a ſtriking inſtance to the contrary. Of the countries which, like their own, do not produce corn, wine, and oil, they entertain but a mean opinion. They picture to themſelves the miſery of the inhabitants of Northern climates, who ſhudder in the midſt of froſt and ſnow, whilſt they themſelves are baſking in their green fields. Theſe circumſtances, and the affectionate attachment they have for their King, endear them to their native ſoil. They centre a great portion of their happineſs in the fine climate with which nature has bleſſed them, and the abundance of delicious fruit the ſoil yields with little labour. Under every misfortune they are ſure to find conſolation in religion; and next to theſe divine favours, muſic is the greateſt ſolace of their lives: it diſſipates the ſorrows of the poor man, and refines the ſentiments of the rich; life glides on agreeably amidſt ſuch endearing ſcenes. It would be vain to perſuade a Portugueſe that he could enjoy ſuch happineſs in any other part of the globe: he is nurtured in this opinion, and if chance or misfortune ſhould impel him into a foreign land, he pines as if in a ſtate of captivity.

A ſhort time before I left Liſbon I dined at a Spaniſh ordinary, near the convent of St. Francis, in company with a gentleman who was a native of Malta, and a Knight of that Order. The univerſality of his information, and the liberality of his remarks, induced me to requeſt his opinion reſpecting the Portugueſe. Theſe are his obſervations on that head, as nearly as I can recollect:

" There are no people in Europe, Sir, whoſe real character is leſs known than thoſe of Portugal; for as their language is but little ſtudied or underſtood, our knowledge of them is derived chiefly from the Spaniſh writers, and a Spaniard is rarely known to ſpeak favourably of the Portugueſe. The latter, on the contrary, whatever might be their real opinion of the former, are induced by the precepts of Chriſtian charity to ſpeak reſpectfully of them. Of this we have a ſtriking inſtance in Joſeph Texera, a Portugueſe Friar of the Dominican Order. This Friar lived in the ſixteenth century, and was confeſſor to Don Antonio, heir preſumptive to the crown of Portugal, whom he followed into France. He there declared from the pulpit, in one of his Sermons, *that we are bound in duty to love all men, of whatever religion, ſect, or nation, even the Caſtilians.*

" From the political enmity which for ages have ſubſiſted between the two rival powers, it is probable that the accounts we receive of the Portugueſe through the medium of the Spaniards are not altogether to be depended upon. On the other hand, if we take the character of the Portugueſe from the native writers, we ſhall imagine they poſſeſs not only all the good qualities in exiſtence, but are

 exempted

exempted from all the bad ones. This is like a painter vainly attempting to produce a fine picture without shadows.

"From the best information I can collect, the ancient Portuguese have been a brave, active, and generous people. At a time when the other nations of Europe were sunk in sloth and ignorance, they were employed in propagating Christianity, in extirpating Infidelity, and enlarging our knowledge of this sphere.

"Necessity, the parent of action, was the source of all their great enterprises; attacked on one side by a powerful and restless neighbour, on the other by the Moors, who had long infested the country, their incursions and conspiracies required the exertions of every sinew of the state to preserve its independence. At length the horde of Infidels were expelled, and the pride of the Castilians humbled.

"In the reign of John the First, when the Portuguese found themselves secure from foreign or domestic foes, their troops then inured to fatigue, and their Captains, animated by military fame, pursued the Barbarians into Africa. Their contests in this quarter, though unprofitable, and almost ruinous to the state, were ultimately attended with consequences very fortunate for the powers

of

of Europe; as they diffused a spirit of enterprise which afterwards led to all the modern discoveries in navigation.

"The Lusitanian soldiers were brave and hardy, innured to all the hardships of war, fatigue, hunger, and thirst, which they bore with great patience in the hottest climates. In the field their courage bordered on rashness; their natural impetuosity could never be restrained even by the most rigid military discipline; they were too ambitious of signalizing their valour out of the ranks, by which they sometimes caused their defeat in deranging the order of battle; but when they fought in a phalanx, the enemy found them invincible.

"The riches of Asia, the relaxation of discipline, together with the ignorance and rapacity of the Governors of India, at length corrupted the manners of the soldiers, and defaced every trace of their ancient character.

"Every department of the state was hastening to ruin, when King Sebastian ascended the throne; in him, as their last refuge, were centered the hopes of the people; and the tokens of virtue and courage he had given them in the early part of his life, seemed to promise the accomplishment of their expectations: he certainly inherited a great portion of the valour of his ancestors, though time evinced that he possessed but very little of their prudence. No Prince

Prince was ever more enamoured with a love of fame, nor ſought a more indirect road towards the attaining of it. The happineſs of his people is what conſtitutes the real fame of every Monarch; yet this was the leaſt of Sebaſtian's purſuit. The vain glory of excelling in arms occupied his ſole attention, and that glory he promiſed to himſelf in the plains of Africa: but, alas! he, and the greater part of thoſe who accompanied him thither, found there not laurels, but an untimely grâve.

" The death of this Prince would have been the leſs regretted, if he had not left a ſucceſſor to fill the throne who was in the decline of life and underſtanding, without energy, without abilities to heal the bleeding wounds of his expiring country. Providence, apparently, ſeeing its diſſolution approach, ſent a Cardinal King to give it the dying benediction. Thus we find that ſtates, like individuals, have their infancy, maturity, and decline; and what is not a little remarkable of this, it commenced with a Henry, and with a Henry it expired. The firſt was a hero and a ſtateſman, the latter poſſeſſed neither of theſe qualities, nor ſupplied the want of them by his wiſdom.

" Philip the Second now appended the crown of Portugal to that of Spain. It had been the invariable policy of this Prince, and of his ſucceſſors, to render Portugal ſubſervient by reducing its reſources, which they were carrying into effect every day, till at length the Portugueſe, no longer able to bear the chains of their foreign maſters, revolted; and, by their reſolution and unanimity, ſupplied the want of forces in caſting off their bondage; and ever ſince, the kingdom is gradually advancing to proſperity under its native and lawful Sovereigns.

"It is evident, however, that the advancement of the country is by no means proportionate to its vaſt reſources; nor is the ancient military ſpirit of the people yet revived. Some remains of the courage of their anceſtors may ſtill linger among them; but the contempt in which they hold the profeſſion of arms is ſufficient to extinguiſh every ſpark of military enterpriſe. For ſeveral years paſt they have admitted officers into the regiments of infantry without talents or education, whoſe ignorance multiplied abuſes and relaxed diſcipline. The abuſe at length advanced to that degree, that officers were appointed from among the domeſtics of noble families. When Count de Lippe was appointed Commander in chief of the forces of the kingdom, he endeavoured to eſtabliſh the dignity of the profeſſion. One day he happened to dine with a Portugueſe Nobleman, who was a Colonel in the ſervice; one of the ſervants who attended at table was dreſſed in an officer's uniform: on inquiry, he found this attendant was a Captain in a regiment of infantry; on which the gallant Commander immediately roſe up and inſiſted upon the military ſervant's ſitting at table next himſelf.

"It

"It has always been the policy of the wisest Generals to preserve a degree of honourable dignity in the army; for pride is as commendable in a soldier as humility in a priest; but servility and military spirit are incompatible. This was the Count de Lippe's maxim; and such was his zeal for the honour of the profession, that he declared openly it was a dishonour to an officer not to demand, or refuse to give, satisfaction for an offence.

"Since the reign of Joseph the First, there has been a great change for the better, not only in the army, but in almost every other department of the state. When that Prince ascended the throne, agriculture and manufactures were so much neglected, that the people depended upon foreign nations for food and raiment; the arts were despised, and the revenues unproductive. The English, pursuant to the Methuen treaty, supplied the Portuguese with woollen cloths, in exchange for which they were to receive the wines of the country. The encouragement held out by this treaty for the growth of wine, and the facility which long experience has given the Portuguese in that branch of husbandry, induced the farmers to neglect the cultivation of corn, and convert their fields into vineyards; thus the grape increased in proportion as the grain diminished.

"This was partly the state of Portugal when King Joseph appointed Senhor Carvalho, afterwards Marquis de

 Pombal,

Pombal, his Prime Miniſter. The adminiſtration of this great ſtateſman forms an epoch in the annals of Portugal. He endeavoured, and not in vain, to direct the attention of the people to their real intereſt; the landholders were compelled to diminiſh their vineyards, and appropriate a third part of them to grain and other ſpecies of culture. This wiſe regulation was attended with ſuch ſalutary effects, that to this day it is conſidered one of the moſt beneficial acts of his adminiſtration.

" As the natural reſult of agriculture is population, he prepared employment for the riſing generation, by eſtabliſhing manufactories of different kinds; induſtry thus excited, the country began to wear a new face; the merchant engroſſed the trade heretofore carried on by foreigners, and the farmer fed and clothed himſelf and his family with the produce of his native ſoil.

" The Marquis's efforts, thus far crowned with ſucceſs, urged him to further exertions; he endeavoured to propagate a ſimilar ſpirit of induſtry among the Coloniſts, who had long felt the inertia of the mother country. But knowing how vain it was to expect either activity or induſtry from a people groaning with the chains of ſlavery, he publiſhed an edict, whereby the inhabitants of Brazil, and of the other colonies appertaining to the crown, were to be reſtored to their freedom, and to enjoy the ſame immunities as the natives of Portugal. An act ſo replete

3 with

with justice and humanity, is sufficient to expiate many of the political sins imputed to the Marquis de Pombal, and is a lasting honour to Portugal, which was the first among the modern nations of Europe that enslaved mankind, and the first that set the humane example of their emancipation. It was also the first that taught Europe navigation and commerce upon a comprehensive scale: had not Prince Henry existed, we should not, probably, have ever heard of Columbus. *It is to the discoveries of the Portuguese in the old world* (says Voltaire) *that we are indebted for the new.* They were, in fact, the first that explored the coast of Africa, that suggested the existence of the Western world, and discovered the road to India. A people who have been thus early in so many enterprising pursuits, and exhausted their vigour when most of the surrounding nations were but waking from their slumber, might reasonably be allowed to take a respite. They are now but commencing their career anew; and it must be left to time to determine whether they will ever more re-establish the once respectable name of Lusitanians."

 The

The following observations on the state of the weather, I am indebted for to my friend the Reverend Herbert Hill, Chaplain to the British Factory at Lisbon.

*Extracts from Meteorological Observations, made at Lisbon in the Years* 1783, 1784, 1785.

| | | 1783. | 1784. | 1785. | |
|---|---|---|---|---|---|
| Fair weather | Days | 171 | 157 | 155 | The general number of days of fair weather is supposed to be 200. |
| Cloudy and showers | —— | $106\frac{1}{2}$ | 132 | 127 | |
| Settled rain - | —— | 88 | 67 | 83 | |

Quantity of Rain mark'd by lines, 12 to a French inch.

| | Jan. | Feb. | Mar. | Apr. | May. | June. | July. | Aug. | Sept. | Oct. | Nov. | Dec. |
|---|---|---|---|---|---|---|---|---|---|---|---|---|
| 1783— | $52\frac{1}{2}$ | 25 | $46\frac{1}{2}$ | $8\frac{1}{2}$ | 21 | $12\frac{1}{2}$ | 0 | 1 | 4 | $37\frac{1}{2}$ | $42\frac{1}{2}$ | 79 |
| 1784— | 32 | 44 | 91 | 41 | 8 | 0 | 0 | 0 | 6 | 45 | 30 | 106 |
| 1785— | 61 | 45 | 46 | 35 | 27 | $0\frac{1}{4}$ | $0\frac{3}{4}$ | 15 | 34 | 27 | 21 | 76 |

1783, medium $27\frac{1}{2}$ }
1784, —— $33\frac{1}{2}$ } Polegadas, or Inches—it ought to be, as is
1785, —— $32\frac{1}{4}$ } supposed, only 23 Polegadas.

State of the Thermometer, medium heat supposed to be 63°.

1783—medium heat for the year, about 56.

| | Jan. | Feb. | Mar. | Apr. | May. | June. | July. | Aug. | Sept. | Oct. | Nov. | Dec. |
|---|---|---|---|---|---|---|---|---|---|---|---|---|
| 1784— | 54 | 55 | 57 | 57 | 67 | 70. | 73 | 73 | 71 | 60 | 54 | 51 |

the medium therefore is 62, notwithstanding the thermometer on June 15 was at 97, on July 16 at 99, on August 13, for two hours, at 106, and the day after at 103, on December 4. it was at 30°.

1785—the mean heat was $62\frac{1}{4}$, the thermometer never rose higher than 94, expressed by decimals, the mean monthly heat was

| Jan. | Feb. | Mar. | Apr. | May. | June. | July. | Aug. | Sept. | Oct. | Nov. | Dec. |
|---|---|---|---|---|---|---|---|---|---|---|---|
| 539 | 522 | 562 | 620 | 655 | 710 | 745 | 704 | 696 | 639 | 545 | 522 |

State

State of the Barometer, mean height at the sea 28 Polegadas, 2 Lines, for elevated situations—1 Line equal to 73 Feet.

| | | | |
|---|---|---|---|
| 1783—28.2½ | 4 Feb. 16 and 19 Dec. | 27.5 | 2 Nov. |
| 1784—28.7 | 21 April | 27.5 | 27 Dec. |
| 1785—28.6 | 9 January | 27.6 | 17 Feb. |

Variation of the Needle was observed about the latter end of the year 1785 to be about 23°, or somewhat more.
——— 1789 ——— 23½.

1777, was remarkably wet.
1779 and 1782, the quantity of rain only 20 Polegadas.
1783, it rain'd 240 times in 124 days—Measured by time, it rain'd 572 hours, or 24 days.
1784, ——— 384 times, or 23 days.
1785, ——— 232 times, or 19 days.

1782, February 19, it snow'd.
1783, February 18, and March 12, it hail'd.

*Observations for* 1781.

| | Days. | | Pol. | L. |
|---|---|---|---|---|
| Fair weather | 200 | Quantity of rain | 23 | 7 |
| Cloudy - | 88 | Dec. 6. to Dec. 27. | 9½ | |
| Rain - | 77 | 18 only - | 18 Lines. | |

| | | | | |
|---|---|---|---|---|
| Therm. | 11 July | 99° | mean height of the year | 63° |
| | 19 Jan. | 34° | | |
| | | Pol. L. | | |
| Barom. | 9 Dec. | 27 5 | ——— | 28 2 |
| | 29 ——— | 28 8 | | |

Number

*Number of Marriages, Births, and Deaths registered at Lisbon in the Years 1788 and 1789.*

| | Anno 1788. | Anno 1789. |
|---|---|---|
| Marriages - - | 1560. - - | 1598. |
| Births - - | 7041. - - | 6561. |
| * Deaths - - | 5454. - - | 5386. |

## *Of the Portuguese Jews.*

The late Lord Tarawley appears to have entertained a singular opinion of the inhabitants of Portugal, when he asserted that they were composed of Jews and Sebastians. One class of these, he says, expect the coming of the Messiah; the other, King Sebastian. Which of these two parties have the stronger faith I leave the reader to conjecture; but I must observe, with his Lordship's permission, that there is a third party in Portugal, which includes almost every individual in it, who expect neither until the Millennium. There might, indeed, be still a few in the kingdom who are in expectation of the Messiah; but even these few are obliged to confess that he is already come.

Among the Jews of this country were formerly to be found men of great talents. The celebrated edition of the Bible, which was published at Farrara in one thousand five hundred and fifty-three, was translated by a Portu-

* The Friars, Nuns, and their domestics, are not included in the list of deaths.

guese

gueſe Jew; it is rendered nearly word for word with the original Hebrew text into a ſort of corrupt Spaniſh, then uſed in the Jewiſh ſynagogues. Such words in the tranſlation as are not in the original are marked with aſteriſks. This work was reprinted in fine characters at Holland in one thouſand ſix hundred and thirty; but many of the words were altered, with a view to render them more intelligible, and ſeveral of the aſteriſks were omitted. The firſt edition is become very ſcarce.

In the reign of John the Firſt they had their ſynagogues and Rabbins in Portugal; and John the Second and Emanuel tolerated them at the commencement of their reigns. *Duarte Nonnez*, a Jew, who was baniſhed from Portugal, his native country, in the ſixteenth century, was preferred by the Catholic King to be a privy-counſellor on account of his great abilities, though all of that perſuaſion were formerly baniſhed from Spain.

The following account of their expulſion from Portugal is chiefly extracted from Oſorio, Biſhop of Silva, whoſe relation is eſteemed the moſt correct extant; as he had the beſt information on the ſubject, and was an eminent and impartial hiſtorian, as well as a Chriſtian philoſopher.

Their Caſtilian Majeſties, Ferdinand and Iſabella, having conceived an averſion to this people, who were charged with many acts of impiety againſt the Chriſtian religion, baniſhed banifhed them from their dominions in the year one thoufand four hundred and eighty-two. They difperfed into different places, but the greateft part fled to Portugal. John the Second gave them fhelter, on condition that each fhould pay him eight Ducats, and quit the kingdom at a limited time, otherwife they fhould become flaves; he was bound to furnifh veffels to tranfport them wherever they thought proper, and to give full liberty to all who had a mind to depart.

Whilft King John's ftate of health permitted him to difcharge the affairs of the kingdom, he was careful in performing his promife; he gave orders to commiffion veffels to tranfport them wherever they defired, and commanded that none fhould moleft them. His orders, however, were not attended to, for the captains and feamen treated them in the moft cruel manner, keeping them cruifing backwards and forwards on the ocean till all their provifions became exhaufted, and were conftrained to buy of the captains at fo exorbitant a rate, that on landing they were ftripped to the very fhirts; nor did their wives and daughters efcape the violence of thefe tyrants, but became victims to their luft.

The reft of the Jews who remained in Portugal, partly alarmed with the apprehenfions of fuch barbarous ufage, and partly hindered by want of money to procure neceffaries for the voyage, remained in the kingdom till the time prescribed had elapsed, and thus forfeited their liberty. Whoever now wished to have a Jewish slave petitioned the King, who generally assigned them to such persons as he knew to be of a mild and merciful disposition, and disposed to lighten the chains of the miserable wretches. This happened a short time before the death of John; but it was the general opinion, especially of those who had been most conversant with the King, that, had he lived a little longer, he would have given them their freedom upon easy terms.

Such was the situation of the Jews when Emanuel began his reign. This Prince being sensible that necessity, not choice, caused them to continue in Portugal after the limited time, generously restored them to their liberty. Induced by a grateful sense of such extraordinary benevolence, they offered him a large sum of money, which he refused; being resolved to gain their affections by kind treatment, and by degrees to convert them to the Christian faith.

The peace, however, of the unhappy Jews was of short duration: the clamour raised against them throughout the nation induced the King to take the matter again into consideration. His council was divided in opinions, whether the Jews, who had been driven out of Spain, and taken up their residence in Portugal, should be banished from thence or allowed to remain. In the mean time, the King and Queen of Caſtile ſent letters to Emanuel, earneſtly intreating that he would not ſuffer ſuch a perverſe people, ſo much under the diſpleaſure of God and the odium of men, to remain in his dominions.

Emanuel looked upon this as a point of the utmoſt delicacy. Some of his counſellors were of opinion that they ought not to be exterminated, ſince the Pope himſelf had permitted them to dwell in his territories. Induced by his example, ſeveral ſtates in Italy, and many Chriſtian Princes in Germany, Hungary, and other parts of Europe, had alſo granted the ſame liberty, and allowed them to carry on trade and buſineſs of all ſorts. Beſides, (ſaid they,) their baniſhment can never reclaim them; for wherever they go they will carry their perverſe diſpoſitions. A change of country will never effect a change of ſentiment in their depraved minds. Should they paſs into Africa, on being driven from hence, which is not improbable, all hopes of their converſion muſt be loſt. Whilſt they live among Chriſtians, many of them will be influenced by friendſhip and example to embrace the Chriſtian faith, as ſome have already done, which can never be expected when they come to be mixed with blind and ſuperſtitious Mahometans. Beſides, it will be very detrimental to the public intereſt, if thoſe people, ſome of whom poſſeſs conſiderable riches, carry their wealth to the Moors, and teach our enemies the arts they have learned in our nation.

On

On the other hand, thoſe of a different opinion affirmed, that the Jews, not without reaſon, had been baniſhed from Spain, France, and many places in Germany, by Princes who ſet a leſs value upon the increaſe of their revenues than the intereſts of religion: they perceived the dangerous conſequences of allowing ſuch a people to remain in their dominions; that they were apt to impoſe on the ſimple and infect the illiterate with their pernicious doctrine; that it would be very imprudent to put the leaſt confidence in men ſo inveterate againſt our holy religion, who were bound by no ties or obligations, but ready to ſacrifice every thing to their intereſt, pry into the ſecrets of the ſtate, and give intelligence to our enemies. It would likewiſe (ſaid they) be more eligible to baniſh them immediately when they can only carry away the wealth they have ſcraped together in other countries, than to allow them to remain longer, and then to diſmiſs them, after they ſhould have amaſſed conſiderable riches.

Emanuel was influenced by the latter opinion, and decreed, that all the Jews, and Moors likewiſe, who had refuſed to embrace the Chriſtian faith, ſhould quit his dominions; and fixed a day, after which all thoſe who remained in Portugal were to loſe their liberty.

When the day approached, they began to prepare for their departure. Emanuel was greatly afflicted to think that ſo many thouſands of people ſhould be driven into banishment; and was desirous, at least, to convert their children. For this purpose he devised a scheme, which, in fact, was contrary to all justice and equity, though eventually attended with good consequences to the kingdom. He ordered all the children of the Jews, under fourteen years of age, to be forcibly taken from their parents, that they might be educated in the Christian faith; an order which, in the execution, was attended with the most affecting circumstances.

What a moving spectacle was this to behold! Children torn from the embraces of their screaming mothers; others dragged from the necks of their weeping fathers, and affectionate brothers and sisters, about to be separated for ever. The city of Lisbon was filled with cries and lamentations; even the spectators could not refrain from tears. Fathers and mothers, moved with indignation, were commonly seen to lay violent hands upon themselves, and precipitating, out of love and compassion, their infant children into wells and pits, to avoid the severity of this decree.

There was still another calamity that bore hard upon the unfortunate victims; such as were desirous of leaving the country had not the liberty of so doing. The King was so intent upon making converts of them, that he resolved, partly by rewards, partly by necessity, to invite or compel them to embrace the Christian faith. By agreement he was to have provided them with ſhipping, and to allow them to depart unmoleſted; but this he put off from time to time, and obliged them to reſort from all quarters to Liſbon, to be ſent abroad, though at firſt he promiſed three different ports for their departure.

The time was ſo protracted by theſe delays, that the day fixed upon had elapſed, and all who remained forfeited their liberty. Thus haraſſed, they at length affected to become Chriſtians; by which they were reſtored to their liberty, and recovered their children. The King gave them great encouragement, ſo that many of them lived contentedly in the Portugueſe dominions. "Upon whoſe faith, (ſays "Montaigne,) as alſo that of their poſterity, even to this "day, few Portugueſe can rely, or believe them to be real "converts, though time and cuſtom are much more po-"tent counſellors in ſuch changes, than all other con-"ſtraints."

Such were the methods uſed to bring about the converſion of the Jews; but ſurely it muſt be confeſſed to be unwarrantable. Will any one pretend to maintain, that it is conſiſtent with the principles of common juſtice, or of religion, to force perverſe and obſtinate minds into a belief of things which, in reality, they reject and deſpiſe? Can any one pretend to hinder the freedom of the will, or fetter the underſtanding? It is impoſſible, and directly averſe from the doctrine of Chriſt. He does not

take

take pleaſure in any thing that proceeds from force or conſtraint; he is pleaſed only with a voluntary ſacrifice flowing from the heart. He does not command violence to be offered to the underſtanding of men, but to invite them by reaſon and gentleneſs to the contemplation of true religion. Beſides, what is more preſumptuous than for a mortal to take upon him to do what the Divine Spirit only can effect. It is He alone who is able to enlighten and purify the minds of men; and ſuch as He finds not altogether perverſe and repugnant to His holy influence, He removes from darkneſs to the light of Chriſtianity.

That many of the Jews were not ſincere in their converſion has been often evinced ſince the above period, by the numbers that have ſuffered perſecution, or quitted the country to avoid the rigour of the inquiſition. The greateſt part of them have ſettled in England and Holland; and among the Jews who reſide in theſe countries, thoſe of Portugal are ſaid to be the moſt reſpectable characters. I know one of them in this country who is much reſpected and eſteemed by all who know him for his amiable qualities; he is kind and affectionate to his relations, and warmly attached to his friends, among whom are people of various ſects, Jews and Gentiles. If many of the deſcription of Mr. Rebello of Hackney have been baniſhed from Portugal, the loſs muſt be very great indeed.

And yet, notwithſtanding the perſecutions they have ſuffered, the love of that country is ſo rooted in their nature, that many of them have been known to import earth from Liſbon, and enjoined their ſurviving friends, as their laſt dying requeſt, to depoſite it along with their corpſe. This is literally carrying the love of country into the grave. There is ſomething in the air and ſoil of Portugal ſo congenial to the diſpoſition of the Iſraelites, that when once accuſtomed to it, neither time, nor change, nor perſecution, can alter their affections for it. Luſitania, in ſhort, is their favourite land; their Salem; for which they mourn wherever fate compels them to ſtray, like their anceſtors of old on the banks of the Euphrates, who hung their harps on willow branches, and ſighed for their beloved Salem.

*Father Lewis de Souſa.*

It is to the pen of this Father that I am indebted for the hiſtory of the Royal Monaſtery of Batalha, of which I have given a tranſlation in my account of that ſtructure. Amongſt the hiſtorians of Portugal, he holds the firſt rank in point of ſtyle and veracity. As the circumſtance which induced him to ſeclude himſelf from the world and become a friar is rather ſingular, a ſhort account of it may not be unacceptable to the reader.

In one thouſand five hundred and ſeventy-eight, when Don Sebaſtian, King of Portugal, was defeated and ſlain in a pitched

pitched battle againſt Muly Moloch, Emperor of Morocco, many of the Nobility of Portugal who accompanied him ſhared the ſame fate, and others who fell into the enemy's hands were made captives.

Amongſt the Gentlemen who accompanied King Sebaſtian in this unfortunate expedition, there was one whoſe name the biographer has omitted; it was included, however, in the return of the ſlain. When his wife who reſided in Liſbon received the intelligence, ſhe nevertheleſs entertained hopes that it might have been a miſtake, and that Heaven would yet favour her with a ſight of him.

Under this pleaſing expectation ſhe remained ten years, notwithſtanding the repeated accounts ſhe received from the agents employed to redeem the captives confirmed the relation of his death. Her friends, who were convinced of the truth of it, entreated her to relinquiſh the idea of ever ſeeing him, and to enter once more into the marriage ſtate.

Souſa, at this time, moved in the firſt circles of faſhion: his company was much ſought for, as he was an excellent ſcholar, as well as an accompliſhed Gentleman, he paid his addreſſes to this Lady: her incredulity reſpecting her huſband's death, at this time, began to give way, and ſhe was prevailed on by her relations to give him her hand. Accordingly they were married, and lived together in the greateſt

greateſt harmony; but it was of ſhort duration: a merchant from Africa arrived in Liſbon, ſought out the Lady, and informed her, that he was charged with a commiſſion from her huſband who was in captivity, and relied upon her affections to expedite his releaſe.

The unfortunate woman, quite overwhelmed with ſhame and ſurpriſe in this affecting dilemma, aſked de Souſa's advice, who was alſo aſtoniſhed at the news. As he was a prudent and conſcientious man, he reſolved to be guided in a matter of ſuch delicacy by the pureſt dictates of honour.

In the firſt place, in order to aſcertain the fact, he had recourſe to an ingenious expedient; he conducted the meſſenger to a picture gallery in his houſe, told him that a portrait of the Gentleman whom he affirmed to have ſeen was in the collection, and requeſted him to point it out as a proof that there was no miſtake in his declaration. The merchant endeavoured to excuſe himſelf, ſaying, that a long ſtate of ſervitude and cruel treatment had made ſuch a change in the captive Gentleman, that he doubted if his moſt intimate friends could recognize him were he preſent; nevertheleſs, ſays he, ſome leading features induce me to think that this is his portrait, pointing to the identical one. Souſa, from this and other collateral circumſtances, was now convinced of the truth of the whole, and applauded the merchant for his humanity.

 This

This affair affected Sousa very much; he deliberated with himself in what manner to act; at length he resolved, having no children to provide for, to retire from the world, and seclude himself in a monastery. The wife approved the resolution, and as a proof of her grief and affection, retired also into a nunnery near Lisbon. But previous to their seclusion, they used every means in their power, to rescue the unfortunate Gentleman from captivity.

Sousa now entered into the Dominican order, and lived in the convent of Bemfica near Lisbon. The Fathers of this order, desirous of completing the history of their foundation, thought this a favourable opportunity, and knowing Sousa to be a man of great talents, they requested him to undertake the task, and perfect what Cacegas, a friar of the same order, had begun. He accordingly set about it, and after many years labour, published it in the year one thousand six hundred and nineteen, under the name of Cacegas, and his own; thus, from his extreme modesty, dividing the honour of the work, the whole of which he could justly claim as his own; but posterity has done justice to his memory, and Cacegas's name is now remembered only through Sousa's works.

His facts are said to be accurate and well arranged; his deductions natural and solid; his style throughout is simple and nervous; and what adds greater honour to his memory, he was a man of exemplary piety and humanity.



In

In the year one thouſand ſeven hundred and ninety, Father John de Souza, who we before mentioned (page 154 and 199) publiſhed a curious collection of papers, entitled *Documentos Arabicos*, which he tranſlated into Portugueſe, by permiſſion of her Majeſty, from the original Arabic manuſcripts, depoſited in the royal archives of Liſbon. They chiefly conſiſt of copies of letters that paſſed between the Kings of Portugal and the tributary Princes of India in the ſixteenth century. We ſhall attempt to render one of them into Engliſh from the Portugueſe verſion, which is written in the true ſpirit of the adulatory ſtyle.

## *A Letter from the King of Melinda, to Emanuel King of Portugal.*

" With the moſt profound reſpect, exalted and honourable expreſſions, praiſes, ſalutations, and greetings from an humble and faithful ſervant, (who implores forgiveneſs from the majeſty of God,) the Xeque Wagerage, to the preſence of the moſt illuſtrious, happy, eſteemed, ſincere, praiſe-worthy, protecting, permanent, and invincible Monarch Emanuel, to whom appertain every kindneſs, favour, and honour. His name is celebrated by the people of every region; his beneficence is perpetual, and his fame everlaſting. Lord of the ennobled court, of the kingdom of diſcoveries, and of the palace of treaſures. His ſubjects are victorious, his caſtles formidable, his garriſons fortified, his batteries elevated, his walls decorated, his ſtreets

 ornamented,

ornamented, his houſes lofty, his palaces admirable, his people juſt, his clergy humble, his monks learned, his conſtitution eſtabliſhed, his ſubjects enterpriſing, his gates defended, his heroes intrepid, his cavalry valiant; one of them would fight a hundred warriors. To his city are diſpatched fleets deeply laden; his preſence bows the head and bends the knee; he is the fountain of commerce in every city and kingdom. The equity of his adminiſtration enriches the poor, and ſhortens the days of his enemies: whoever ſeeks to find a blemiſh in him, will ſeek in vain for what the eye never ſaw, nor the ear ever heard; he is the ſource of goodneſs and honours, the diſpenſer of titles, the ſtem of nobility, the centre of the univerſe, the pillar of power, the munificent protector of the virtuous and meritorious, the King of regions, the crown of greatneſs, the diadem of liberality, whoſe forces have ſubdued Sinde, India, Perſia, Arabia, Egypt, Syria, Yeman, and all the provinces of the univerſe. His voice brings the inſolent to ſubjection, and his aſpect humbles the proud; an example beyond emulation; his name is praiſed amongſt men, becauſe he raiſes up the poor. When he ſits on his throne every eye is dazzled with his glory; his cuſtoms are agreeable, his authority nerves the arm of the warrior, his fame reſounds from pole to pole, his preſence is more beautiful than the full moon, his graces refreſh like the dew of ſpring, his determinations are as fixed as fate, his name extends to every part of the earth, his beneficence diſtinguiſhes him at all times and in all countries: ſuch is King Emanuel; the great God perpetuate his reign, and preſerve him from the envy and artifice of his enemies. Amen.

"This is to give thee to underſtand, moſt dear and ſincere friend, that the writer is in good health, and anxious to know the ſtate of thine, and of all that belong to thee. May the Lord preſerve thee, and all that is thine! He would have come in perſon to thy noble preſence; but being occupied in rearing his ſons, and providing them with ſervants and ſlaves, who, together with their father, is thy ſervant and ſlave; and never ceaſes to pray to God, by day and night, to crown thee with honour, riches, and glory. His perſon and property have been entirely devoted to thy ſervice, from the firſt time he has ſeen thy ſubjects to the preſent hour, as they can inform thee. He implores thy protection and friendſhip, to the end that he may be honoured and eſteemed by thy people. He begs thy permiſſion to ſail in his own ſhip once a year to Goa and Moſambique, to provide neceſſaries for thy uſe.

"Having contemplated all that this world could hitherto boaſt of, he never could diſcover a monarch more powerful, nor an empire more happy than thine. It has pleaſed God to ſhower his bleſſings in abundance on thee, and it is to him alone thoſe bleſſings muſt be aſcribed.

"In

"In ancient days, be it known to thee, O King, there lived a generous man, named Halem, who was the very essence of liberality, and had riches adequate to his munificence; in all his life he was never known to refuse any request: it is related that a man who wanted to try the extent of his liberality, made a journey for that purpose to his house. Halem asked what brought him hither. I came, said he, to demand thy head. What claim hast thou to my head, replied Halem? Listen to me, quoth he; there lives a King in my neighbourhood, who gave me a thousand pieces of gold to permit him to wear his head. Halem immediately retired to his chamber, brought out a thousand pieces, and says to the man, as he extended his neck, Here, friend, take your choice, my head or the money: the man accepted the latter, and went away.

"Thy servant now, O King! repeats a similar experiment; as thou art the most liberal Sovereign among the Kings of the earth, I figure to myself thy mighty power and resplendent qualities; and my friends, who have weighed thy grandeur with all others, agree that Alexander and Cæsar were even as dust in the balance compared to thee, because all the treasure of the globe is at thy disposal; thy generosity, therefore, however great, can never lessen thy wealth; remember then, O King! that, of all others, I am * the most deserving of thy favours.

* He speaks of himself promiscuously in the third and first persons singular.

"Thy

"Thy ſervant, the Xeque Wagerage, implores thee to look with an eye of compaſſion and clemency on the inhabitants of Melinda, and if they be found worthy of ſo great a favour, it will raiſe them in the eſtimation of ſurrounding nations, and entitle them to their praiſe, reſpect, and protection; and as the Xeque of Melinda never yet viſited Moſambique, he expects that thou wilt condeſcend that he ſhould go thither; and if any perſon, whether Portugueſe or Muſſelman, ſhould preſume to dictate to him, or reſiſt his authority, he ſhall reply, that ſuch is King Emanuel's pleaſure, which is the manner he now commands and determines all matters in Melinda; becauſe the authority of Monarchs is unlimited: he alſo deſires, when the Xeque of Melinda is at Moſambique, that orders will be given to the Portugueſe not to offend him, but conſider him as the organ of the King, and inveſted with his power. He will take cognizance of thoſe who have always co-operated to exalt thy name, intereſt, and reputation; of this teſtimony ſhall be given by thy ſervants Simon de Andrade, Franciſco Pereira, Fernando de Freitas, Gaſpar de Paiva, Antonio da Coſta, and all the reſt of the Chriſtians, as well as Muſſelmen of Mozambique.

"In fine, be aſſured, O King! that myſelf, my ſons, and my property, are devoted to thy ſervice, and ſhall continue ſo to the laſt day of my life; therefore I implore

implore thee to accede to my ſupplications. Peace be with thee!

"Know, O interpreter of this letter! that the Xeque Wagerage warns thee to read this narrative to the King in a proper and becoming manner, without adding or diminiſhing ought; ſo that it may appear to all, that the Sovereign was delighted with its contents. He will pay thee thy cuſtomary fees; be careful, therefore, in doing juſtice to it, and God will reward thee. Twenty-eighth of Zulcade nine hundred and twenty-one of the Hegira; which correſponds to the thirtieth of September one thouſand five hundred and fifteen."

*Note by De Souza.*

The Xeque Wagerage was Lord of Melinda when Vaſco da Gama concluded a treaty of alliance with him, in the year fifteen hundred; in conſequence of which, that Prince ſent an Ambaſſador with Vaſco da Gama to Portugal, with a rich preſent to King Emanuel. This Ambaſſador returned to Melinda in the ſhip of Pedralves Cabral, and brought with him a letter and a preſent from King Emanuel to his friend the Xeque.

*Vide Chron. part 1. 42. et ſeq.*

*Cintra.*

*Cintra.*

The name of a mountainous country, about twenty miles Weſt of Liſbon. That part of it which is called the Rock of Cintra is well known to all navigators, from its being ſituated at the Weſtern extremity of Europe. In the writings of the ancient geographers, it is called the Promontory of the Moon; by others, *Oliſiponeſe*; probably on account of its vicinage to Liſbon; but according to Strabo, it was formerly named *Hierna*.

Nature apparently threw up the mountain of Cintra as a formidable barrier to ſtay the waves of the Atlantic Ocean, and to mark the Weſtern termination of her works in the European world. The height of the loftieſt part of it above the level of the ſea is computed at upwards of three thouſand feet. Every morning its ſummit is enveloped in clouds, and in the evening, long after night has obſcured the vallies, it retains ſome glimmering of daylight.

On its apex there is a monaſtery of the Order of Saint *Jeronimo*, whoſe Weſtern front ſtrikes every ſpectator with awe, as it appears hanging over an aſſemblage of lofty ſhattered rocks.

From the village of Cintra, which is ſituated at the foot of this mountain, on the Weſtern ſide, I ſpent two hours in climbing up to the monaſtery. It was founded by King Emanuel at the beginning of the ſixteenth century. The architecture is of a ſpecies of Gothic, not purely Norman nor Arabian, but a compound of both: the whole is built of a greyiſh ſtone of the granite kind, and the vaults of the church, chapter-houſe, and ſacriſty, are conſtructed of the ſame materials, and formed into divers compartments by ribs and croſs ſpringers; the chapter-houſe, particularly, exhibits a fine ſpecimen of this kind of vaulting.

In the church is a curious *ſacrarium* of alabaſter, ſaid to be the work of an Italian. Whoever was the artiſt, he appears to have poſſeſſed but ſlender abilities as a ſculptor. One of the Friars placed a lighted candle in the inſide of it, and cloſed the aperture; yet, from the tranſparency of the ſtone, it emitted light ſufficient to read by.

Probably it was of this kind of ſtone that the Temple of *Fortuna Seia* was conſtructed, of which Montfaucon ſpeaks in his *Diarium Italicum*.

"Pliny informs us, that Nero built the Temple of *Fortuna Seia*, on the ſpot firſt dedicated to her by *Servius Tullius*, of a ſort of ſtone found in Cappadocia, as tranſparent as glaſs. Hence it was called *Phengites*, from the Greek word *Phengos*; that is to ſay, brightneſs.

"I have met ſome who hold Pliny's relation of this temple as fabulous; but indeed there is nothing in it incredible; for daily experience evinces the truth of as improbable matters. In the church of *Saint Minias*, at Florence, there are windows of alabaſter, inſtead of glaſs; a table of which fills each aperture, though fifteen feet high, and yet the church is ſufficiently luminous. Were the alabaſter column ſtanding in the *Vatican* library cut into tables, it would be almoſt as tranſparent as glaſs."

To return to the monaſtery. Here is an hoſpitium for the accommodation of pilgrims who viſit this church to perform nevenaries; that is to ſay, nine days devotion; and alſo for thoſe who come to celebrate vigils.

The number of Friars who formerly inhabited the monaſtery amounted to thirty; at preſent they are reduced to four. Were I one of the Order, I ſhould wiſh to paſs my days among them; for I never ſaw a more charming ſituation for meditation, more ſequeſtered from the concerns of life, or better adapted for diſpoſing the mind to the contemplation of another life.

Hence I do not wonder at the relations handed down to us from paſt ages, of ſo many mighty things having been achieved on mountains; they are the fitteſt theatres, on many accounts, for performing great exploits.

Indeed it is almoſt impoſſible for an inhabitant of this place not to act and think different from thoſe who dwell in a valley. The ſounds and proſpects peculiar to it are very favourable to reflection, particularly of a ſtormy day, when the murmurs of ſurges, and the howling of tempeſts, fill the mind with a ſympathetic ſadneſs. Whereever we turn our eyes, the mind is ſtruck with the awful works of Nature: on one ſide is the diſtant ocean, whoſe evanid ſurface blends with the blue horizon; beneath, the deep valley ſtrikes one with the appearance of an auguſt cavern: the ſhattered ſtate of the impending rocks on the declivity of the mountain, torn as it were aſunder, and every where burſting from the ſoil, threaten at the leaſt ſhock to tumble down and deſtroy the village.

About thirty years ago a foreign gentleman diſcovered a mine of loadſtone in this mountain. What ſuggeſted the idea of it, were the herbs that grew immediately over it, which were of a pale colour, and more feeble than the adjacent plants of the ſame ſpecies. Having dug about ſix feet deep, he found a fine vein; but as the mountain is a maſs of disjointed rocks and clay, he could not proceed farther, without propping as he excavated. Government, therefore, apprehending the produce would not defray the expence, ordered it to be ſhut up.

On

On the Weftern fide of the mountain are feen the remains of fome ancient walls, which are built partly on the rocks, and partly conftructed over the cavities. Subterranean paffages and fragments of ancient tombs are faid to have been found here; but hitherto no account of them, nor of the other veftiges, have been given to the public. Whether they are Roman or Moorifque I could not learn; but moft probably they appertain to the latter, or at leaft parts of them, as there are the remains of an ancient building, fuppofed to have been a mofque ftill extant. A fmall apartment to the rear of it is vaulted and ornamented with ftars painted on an azure ground; and the walls ftill retain fome veftiges of Arabic characters.

The fineft piece of antiquity about the place is a quadrangular monument, fuppofed to have been a Moorifque bath; it is fifty feet long by feventeen broad. Annexed is an interior view of it; Plate XII. The walls are built of hewn ftone, with three pilafters at each fide, which are continued in arches, as bands to the vault, with which it is covered.

The water of this bath is four feet deep; and what is very remarkable, it neither increafes or diminifhes, Winter or Summer, though it has no apparent fource; and notwithftanding it is never cleaned, yet it is always tranfparent, and the fides and bottom are free from weeds or

fediment,

sediment, which, according to Vitruvius, are the surest signs of the salubrity of water.

There is a tradition among the common people, that treasures are hidden beneath the above ruins; and that under this bath are interred a Morisque King, with his treasures, in a tomb of brass, guarded by evil spirits. And not only the common people, but also those who, from their situation in life, ought to know better, give credit to these ridiculous tales.

The village of Cintra, and the different villas at the foot of the mountain, are supplied with water from its summit, by means of little conduits formed along its sides. How this water is collected on the mountain, has given rise to various conjectures: some imagine it to proceed from the distillations of the clouds, which, as we observed before, envelope it morning and evening; but it is evident that an hour of meridian sun, in Summer, will exhale more vapours in this country, than is imbibed by the highest mountain in the course of a night. Others conjecture that the latent moisture is drawn upwards by some magnetic properties of the mountain, in the nature of a siphon; but, strictly speaking, there is no water to be found here on the very summit. The convent, which is seated on the mountain, is supplied by a well, which I compute to be sixty or seventy feet deep; now this is the highest

highest water to be found in this mountain; and the same depth below the surface of the earth is sufficient, generally, to ascertain water in plains: of course, the same cause by which water is impelled to ascend in the latter, will apply to the former. We may also add, that in mountains the interspaces of the rocks may be considered as so many tubes through which water ascends, as in the shafts of wells, owing to its volatile and porous nature; for it is computed to have forty times more space in it than matter: we find a similar effect produced by a cloth partly immersed, and partly hanging over the side of a vessel with water, which it draws out as effectually as a siphon.

At the foot of the above mountain, contiguous to the village of Cintra, is a palace, wherein the Royal family used formerly to reside during the Summer season, on account of the amenity of the place, and the salubrity of the air; for though it is but sixteen miles distant from Lisbon, yet I was assured by a Gentleman, who occasionally resided here for many years, and kept a register of the weather, that he found it, on an average, eight degrees colder in the month of July than the capital.

Notwithstanding this and many other advantages which Cintra possesses over any other part of Portugal, it is but little resorted to by the natives. The palace is entirely deserted, and has not, I believe, been much frequented since the death of Alfonso VI. who ended his miserable life in

it,

it after a close confinement of seven years. The floor of the apartment wherein he was immured, which is paved with tiles, is broken and worn in many parts, from his steps; for he was continually walking in it, or taking snuff, his chief amusements.

The principal crime laid to the charge of this unfortunate Prince was impotency; for this he lost his crown, his wife, and his liberty. He reigned five years, was imprisoned fourteen; eight of which he passed in the island of Tercera, and the remainder here. He died in one thousand six hundred and sixty-nine, in the forty-eighth year of his age; and in three months after died his wife, who married his brother Peter the Second.

This palace, apparently, has been raised by piece-meal, for it is very irregular throughout; the architecture is chiefly Arabian: the ornaments that accompany the windows represent interlaced branches of trees deprived of the leaves, and as though some of the shoots were lopped off. I have given a representation of one of them in the introduction to my description of the monastery of Batalha. Over the kitchen are raised two lofty cones for chimnies, which resemble the shafts of our glasshouses: the apartments are numerous; but the communication from the one to the other is not very convenient. The principal ornaments about it are fountains, which are constantly supplied from the mountains with excellent water: there are

no

no gardens annexed to it on account of the precipice to the rear.

Alfonſo the Fourth, at his acceſſion to the throne, paſſed a month here together in hunting the wild beaſts, which, in his time, roved in numbers about theſe mountains. The ſevere reproof he received from one of his ſubjects on that occaſion deſerves to be recorded.

Whilſt the King was enjoying the pleaſures of the chace with his favourites, the affairs of the ſtate were conſigned to men who ſtudied their own intereſt more than that of the public. The Nobility, perceiving the abuſes of the Miniſters, and the Sovereign's inattention to the duties of his crown, held a council at Liſbon, to which they invited the Prince. He accordingly appeared; but, inſtead of attending to their deliberations, he proceeded to recite his adventures at Cintra, with all the levity of a young ſportſman. When he had finiſhed his narrative, one of the Noblemen ſtood up, and thus addreſſed the King:

"Sire,—Courts and camps were allotted for Kings, not woods and mountains. When buſineſs is ſacrificed to amuſement, the affairs even of private perſons are in danger; but when pleaſure engroſſes the thoughts of a King, a whole nation muſt inevitably be conſigned to ruin. Sire, we came here, not to hear the adventures of the chace, which are intelligible only to grooms and falconers, but to consult the welfare of the people. Your Majesty will find sufficient employment in attending to their wants; and if you will remove the grievances with which they are oppressed, you will find them dutiful and obedient subjects, if not——here the King starting up in a rage interrupted him, saying, *if not*, what then?——If not, resumed the Nobleman in a firm tone, they will look for a better King."

Alfonso hastened out of the room, and in the highest transport of passion expressed his resentment; but as passion always begins in folly and ends in sorrow, his rage soon abated, and he returned with a serene countenance to the assembly, whom he thus addressed:

"I now perceive the truth of what you have just advanced. A King, who will not perform the duties of his throne, cannot have affectionate subjects. Remember, that from this day you have to do, not with Alfonso the sportsman, but with Alfonso the Fourth, King of Portugal." His Majesty did not fail to adhere to his promise. He afterwards became one of the best Kings that ever reigned in Portugal.

The Marquis de Marialva has a mansion near this village, where the Royal family honoured him with a visit on the month of Auguſt laſt. In the evening they were entertained with an excellent concert, conſiſting of upwards of forty performers, among whom were ſome eminent muſicians. Her Majeſty was dreſſed in black. His Royal Highneſs the Prince of Brazil ſat on her right hand, and the two Princeſſes on her left: all were dreſſed in the plaineſt manner, ſuch as every perſon muſt admire who has a juſt ſenſe of true greatneſs. They were attended by ſeveral of the Nobility and Miniſters of ſtate.

The noble hoſt begged her Majeſty's permiſſion to hear an officer of the guards play a ſolo upon a Jew's harp; which being granted, he entered the room fully equipped as on duty, and played a difficult piece in a maſterly manner, inſomuch as peculiarly to arreſt the attention of the Royal viſitants. Next appeared a beautiful girl, about nine years of age, dreſſed in all the tinſel of theatric pride: ſhe ſung an euloge to the Queen; and, at the ſame time, danced a kind of alemande. Her voice was clear and melodious, her action graceful and ſentimental. She did not appear embarraſſed in the leaſt at the preſence of the Sovereign, whoſe power, magnificence, and virtues, ſhe was extolling to the ſkies.

A dance followed after this between a black girl, a native of Africa, and a dwarf belonging to the Marquis de Marialva: the African is named Don Roſa; ſhe lives with her Majeſty, at whoſe feet ſhe ſat during the concert. I obſerved, at different times, that ſhe ſpoke to the Queen, and reſted her hand upon her lap: this inſtance of Royal condeſcenſion to one of that perſecuted race, deſerves to be recorded for the honour of human nature.

About nine o'clock, two of the moſt eminent performers on the violin played a duet: after which the Royal family withdrew to the gardens, where a grand exhibition of fire-works was prepared and played off, under the inſpection of a Prieſt of Cintra.

When this was over, the Royal gueſts ſat down to ſupper, in a ſuperb ſaloon, decorated with green boughs, ſome bearing bloſſoms and others fruit. The table was laid out with all the elegance imaginable. There was alſo a table for the Nobility, Miniſters, and Officers of the guards, and another for the Maids of Honour, in ſeparate apartments. The princely ſtyle in which every thing was conducted, reflects great honour on the well known taſte and hoſpitality of the noble Marquis, whoſe character reſts upon a ſtill more exalted baſis, his attachment to his Sovereign and country, his moderation in all his actions.

About ſix miles South-weſt of the village of Cintra, are ſome veſtiges of a ſtructure, ſuppoſed to have been a temple dedicated to the ſun and moon. *Nunez de Leaõ*, who

who has publiſhed a ſhort deſcription of Portugal, ſays, there remains ſome fragments of it bearing the two following inſcriptions:

SOLI . ET . LUNAE .
CÆTIUS . ACIDUS . PERENNIS .
LEG . AUG . PRO . PROVINCIAE .
LUSITANIÆ .

SOLI . ÆTERNO . LUNÆ . PRO . ÆTERNITATE .
IMPERII . ET . SALUTE . IMPER . CAI .
SEPTIMII . SEVERI . AUGUSTI . PII . ET . IMP .
CAOS . M . AURELII . ANTONINI . PII .
ET . JULIA . —— AUG . — M . —— CÆS .
ET . JULIÆ . AUG . MATRIS . CÆS . DRU .
SUS . VESTER . SICILIANUS . VIATOUS .
AUGUSTORUM . T . Q . JULIUS . SATURNI .
ET . ANTONINUS .

According to Florian de Campo, a continued chain of mountains extends from this place, under the Atlantic Ocean, to the Iſland of Madeira, which is diſtant one hundred and fifty leagues from thence. As it is eaſier to make aſſertions of this kind than to prove them, an author, who is fond of the marvellous, may advance them at pleaſure, without apprehenſion of being refuted by ocular demonſtration. Very few, however, who have ventured into the chaos of conjecture, have ſucceeded better than Huygens; his famous hypotheſis gives us a ſublime idea of the immenſity of ſpace, and of the ineffable works of the Omnipotent Being; beſides, it is not improbable, as he obſerves, *that in the regions of infinity there may be ſtars whoſe light is not yet travelled down to us ſince their firſt creation.*

But to return to our ſubject. Here is a rock called *Pedra da Alvidras*, whoſe height above the ſea, which is at the foot of it, apparently is not leſs than two hundred feet; and though it is very ſteep, and the ſurface ſmooth, yet I am informed that the neighbouring labourers, without ropes or apparatus of any kind, deſcend to the bottom of it to fiſh, each carrying a rod and a baſket, and clamber up the ſame route. They often perform this taſk for a ſmall preſent, to amuſe, or rather to terrify, thoſe who viſit the place. The leaſt ſlip would be fatal to them, as they muſt inevitably be daſhed to pieces againſt the ſharp projecting rocks beneath. I have not heard, however, that any have fallen a ſacrifice to their temerity.

What a ſtriking inſtance is the above of the effects of education. A ſoldier would ſooner undertake to face the mouth of a loaded cannon, than to follow ſuch a daring example; yet theſe people, who are accuſtomed to it from their infancy, appear diveſted of fear on this occaſion, though, perhaps, they dare not venture by night to a place reputed for the haunt of ghoſts or goblins.

A fine valley, called Collares, extends between this and the village of Cintra. It may be called the Golden Vale of Portugal; for it is one of the richeſt and beſt cultivated ſpots

ſpots in the kingdom. The greater part of it is planted with fruit-trees, particularly orange; and though they are ſo cloſe together, that their boughs intertwine, yet they bear vaſt quantities of delicious fruit.

The fruit and green markets of Liſbon are chiefly ſupplied from this luxuriant garden. Muſk and water-melons grow in it in ſuch abundance, that the inhabitants ſell them during the ſeaſon for leſs than a penny a piece.

Of the peculiarity of the ſoil about this diſtrict, Carcavella furniſhes a ſtriking inſtance; where there is a vineyard, of no conſiderable extent, that yields grapes different from thoſe of any other part of the kingdom; its wine is well known all over Europe, but I believe its name is better known in general than its flavour; for it is not poſſible that ſo limited a ſpot can yield one half of the wine ſold in London alone under the denomination of Carcavella, or Calcavella, as it is improperly called.

### *Cork Convent.*

This Convent, or Hermitage, is partly burrowed between the rocks, which ſerve as vaults to the church, ſacriſty, and chapter-houſe, &c. and partly built over the ſurface. The ſubterraneous apartments are lighted by holes cut obliquely in the rocks, and lined internally with cork, to guard againſt the humidity. Hence it is called the Cork Convent. It is inhabited by about twenty hermits of the moſt rigid

rigid Order of Saint Francis. They are governed by a Prior, and live chiefly on fiſh, fruit, and bread: each has a ſeparate cell, about the ſize of a grave, furniſhed with a mattreſs; yet one of their community who lately died, named Honorius, thinking the meaneſt of theſe cells too luxurious a habitation, retired to a circular pit at the rear of the Hermitage, not larger than Diogenes's tub, for it is but four feet diameter; and here, after a reſidence of ſixteen years, he ended his peaceful days at a good old age. The floor of it is ſtrewed with leaves, which ſerved for his bed; and the rugged ſtone, which he uſed alternately as a pillow and ſeat, is ſtill to be ſeen there. Theſe inſtances of ſelf-denial ſhew us into what a narrow compaſs all human wants might be reduced, and evince the truth of the poet's aſſertion:

Man wants but little here below;
Nor wants that little long. *Goldſmith.*

A Portugueſe nobleman, well known for his poetical taſte, wrote a few lines extempore, deſcribing the beauties of this enchanting country, during my reſidence there. I have thus attempted them in Engliſh:

*Deſcription of Cintra.*

'Cintra, whoſe mountains ſeek the ſkies,
Thy vallies deck'd in living green;
Thy flowrets rob'd in varying dies,
With grottos form'd by Fancy's queen.

Refreſhing rills that never fail,
When Phœbus ſhoots his brighteſt beams;
Whilſt balmy odours load each gale,
And nodding fruits ſurvey the ſtreams.

Here Zephyr courts each opening flower,
And birds that charm, of every ſong;
Here echo dwells in mazy bower,
And love that liſts the whole night long.

*Penha Verde*,

Formerly the reſidence of Don John De Caſtro, is now inhabited by one of his deſcendants. Here that great man paſſed the ſhort intervals that peace permitted his abſence from the field or the ocean; alternately employed in ſtudy and cultivating his gardens. To evince his indifference for any emolument that might ariſe from theſe plantations, he cauſed them to be ſtripped of every fruit-tree, and had ſterile ones planted in their place.

Penha Verde, for its extent, is the beſt ſituated for diverſity and proſpect of any villa in the kingdom; the country on every ſide preſents a wild aſſemblage of ſtriking ſcenes; mountains and vallies interſperſed with rocks, wood, and water; little temples and grottos are conſtructed in divers parts of the gardens: the former is furniſhed with altars, which Don John uſed often viſit to pray; a duty which

 he

he ſtrictly obſerved, whether in peace or war; for he juſtly conceived that piety is not incompatible with true courage. To a man of his caſt of mind, there cannot be a more appropriate reſidence: as the greater part of his life was ſpent among ſcenes of the moſt tumultuous nature, in Europe, Aſia, or Africa, the wilds of Cintra ſerved but to fan that ſpirit of enterpriſe which animated him till the laſt hour of his life.

The actions of this celebrated character have been recorded by different writers, particularly Jacinto Freyre de Andrade, who has publiſhed an account of his life; and they all allow that he deſerves to be claſſed in the firſt rank of Chriſtian heroes. A man who, by his precepts and example, contributed ſo much to the advancement of public and private virtue, and left to poſterity the moſt illuſtrious inſtances of courage, probity, and patriotiſm, is entitled to a more honourable niche than I can beſtow him among theſe trifling fragments. The ſketch that I am about to offer of his memoirs is collected, partly from thoſe eſteemed the beſt Portugueſe writers, and partly from the oral tradition of well-informed people.

*Don*

### *Don John de Castro.*

Don John de Castro was born at Lisbon in the year one thousand five hundred, of an illustrious family. In his youth he appears to have made great progress in mathematics, under the celebrated Peter Nonnius, one of the ablest professors of that science of his time. Fired with the military fame of his countrymen, he was determined to share the laurels which they were then reaping at Tangiers, the seat of martial achievements; for this purpose he departed secretly from his parents at the age of eighteen, and soon after appeared at Africa in the front of battle. His valour and prudence did not pass unnoticed here, for he was knighted in the field by Don Edward de Menezes, the Governor of Tangiers.

After serving nine years in this place, he returned to his native country, where he was received by his Sovereign and fellow-citizens with every mark of distinction to which his services justly entitled him: conscious, however, that he had only done his duty, his mind was not to be diverted by the applause of the moment. He retired to the solitary rocks of Cintra, not to repose on his laurels, but to promote the farther welfare of his country, by the application of an active and capacious mind to the studies necessary to constitute a great commander.

As his health, which had been injured by wounds and fatigue, began to mend, he was impatient to put the plans he had deviſed in the cloſet into execution, which, in a ſhort time, he partly accompliſhed in various engagements by ſea under his command.

The tranquillity of affairs in Africa now afforded him an opportunity of diſplaying his talents in another quarter. He ſet out for India as a volunteer, and accompanied *Eſtevaon de Gama* in his expedition to the mouth of the Red Sea. The King ſent out orders to the Governor of Goa, to pay him a thouſand *cruſados* annually as long as he remained in that country: but Don John refuſed this bounty, thinking it more honourable to live frugally on his own ſcanty fortune, than be ranked among the needy penſioners of the crown.

During the intervals of repoſe in this expedition was Don John employed in making charts, and taking obſervations of the bays and coaſts along the Straits of Suez. He is ſaid to have made many judicious obſervations on the Red Sea, and on the cauſe of the overflow of the Nile. Theſe, together with other pieces written in the courſe of his voyages, he dedicated to the early companion of his ſtudies, Don Lewis, brother to the King.

But there is one thing ſtill more remarkable of him in that expedition, though, perhaps, not generally known.

At

At his return he is ſaid to have brought to Portugal the firſt orange-tree ever ſeen in Europe, and from which originated all that valuable fruitage we poſſeſs at this day. The ſervice he rendered mankind by this act alone entitles him to the gratitude of poſterity; and he himſelf was not ſo dazzled with the love of military fame, as not to eſteem this gift to his country as the greateſt of all his actions.

And here it may be reaſonably aſked, why a perſon of his diſtinguiſhed talents was not inveſted with ſome important command in Aſia? But his biographer thus reſolves the queſtion: In his days, as at preſent, the Sovereign's favour was but too often obtained through the influence of favourites; and as Don John was not of an obſequious diſpoſition, and too proud to derive any diſtinction from the minions of a court, it is not matter of ſurpriſe that he remained ſo long neglected.

The time, however, arrived when the King, waving all conſiderations of miniſterial influence, reſolved to reward one faithful ſervant, in Don John de Caſtro, who had never aſked him a favour, nor ever denied his ſervices in his country's cauſe. His Majeſty ſent for him ſhortly after his arrival from India, and appointed him Governor of all his territories in the Eaſt. He accordingly ſet out with the general wiſhes of the nation, to take

upon

upon him this important command, on the ſeventeenth of March one thouſand five hundred and forty-five.

Having arrived at the ſeat of government, he found innumerable difficulties to ſurmount; an expenſive war had exhauſted the treaſury, and the troops were ſunk into effeminacy and diſſipation. Don John, however, was not to be intimidated by ſuch diſcouraging circumſtances. He immediately ſet about reforming every department of the ſtate, civil and military, and in a ſhort time reſtored œconomy to the one, frugality and diſcipline to the other; he himſelf was the firſt to ſet the example in each, thereby enforcing his precepts by his practice.

But the moſt difficult part of the taſk was to reform the ſoldiers from their depraved habits; and in accompliſhing this, he might be ſaid to have cheated them into diſcipline; for the only means he employed was emulation, of all other means the moſt congenial to the pride of a ſoldier. For this purpoſe he introduced every manly exerciſe that could brace the ſinews and baniſh effeminacy: military evolutions, feats of horſemanſhip, wreſtling, racing, throwing the bar, &c. indeed it may be ſaid that he revived the emulation of the Olympic games in the plains of Goa. The moments of repoſe were ſparingly counted to every ſoldier, and out of theſe they were obliged to devote a certain time in ſcouring and brighten-

ing

ing their armour, which heretofore had been covered with ruſt. An army thus inured to every hardſhip, and the ſcorching rays of a vertical ſun, were impatient to be led into the field of battle; their warlike appearance ſtruck the enemy with terror, and victory in every conflict declared in their favour. What a ſtrange appearance a legion of ſuch brave ſun-burnt fellows would make among the modern Portugueſe, who eſtimate men by their indolence, by the fairneſs of their ſkin, and the delicacy of their fingers!

Of the ſeveral engagements in which our hero diſtinguiſhed himſelf, we ſhall, for brevity's ſake, notice but the one which contributed moſt to exalt his military reputation, and that was at the relief of Dio. The King of Cambaya, with all the forces of his kingdom, laid ſiege to this fortreſs, aſſiſted by a numerous army from the Grand Sultan. During ſeveral months the gallant Don John Maſcarenhas defended it with a handful of men againſt the enemy, who are ſaid to have been upwards of fifty thouſand in number, and had ſixty pieces of braſs cannon. The command of this army was given by the Sultan to Cogé-Sofar, the ableſt general in his dominions. Having drawn up his forces before the fortreſs of Dio, he addreſſed them to this effect:

"Friends and companions, It is almoſt unneceſſary for me to mention how you ought to deſpiſe that handful of Portugueſe

guese before you; they are scarcely five hundred in number, without possibility of receiving any reinforcement by land, and the winter cuts off their prospects of succour by sea. Our incessant attacks will constantly employ them on the walls, or in repairing the breaches of our cannons; fatigue will overpower them, and they must necessarily yield; for they will not have one soldier in reserve. Behold, my friends, to what a scene of glory I have brought you, to humble the pride of the insolent *Christians*, the sworn enemies of our Prophet, and to avenge the blood of your relations and friends, whose bones are interred beneath the ground you stand on. Hark! methinks I hear them groaning with their wounds, and calling on us to purge the land of these impious barbarians, the murderers of the great Badur."

When he had finished his speech, he sent a message to the Governor of the fortress, threatening, if he did not accept of the terms offered in it, to put every man in the garrison to the sword. Mascarenhas returned for answer, "That the Portuguese were not accustomed to receive laws at the point of the bayonet, and that he would agree to none different from those which already existed relative to the garrison of Dio. If Cogé Sofar did not accept of these conditions, he must accept of worse, which should be written with the blood of his Janizaries."

Don

Don John de Caſtro, who at this time was at Goa, loſt not a moment in preparing for the relief of the beſieged; he equipped nine ſmall veſſels for that expedition, in which he told his ſoldiers none were to be admitted but his favourites. Then calling for his ſon Ferdinand, who was but a private ſoldier, he addreſſed him in the preſence of the troops, in the following manner:

"I ſend you with this relief to Dio, which is now beſieged by an army of Turks; and I charge you to do your duty as a ſoldier, otherwiſe I ſhall no longer acknowledge you as a ſon. Let no conſideration of family diſtinction betray you into error; for remember that all men by birth are equal, and that you are not entitled to the leaſt pre-eminence over any of your companions, but in proportion as you excel them in acts of valour and virtue. Let no man, therefore, ſurpaſs you in obedience to the commands of your Captain, in zeal for your Sovereign, and love for your country. Go then, in the name of God, and purchaſe honour for yourſelf, and either return to me victorious, or not at all."—In this collateral manner was Don John wont to animate his troops, and to curb the pride of the young Nobility.

The fleet having arrived at Dio, the Governor received a very friendly letter from Don John, wherein, among other things, he mentioned how much he envied the glorious poſt he filled, a poſt much more honourable than

 that,

that of Governor of India. I ſend you (ſaid he) with this relief my ſon Ferdinand, who, I truſt, will be ſurpaſſed by none in affection to your perſon, and obedience to your orders: if the boy ſhould ever return to his native country, with what exultation will he relate, among the vanities of old age, the honour of having ſerved as a ſoldier under the brave Don John Maſceranhas.

As ſoon as the troops were landed, the Governor aſſembled his men in the parade, and addreſſed them thus: " Behold, my brethren, theſe Turks and Janizaries, who vainly attempt to recover the honour they have loſt in the firſt ſiege againſt this fortreſs; but theſe are not more conſiderable than thoſe who were vanquiſhed, nor we leſs than the vanquiſhers. What! have thoſe brave Portugueſe who conquered them carried every fame into the grave, and left us none to tranſmit to poſterity? No, my brethren, let us convince the world that we are not leſs brave than they. We have not ſailed five thouſand leagues to become ſlaves to infidels, and to tarniſh the renown of our country. We want for nothing: our proviſion and ammunition will hold out until ſuccour arrives; and though at this ſeaſon the ſeas are difficult to encounter, yet have we a Don John de Caſtro, who, I pledge myſelf, will make his way through the waves, with his ſword in his mouth, to come to our aſſiſtance. If any thing could inſpire men with true courage, it is the glorious cauſe in which we are engaged; the honour and intereſt of our

King

King and country, our property, our lives, and what is ſtill more dear to us, our holy religion. Let every ſinew then be exerted againſt that hord of barbarians that would rob us of all theſe invaluable conſiderations, and we cannot fail to be victorious if we are unanimous; for though our number is but ſmall, our power is great, for the God of victories aſſiſts us."

By this and other well timed diſcourſes, Don John Maſceranhas ſo animated his men, that he performed prodigies of valour during the eight months that he ſuſtained this deſperate ſiege. At length Don John de Caſtro arrived, and brought with him all the Portugueſe forces he could collect in Aſia. The troops of the garriſon now amounted to about four thouſand, including ſeamen and auxiliaries; with theſe he reſolved immediately to terminate the ſiege.

On the evening previous to his making the attack, he diſtributed his army into four columns, giving the command of one to Don John Maſceranhas, another to his eldeſt ſon, Don Alvares de Caſtro, a tried veteran; Don Manuel de Lima led the third, and the fourth he reſerved for himſelf. Next morning, at break of day, he ordered a public maſs to be celebrated in the midſt of the parade, at which he himſelf, and the greateſt part of the garriſon, received the ſacrament. This ſolemn ſervice being over, he addreſſed the men in an animated ſpeech: and to convince

 them

them that there was no alternative but death if they did not conquer, he commanded the gates of the fortreſs to be taken down and burnt. After this every man reſumed his poſt: the ſignal being given, they ſallied out, ſword in hand, and completely routed the enemy. Five thouſand Moors are ſaid to have periſhed in this day's engagement, together with Ramaçaon their General, and ſeveral other Moors of diſtinction. Cogé Sofar, the father of Ramaçaon, had been killed ſome time before, as was alſo Juxarcaon. Another General of the ſame name was taken priſoner, together with ſix hundred men. Forty pieces of cannon, and ſeveral ſtands of colours, alſo fell into the hands of the victors, beſides a conſiderable treaſure found by the ſoldiers in the town contiguous to the fortreſs which was delivered up to plunder.

We ſhould not forget to mention a circumſtance, which, in a great degree, contributed to forward the above victory. During the engagement, Father Caſal, the chaplain of the garriſon, carried a crucifix on the point of a ſpear, with which he appeared wherever the combat was moſt obſtinate, animating the men. It happened that the column under Alvares de Caſtro was overpowered, and thrown into diſorder, and all his entreaty to rally them was in vain. The Prieſt, however, effected what the General could not; he ſhewed them the crucifix which a weapon had ſtruck and thrown into a reclined poſture, exclaiming, at the ſame time, *ſacrilege, ſacrilege. Oh! ſoldiers of Chriſt, re-*

*venge the ſacrilege!* on which the ſcattered ſoldiers, animated with an enthuſiaſtic rage, advanced to the charge, and determined the battle.

In conſequence of this important victory, the Portugueſe poſſeſſions in India were ſecured for the preſent; but Don John, who never left any thing to chance which he could effect by foreſight, reſolved to follow up the advantage he had recently obtained without loſing a moment. In the firſt place, he ſet about rebuilding, upon a new conſtruction, the garriſon of Dio, as the old one had been nearly demoliſhed by the enemies cannon; but this object was not to be accompliſhed without money, and the treaſury was quite exhauſted; as to himſelf, he had nothing beſides his ſword and helmet. Having in vain tried ſeveral expedients to raiſe ſupplies, he at length thought of one, which may appear rather ſingular at the preſent day: he reſolved to depoſite the bones of his beloved ſon, Don Ferdinand, who had fallen in the ſiege, for the ſum he required. Accordingly he ordered the grave to be opened and the body raiſed: he embraced it tenderly, ſaying, whilſt the tears guſhed from his eyes, my ſon, thou art dear to me even in death; but my duty commands me to ſtifle the feelings of nature, when my country's ſafety is at ſtake. As the corpſe ſcarce exhibited any marks of excarnation, his officers prevailed on him to permit it to be re-interred; and in lieu of it, he ſent a lock of his own muſtaches to the inhabitants of Goa, as a ſecurity for

for the ſum of twenty thouſand pardaos. They immediately advanced more than he required, as a free gift, and returned the honourable pledge by a ſpecial meſſenger, who was alſo charged with a letter highly expreſſive of the deep ſenſe they entertained of his patriotiſm.

Some idea of this great man's character may be conceived from theſe faint ſketches: to enumerate all the meritorious acts of his life, would exceed the limits we preſcribe to this work; we ſhall therefore paſs them over, and haſten to a ſcene that crowned his glorious career.

The account of his victory having reached the King his maſter, he appointed a day of ſolemn thankſgiving. The Pope and ſeveral Princes congratulated him on the occaſion, and every one in the kingdom received the news with demonſtrations of joy except the Queen; ſhe too had no objection to the victory, but envied the honour of the victor, becauſe he was received in triumph at his happy return to Goa. This gave her Majeſty ſuch umbrage, that ſhe obſerved, *Don John de Caſtro conquers like a Chriſtian, but triumphs like a Heathen.*

In his letters to his Majeſty he ſolicited leave to return home, entreating, at the ſame time, if he approved his ſervices, that he would grant him two acres of ground, or rather rocks, which border on his little villa at Cintra. The latter the King granted, but refuſed the former; aſſuring

assuring him of the high estimation in which he held his services, and requesting him to continue his command three years longer. Hitherto Don John had only the title of Governor of India, but now the King salutes him, *Vice King and Friend.* He lived, however, but a short time to give lustre to these honours. He was attacked by a violent sickness, and expired in a few days in the arms of his confessor, in the forty-eighth year of his age, and third of his administration in India.

A short time before his dissolution, he assembled in his chamber the Magistrates of Goa, and the different Officers of State, to whom he delivered up the government. After which he addressed them in the following speech:

" I am almost ashamed to tell you, Gentlemen, that the Viceroy of India, expiring with wounds and fatigues on this bed of sickness, is in want of the necessaries which even a private soldier finds in an hospital. You are sensible, that as long as there was an enemy to subdue, I have not been sparing of toil or fatigue in every thing which tend to the glory of our King and country; and now, that we have subdued our foes, and established an honourable peace with all the powers of the East, a worn out soldier, who has contributed so often to your victories, has some claim to your regard. It is probable, that in a short time I shall be no more; and short as I am likely to exist, I have not wherewithal to support or nourish me;

 for

for I have laid out to the laſt ſhilling in relieving the wants of my brother ſoldiers, and have left nothing to relieve my own; nay, not ſo much as would buy a fowl for my dinner. I requeſt, therefore, that you will provide a perſon of your own to provide a frugal maintenance for me out of the King's revenue. I alſo requeſt, that you will order me a change of bed-linen, as I have not a ſecond quilt to my bed." Then raiſing himſelf up, with the aſſiſtance of his confeſſor, the venerable Xavier, he laid his hand on the Goſpel, and ſolemnly ſwore on it to the truth of what he had juſt advanced; and deſired the Secretary of Goa to take minutes of it, and enter it on the journals of the Council of State, in order that, if the fact was not found as he had ſtated, his memory and his poſterity might be branded with infamy. We ſhall only obſerve, that time evinced the truth of every word he uttered in his laſt moments; for all the money found in his cabinet did not exceed a *vintem*; that is, leſs than three half-pence.

A few days before he expired, he ordered that his body ſhould be interred in the Franciſcan church at Goa, and tranſlated from thence by the firſt opportunity to the chapel belonging to his villa at Cintra. In all his actions he never loſt ſight of this charming retreat, wherein he hoped one day to paſs the evening of life in ſtudy and meditation, as appears by the letter he wrote after the ſiege of Dio, to the Infante Don Luis, requeſting he would

intercede

intercede with the King for his recal. The Infante, in his affectionate reply, uſes this expreſſion: "After your "performance of the Royal will, I truſt you will cover "the tops of the rocks of Cintra with chapels and tro-"phies of your victories, and long enjoy them in pro-"found repoſe." His remains are now repoſited in the Dominican convent at Bemfica near Liſbon, where his grandſon erected a monument to his memory, with the following inſcription:

D. JOANNES DE CASTRO
XX. PRO RELIGIONE IN UTRAQUE
MAURITANIA STIPENDIIS FACTIS:
NAVATA STRENUE OPERA THUNETANO
BELLO:
MARI RUBRO FELIÇIBUS ARMIS PENETRATO:
DEBELLATIS INTER EUPHRATEM ET INDUM
NATIONIBUS.
GEDROSICO REGE, PERSIS, TURCIS
UNO PRÆLIO FUSIS:
SERVATO DIO, IMO REIPUB. REDDITO:
DORMIT IN MAGNUM DIEM:
NON SIBI, SED DEO TRIUMPHATOR:
PUBLICIS LACRYMIS COMPOSITUS,
PUBLICO SUMPTU PRÆ PAUPERTATE
FUNERATUS.
OBIT OCT. ID. JUN. ANNO M.D.XLVIII.
ÆTATIS XLVIII.

*Sanſkreet Inſcription.*

This inſcriptional ſtone is one of the trophies Don John de Caſtro obtained in India: it is to be ſeen in his garden at Cintra. His Excellency Chevalier de Souſa, the preſent Envoy at the court of Sweden, informs me, that "it was brought, with other antiquities, from India by "the Duke de Bragança, and delivered by him to the "heir of Don John de Caſtro." Lafiteau mentions it from Diogo de Couto.

In the ſame garden is another inſcriptional ſtone, the characters of which are almoſt entirely defaced by the weather. The upper part of it exhibits the emblems of the Sun and Moon; and the repreſentation of a man ſtruggling with a rampant beaſt is ſculptured in bas relief on the foot of it. There is alſo a decapitated centaur of tolerable workmanſhip ſtanding on a pedeſtal near theſe inſcriptional ſtones, which are all the Aſiatic antiquities that remain here at preſent.

Several travellers, who have viſited Portugal from time to time, are ſaid to have copied ſome of the characters of this Sanſkreet Inſcription, or taken impreſſions of a few of them on plaſter of Paris or wax. And the late Reverend Mr. Allen, formerly Chaplain to the Britiſh factory at Liſbon, copied the two extreme lines and middle one.

This, I am informed, was the greateſt progreſs made in tranſcribing it ſince it arrived in Portugal, (which appears to be about the year one thouſand five hundred and ſixty-ſix,) until I made the copy hereunto annexed, in one thouſand ſeven hundred and eighty-nine. *Vide* Plate XIII.

To the antiquary, a ſhort account of the manner in which it has been copied may not be unacceptable; the proceſs was very ſimple. In the firſt place, I prepared as many ſtrips of paper as there are lines in the whole; to wit, ſixty-ſix; on each of which were drawn two parallel lines, leaving a ſpace between, equal to the height of the letters. Theſe ſtrips being placed, one after the other, immediately under the lines, and faſtened with wax at each end; the letters then were drawn on them with a black lead pencil, exactly under the correſponding ones of the prototype. There are many other ways, I am aware, of copying inſcriptions of this kind, ſome of which are very expeditious; but the neceſſary apparatus for that purpoſe I had not at hand; and I doubt, on the whole, if there be any proceſs leſs ſubject to error than the above.

The characters are all ſunk, beautifully cut, and in excellent preſervation; each is two-fifths of an inch in height; the ſpace between each line is one-fourth of an inch. In the copy ſubjoined are preſerved the proportions of the original, both in the detail and general diſtribution.

 The

The defects obſerved in the ſtone are not, for the moſt part, owing to the natural decays of time, but to accidents it received, perhaps, in the carriage; for it is very hard, being of the baſaltes ſpecies, and of a blackiſh hue. Some imagine that the face of it was formerly gilt, and I have noticed in one or two places ſome traces that appeared to juſtify the conjecture.

Hitherto the language in which it is written has been conſidered as Hindoo, and the meaning remained an enigma, though ſome attempts to aſcertain it has been made by the three lines before mentioned, that were copied by the Reverend Mr. Allen. Some account of theſe is ſaid to have been publiſhed by a Profeſſor of Oriental languages in Germany. The information, however, I have received on this head is too imperfect to lay before the public. I ſhall therefore take no further notice of it, ſince it is manifeſt that very little or nothing to the purpoſe could poſſibly be deduced from ſo ſmall and disjointed a portion of the whole. I am happy, at length, to be enabled to lay before the public the purport of this curious inſcription, which has eluded the reſearches, not only of the Portugueſe, but of all the literati of Europe for upwards of two hundred years paſt. And for this I am indebted to the pen of the learned and ingenious Mr. Wilkins, whoſe extenſive knowledge of Oriental literature is a laſting honour to his country. I ſhould not omit this opportunity

 of

of acknowledging my obligations to him for the polite manner in which he undertook this troubleſome taſk; induced by no other motive than that of gratifying public curioſity.

Of the difficulty of making a complete tranſlation, the dilapidations repreſented in the copy are not the only impediments. Some miſtakes, perhaps, might have occurred on my part in tranſcribing it, that renders the interpretation of the remainder not very eaſy. Mr. Wilkins has judiciouſly pointed out the probability of ſuch miſtakes; as may be inferred from his letter; of which we preſent a copy.

S I R, Hawkhurſt, Kent, July 20th, 1793.

I have beſtowed no little labour to decipher the inſcription; and how much of it has been in vain, you may judge from a peruſal of the few ſheets of memorandums which accompany this; and which, though ſufficient to determine the queſtion concerning the intention of it, will not be ſo acceptable as a complete tranſlation; to which there were many inſuperable obſtructions, beſides thoſe which are obvious: ſome of which I will take the liberty to mention. The characters ग g. म m. स s. न n. त t. & व u are perpetually in the place of one another, as are alſo प p; ष sh & श ś; व v. ब b; च ch & र r; द d & ह h &c. This cannot but occaſion very great confuſion. I find alſo the ſingle dot ° and the double ditto

ditto ° very often omitted; both of which are of great importance in *Sanſkreet*.

To the memorandums I have annexed my rough Notes reſpecting the meaſure of each verſe.

The proper name for the Inſcription is *Sāſana*, which ſignifies an *Ordinance*. It is the term given to it in the inſtrument itſelf.

I remain,

SIR,

Your moſt obedient humble Servant,

C. WILKINS.

*To James Murphy, Eſq. London.*

MEMORANDUMS

MEMORANDUMS *of an* INSCRIPTION *in the Sanſkreet Language and Déva-Nagaree Character.* Tranſlated by Charles Wilkins, Eſq.

Reverence to the God SEEVA.

Verſe 1. The meaning very obſcure.

2. Very enigmatical.—A certain Prince diſpenſes bleſſings day and night.

3. Eulogy of the perſon whoſe name appears in the next verſe. States, that he enjoyed riches and happineſs through the bleſſing of the God *Seeva*, who is here called *Kapardee*; that his good fortune was pleaſing to the God with the ſingle tuſk, the good of the three regions of the world, the offspring of the enemy of the incorporeal divinity by whom he was conducted. (*Ganéſa*, the God of Prudence and Policy, the ſon of *Seeva*, (Time,) the enemy of the God of Love.)

4. Part of this verſe unintelligible.—A perſon of the name of *Veeſwa Malla* is repreſented as the jewel of the diadem of Kings, and as a victorious King, giving luſtre to the race of Oolookya. His adminiſtration flowed in a hundred endleſs ſtreams from the prime eſſence of the reſervoir of ſelf-reſtraint.

5. Part illegible. Still relates to *Veeſwa Malla*, and ſomething about pulling up the root of the tree of plenty, not by the thunderbolt, but by means of a certain perſon of the houſehold of the military order, whoſe name was *Raja-nārāyana*.

6. The Lord *Védya Nātha*, who adorns the whole earth, and whoſe mightineſs ſhews compaſſion for the pains and troubles with which ſhe is ſurrounded, placed in him a portion of his own ſpirit.——Second hemiſtic unintelligible.

Verſe

Verſe 7. He had a wife, whoſe title was *Nāgalla Devee*, with a form like the Goddeſs Sree, by whom the Raja had children, who were the confuſion of his enemies.

8. The meaning of this verſe rather obſcure. *Bhooja Pratāpa*, the younger brother of *Pratāpa-Malla*, got poſſeſſion of the government by force.

9. In the firſt hemiſtic *Veeſwa Malla* places the ſon of *Pratāpa Malla* in his ſtead.—The ſecond part of this verſe is imperfect.—Contains ſomething about *Veeſwa Malla's* partaking of holy ſood, with the immortal water which bears the name of his wife.

10. A very obſcure verſe, and, in ſome places, imperfect. *Arjoona*, who is deſcribed a youth of extraordinary abilities, is called *Arjoona Deva*.

11. In his hand he bore the mark of a wheel, and was a protector of his people. A difficult verſe.

12. His offspring, *Sāranga Dēva*, defeats the chiefs of *Goojara*, who are repreſented as overcome with the pride of wealth.

13. He is deſcribed as having been victorious in a battle between the *Yadava* and *Mālava* chiefs, and is compared to the eagle of *Veeſhnoo* (which, in the fable of the elephant and tortoiſe ſtruggling for ſuperiority, came down and carried them both away).

14. His ſon *Nakoolee*, like a divinity, comes from above to ſhew favour to the human race;

15. And to ſhew favour to the race of *Oolookya*, who, for a long time, had lain under a father's curſe.

16. Four inſpired perſons, whoſe names were *Kooſeeka*, *Gārggya*, *Karooſha*, and *Matrēya*, deſcend upon the earth, for the purpoſe of performing certain ceremonies called *Pāſoo-puta-vrata*, and that they were his attendants.

17. The meaning rather obſcure.—Being rendered humble by ſome holy man, he was an ornament to the world which is watered by four ſeas.—Some ſyllables wanting in the firſt foot.

Verſe

Verſe 18. This verſe is alſo defective and obſcure.—From a certain family, ſtated to have been favoured by thoſe four holy men, proceeded the race of *Gārggéya*, a generation of boundleſs minds.

19. The firſt hemiſtic ſtates, that a perſon of the name of *Kārteeka-rāſee* was the deliverer of the family of *Gārggéya*, and chief of the place. The ſecond hemiſtic is imperfect.

20. Imperfect and very unintelligible. *Vālmeekeerāſee* ſeems to be here mentioned as the ſucceſſor of *Kārteeka-rāſee*.

21. The Prince is herein likened to the God *Treepoorāntaka*, and certain great men to other immortals; and it is ſtated that this is recorded upon a ſtone.

22. *Treepoorāntaka* is repreſented as the *diſciple*, or (rather perhaps) the ſucceſſor of *Vālmeekeerāſee*.—The greateſt part of this verſe is very obſcure.

23. Unintelligible.

24. Defective.—Relates to the performance of a pilgrimage.

25. Ditto. ditto ditto

26. Ditto. ditto ditto

27. Ditto. ditto ditto

28. Ditto. ditto ditto

29. Ditto. ditto ditto

30. He meditates on the goodneſs of the God *Rāma*, and viſits *Lankā*, and the dike or bridge ſuppoſed to have been conſtructed during the wars of *Rāma* and *Rāvana*, between the iſland of Ceylon and the continent.

31. Very intricate.—Viſits ſome other holy place.

32. Viſits the river *Saraſwatee* and *Prayāga*.

33. Viſits the city of the God who bears a creſcent, which he adorns. (Banaris.)

34. The illuſtrious *Ganda Vreehaſpatee*, having deſigned it by means of a *Brāhman*, built a magnificent place:

35. Judging, that through the means of the purity of his actions, he ſhould atchieve the greateſt degree of renown, he here rejoiced.' Rather obſcure.

Verse 36. Very imperfect and obscure. It states, that the illustrious *Treepoorāntaka* is also the reflection of the jewel of the diadem of the race of heaven, &c. &c.

37. Obscure.—He bestowed splendid gifts upon some distressed person.

38. Very intricate.—States that Ramā, which means either his wife or his fortune, was the ornament of the world.

39. Very enigmatical. From whose splendid virtues the great men, who delight to sport in the atoms which float in the beams of light issuing from the beauty of the leaf of the sleepy *Ketakee* of the diadem of the Goddess *Saraswatee*, went to adorn the females of the eight points.

40. By which wise man (meaning *Treepoorāntaka*) were founded five temples for burnt-offerings, called *Āyatanas*, to the North of the *Mandapa* (Sarai) of the *Āyatana* of *Sōmēswara*, near the old bell-house of *Sree Bhājee*, and under the protection of the five glories of *Sree Kanta.*

41. The man to whom belongs the excessive magnificence of great minds, who for the happiness of the mother Lady of *Mālhana* *, placed there the Lord of *Mālhana.*

42. The wise man, whose actions are those of the first age, who there constructed an *Āyatana* for the husband of *Oomā*, by name *Gandavreebaspatee.*

43. Who, being the renown of great men, for the happiness of *Oomā* the wife of *Vreebaspatee*, set up the husband of *Oomā.*

44. Here the husband of *Ramā*, called the Lord *Treepoorantaka Ramēswara*, even by his own name, by the favourite name of the protector of the beautiful *Treepoorantēēkā.*

45. Who, being one whose mind was fixed on him on whose diadem is a crescent, placed in the midst of the five *Āyatanas*, the Goddess *Saraswatee*, the God who conducteth to the accomplishment of our wishes, (Ganésa,) and (some others whose names are not easily to be made out.)

* Perhaps the name of the place.

Verse

Verse 46. Seems very incorrect. Who constructed a pillar without the North gate of the place.

47. A person of the name of Jagannātha Kōlanee appointed to clean the Gods every day.

48.
49.
50.
51.
52.
53.
54.
55.
56.
57. All these verses relate to a variety of duties to be performed in the temples, to the offerings ordained to be made, and to the digging of reservoirs for oblations, &c., &c.
58.
59.
60.
61.
62.
63.
64.
65.
66.
67.
68.
69.

70. He gave an *Āyatana* for the use of the *Chātoorjatakapāla*, because a gate had been broken, and had tumbled down.

71. He founded this holy place, and set up this *Sāsana* (ordinance) with his own well-earned wealth.

72. He built the pleasant house of *Srēē* in the midst of the *Āyatana*, and set up a table of his own divine genealogy, for the glory of the illustrious *Ganda-ranaka-vrehaspatee*, and *Sāranga Bhoopatee*.

 Verse

Verse 73. A long laboured verse of four feet of fourteen syllables each, totally unintelligible.

74. Ditto ditto.

75. Ditto ditto.

76. Ditto ditto.

77. In the year of the Æra of *Srēē Veekrama* 1343, 5th of the bright half of the Moon in the month of Măgha *. The great feast of the solemnities of the *Leenga* (Priapus) in the assembly.

*Memorandum of the kinds of Verse the* Săsana *is composed in.*

Verse 1. A long verse of four feet, called Ārya.

2. Four feet of fourteen syllables each, called Vasanta-teelakam, in this form:
— — ◡ — ◡ ◡ ◡ — ◡ ◡ — ◡ — —

3.
4. } Same measure as
5.

6. Four feet of nineteen syllables each, called Sardoolaveekreereeta, in this form: — — — ◡ ◡ — ◡ — ◡ ◡ ◡ — — — ◡ — — ◡ —.

7. Four feet of eleven syllables each, in this form: — — ◡ — — ◡ ◡ — ◡ — —. It is called *Eendravajra.*

8. Ditto ditto.

9. Ditto ditto, but incorrect.

10. Same as second;—one syllable wanting (स) in the first foot.

11. Ditto ditto.

12. Ditto ditto.

13. Is a curious species of verse, called *Ārya*; to compose which, it is necessary that the quantity of the first and third feet be equal to twelve short syllables, the second

* December, A. D. 1286.

foot

foot equal to eighteen shorts, and the fourth to fifteen.

14. Four feet of nineteen syllables.—Seems very incorrect.

15. Four feet of twelve syllables, called *Venastabeela*:

◡ — ◡ — — ◡ ◡ — ◡ — ◡ —.

16. Same as thirteenth,

17. A species of verse of all others the most common, called *Onoostbtoopa*; four feet each of eight syllables. The rule for constructing it is that the fifth syllable in each foot be short, the seventh short in the second and fourth feet, and the sixth long in each foot.

18. Ditto.

19. Four feet of eleven syllables each, the same as seventh. Imperfect.

20. Same as second.

21. Ditto.

22. Same as seventh.

23. Same as second.

24. Uncertain. Many syllables wanting.

25. Same as seventh. Greatest part of the second and third feet wanting.

26. Ditto. Five syllables wanting in third foot, and three in the fourth.

27. A verse of eleven syllables, where the third, sixth, seventh, and ninth syllables are short. Seven syllables deficient in fourth foot.

28. A verse of fourteen syllables to the foot. Seven syllables wanting in the fourth foot.

29. A verse of eleven syllables. Four syllables wanting in last foot.

30. Ditto, in this form:

| | | | |
|---|---|---|---|
| ◡ — ◡ — | ◡ ◡ | ◡ — — |
| — — ◡ — | ◡ ◡ | ◡ — — |
| ◡ | ◡ ◡ | ◡ — — |
| ◡ | ◡ ◡ | ◡ — — |

Verse

Verse 31. A verse of fourteen syllables, the same as second.
32. of 11 syllables to the foot.
33. of 12 ditto.
34. of 8 ditto.
35. of 11 ditto.
36. of 19 ditto. Same as 6th.
37. of 12 ditto. Same as 15th.
38. of 11 ditto. In this form: — ᴗ — ᴗ ᴗ ᴗ — ᴗ — ᴗ —. Called *Rathodḥatā*.
39. of 12 ditto. Same as 15th.
40. of 14 ditto. Same as 2d.
41. of 8 ditto. Seems incorrect.
42. of 8 ditto.
43. of 8 ditto.
44. of 12 ditto. Same as 15th.
45. of 11 ditto. Same as 38th.
46. of 11 ditto. ditto.
47. of 8 ditto.
48. of 8 ditto.
49. Same as 1st and 13th.
50. of 8 ditto.
51. of 8 ditto.
52. of 8 ditto.
53. of 8 ditto.
54. of 9 ditto. Seems imperfect.
55. of 8 ditto. Imperfect.
56. of 8 ditto. ditto.
57. of 8 ditto. ditto.
58. of 8 ditto. ditto.
59. of 8 ditto. ditto.
60. of 8 ditto. ditto.
61. of 8 ditto.
62. of 8 ditto.
63. of 8 ditto.
64. of 8 ditto.

Verse 65. A verse of 11 syllables to the foot. Called *Sāleenee.*
66. of 11 ditto. Same as 7th.
67. of 8 ditto.
68. of 12 ditto. Called *Eendravansa.* In this form:
— — ∪ — — ∪ ∪ — ∪ — ∪ —
69. of 11 ditto. In this form:
∪ ∪ ∪ — — ∪ ∪ — ∪ — —
— — ∪ — — ∪ ∪ — ∪ — —
∪ ∪ ∪ — — ∪ ∪ — ∪ — —
— — ∪ — — ∪ ∪ — ∪ — —
70. of 8 syllables.
71. of 14 ditto. Same as 2d.
72. of 14 ditto. ditto.
73. of 14 ditto. ditto.
74. of 14 ditto. ditto.
75. of 14 ditto. ditto.
76. Uncertain, being imperfect.
Conclusion in Prose.

*N. B.* The verses do not begin with the lines; but their endings may be known by the numbers.

## *Mafra.*

The name of a magnificent edifice, consisting of a church, royal palace, and monastery, is situated in a bleak solitary country, about nineteen miles West of Lisbon, was founded by John the Fifth, in one thousand seven hundred and seventeen.

From the nature and magnitude of this edifice, it may be considered as the Escurial of Portugal; which structure the

5

the Royal founder intended to emulate; it occupies more ground; and the treaſures he laviſhed on it, if properly applied, would raiſe a pile much ſuperior to the Eſcurial in point of architecture; but unfortunately the deſigner of it had neither a mind to conceive, or a hand to execute, a deſign for a glebe-houſe, much leſs a baſilick and Royal palace.

The name of this mechanic was Frederic Ludovici; he was a native of Germany, and a goldſmith by profeſſion. Having amaſſed a conſiderable fortune in executing the gold and ſilver utenſils of the patriarchal church, he was appointed, under the ſpecious title of Architect, to deſign and execute this fabric, through the intereſt of one of his Majeſty's miniſters, with whom his money had greater weight than his talents.

The plan of this edifice forms a quadrangle, meaſuring from Eaſt to Weſt ſeven hundred and ſixty feet, and from North to South ſix hundred and ſeventy feet. In the centre of the Weſt front is a ſort of an Ionic hexaſtyle portico, which leads to the church; at each ſide is a pavilion, one for the accommodation of the Royal Family, the other for the Patriarch and mitred canons. At the rear of the building is a monaſtery with three hundred cells. It has alſo a college, inſtituted in one thouſand ſeven hundred and ſeventy-two, by Joſeph the Firſt. Don Joaquim de Aſſumpçoã, the profeſſor of ma-

 thematics,

thematics, very obligingly ſhewed us the repoſitory of mathematical inſtruments. The library is three hundred and eighty-one palmos long, by forty-three broad, and ſuppoſed to contain between forty and fifty thouſand volumes.

In the dado of the high altar are two large tables of black marble, ſo highly poliſhed, that John the Fifth uſed them as looking-glaſſes before they were ſent hither. Among the ornaments of the edifice are fifty-eight ſtatues of Carrara marble; ſome of which are very well executed. We may form ſome idea of the magnitude of the whole by the number of apartments it contains, which amount to eight hundred and ſixty-ſix. The doors and windows amount to five thouſand two hundred.

The entire of this vaſt pile is vaulted and covered over with flags, forming a platform, whereby we may walk over the ſummit of the edifice. Here I obſerved ſeveral large blocks of ſtones that were ſhivered by lightning. Conductors are erected in the different parts wherein the injuries happened, but no where elſe. The gardens, which are at the rear, are very extenſive, and well-ſtored with a variety of exotics, which the founder imported at a great expence from his poſſeſſions in Aſia, Africa, or America. For a more particular account of this ſtructure, we refer the reader to Father John do Prado's deſcription of it,

 publiſhed

published at Lisbon in the year one thousand seven hundred and fifty-one.

Having been informed by his Grace the Bishop of Beja, that several vestiges of Roman antiquities had been lately discovered in his diocese near the city of Beja, I resolved to make a journey thither, and to visit the city of Evora, which is said to have some valuable ancient monuments.

On the ninth of October one thousand seven hundred and ninety, I set out from Lisbon, and arrived in the evening at Alde Galega, a small village on the East side of the Tagus. Next day, about two o'clock, I reached

*Setuval,*

A city famous for its salt manufactories. Its harbour is said to be the best in Portugal, except that of Lisbon; it is even better sheltered than the latter, and less difficult of approach, but not so extensive. The population of the city is supposed to amount to ten thousand.

Notwithstanding the trade of this place, and the constant intercourse between it and Lisbon, yet there is not a perch of a road to be seen the whole way, which is about six leagues; nor can any find their way in the journey, except those who are in the constant habit of travelling there: every other person must take a guide, or, what will anſwer the ſame purpoſe, one of the mules which is trained to the route.

There is ſaid to be ſeveral valuable pictures, by Henry Corneille Vroom, the celebrated Dutch marine-painter, at a church in the vicinity of this city. This painter having embarked at Holland, with an intent to go to Spain, was caſt away in a gale of wind on the coaſt of Portugal, where his ſhip was daſhed to pieces. Among the fragments of the wreck that were caſt aſhore were found ſome pictures, which were carried to a neighbouring convent. Shortly after, Vroom and a few of his diſtreſſed companions were wafted on the rocks, and conducted to the ſame convent. The Friars, who greatly admired the pictures, were rejoiced to ſee the painter of them: they hoſpitably entertained him and his fellow-ſufferers, furniſhed them with money and clothes, and ſent them to Liſbon. In gratitude for their humanity, Vroom returned to Setuval, and painted ſeveral pictures for the Friars.

At Setuval I embarked in a paſſage-boat, and ſailed up the river Cadaon. On the banks of this river is manufactured all the ſalt exported from Setuval: when prepared, it is piled up in heaps in the form of hay-ricks, and covered with ſtraw or ruſhes, to exclude the rain. The quantity of it produced here, though very great, is but trivial in compariſon to what it is capable of yielding. The river Cadaon is ſo extenſive, and well adapted for

 that

that trade, that one would suppose it competent to supply all Europe with salt; and it is allowed to be superior in quality to any manufactured in Spain, Sardinia, or France.

About ten o'clock at night we reached Alcaçer do Sal, a small town about six leagues from Setuval. Its principal trade consists in salt and fish, with which the inhabitants supply most of the province of Alenteju. They have also rushes here of a particular kind, of which mats, chairs, &c. are made. The territory produces little corn, and the wine it yields is white, and of an inferior quality.

This town in former times was resorted to, during the Summer season, by the opulent Romans who inhabited Beja, Evora, and other parts of Lusitania. They had their villas and baths in it, and a temple dedicated to the goddess *Salacia*. Augustus Cesar made it a free town. The Moors had possession of it from the year seven hundred and thirteen, till one thousand two hundred and seventeen; when Alfonso the Second finally banished them, after reducing the town to a heap of ruins.

I lodged here at an inn belonging to a man who held an office of some importance under the chief magistrate of the town. He entertained me at supper with the best fare his house could afford; viz. beef, eggs, greens, a bottle

bottle of pretty good wine, and a profusion of fruit, pomegranates, olives, grapes, and a musk-melon. No host was ever more desirous of pleasing a guest whom he never saw before, nor ever expected to see again. He took off his sword and sat by me during supper, alternately taking snuff and humming stanzas to the sound of his guitar. Next morning, having hired a mule and a guide for me, he furnished his bill; the amount of which, for supper, wine, bed, &c. was two testoons (one shilling and three halfpence). The remainder of a *crusado* I distributed among his children; and he was so well pleased to see the little ones taken notice of, that he declared, *if ever you come this way again, Sir, myself and my house shall be at your service.*

*October* 21. This morning we passed through a country that exhibits some of the most beautiful scenes that a landscape-painter could wish to behold: scenes whose wild grandeur would invite the pencil of a Salvator Rosa; consisting of lofty hills, rude cliffs, and deep valleys, finely watered, and interspersed with pine and oak trees: here and there a cottage, with a few peasants and cattle, enlivened the scene; and nothing was wanting that the artist could wish for to transfer to the canvas, except the stately ruins. It is extraordinary, that such transcendent prospects do not call forth the exertions of the Portuguese artists to the study of landscape; for there are no professors of that branch of the fine arts in the kingdom, at least I could not hear of, nor meet with one.

Towards

Towards the evening we entered a flat country, without culture, without inhabitants, an unprofitable waſte, which, apparently, for ages, had not been pierced by the plowſhare. In this trackleſs deſert we loſt our way: the guide remained ſome time in ſuſpenſe which courſe to take: at length he begged of me to unlight, took the bridle off the mule, and ſent it before us: we followed the animal, and thus regained our way. Shortly after, we accoſted a troop of carriers who were going to Beja; my guide having bartered with one of them, transferred me to his care the remainder of the journey, and he returned home.

At five o'clock we ſtopped to bait at a well; here the carriers drew up water for their mules with ropes and leather buckets they carried for that purpoſe. Contiguous to this we met a ſwine herd at the foot of an oak: he had juſt threſhed from its boughs a meal of acorns for the briſtly flock which ſurrounded him; a girl who accompanied him was roaſting part of the ſame fruit for their own repaſt, whilſt he played on a ſmall lute.

In the courſe of the evening we met ſeveral herds of this kind feeding on graſs and acorns; hence, probably, ariſes the excellence of the Portugueſe bacon, ſo much eſteemed all over Europe. The fleſh of hogs reared in this manner, muſt certainly be very different in flavour from thoſe fed in cities or ſea-port towns.

During the laſt ſix leagues of this day's journey, I had not ſeen a village, nor even a houſe. Here day and night is equally ſolitary and ſilent: the country appeared to have no claimants except theſe ſwine herds, who roved about it uncontrouled; and the ſtillneſs of nature is ſeldom interrupted but with the ſound of their horns. At nine o'clock we deſcried a light on a neighbouring mountain, which we approached, and there tarried till morning in a lonely hoſtillery.

Shortly after our arrival came in two young Franciſcan Friars from Cadiz, who were going to Liſbon to paſs their noviciate. They appeared very fatigued, as they travelled on foot agreeably to the rules of their order; a mode of travelling they called *riding the capuchins mule.*

Of all the inns I have yet met with, this is the moſt wretched. There was nothing to be had in it but bread and ſour wine, though all of us ſtood much in need of refreſhment: for my own part, I had taken none ſince ſix o'clock in the morning, as the proviſions I had with me were hardened, and rendered unfit for uſe, by the ſcorching rays of the ſun. Whilſt we were contriving how to alleviate our diſtreſs, the keeper of the inn entered with two large hares ſlung to a ruſty fowling-piece, and relieved our anxiety.

The hopes of being ſumptuouſly regaled by this unexpected ſupply gave new life to the wearied Friars, who were

were persuaded that Providence had interposed in their behalf. Their felicity, however, was of short duration; the prospect vanished, and left them amidst their misfortune to reflect on the folly of anticipation. Here was the cause of our disappointment. The elder of the two Friars approached the fire-place where the landlord's two daughters were cooking the hares, which they minced and put into an earthen vessel supported by a tripod. These girls being young and handsome, had tempted the disciple of St. Francis (who was full of youth and vigour like Rabelais' Friar John) to make love to one of them, though he pretended to be devoutly recounting his beads. In short, between piety and beauty the tripod was overset, and the brittle vessel containing the minced hares was dashed to pieces on the hearth.

The only resource now left was to sleep away our hunger like the Laplanders; but unfortunately the situation allotted to us for that purpose was not the most eligible. We were sent to a small office without a door at the rear of the house, on the floor of which was laid a mattress for each of us to repose on. My muleteer cautioned me to be very watchful, as the place was infested with wolves; adding, that he himself would accompany me for safety, but that he could not think of forsaking a comfortable bed he had made up of his sacks in the stable. I slept, nevertheless, very soundly in this doorless chamber, with my sword drawn, till he called me to resume our journey at four o'clock in the morning.

*October*

*October* 22d. Though I did not give much credit to what the muleteer related laſt night reſpecting the wolves, yet this morning I was fully convinced of the truth of it. Shortly after we left the inn, we deſcried one of theſe animals at the diſtance of about three hundred yards; it ſtood for a moment, but fled as ſoon as the muleteers began to ſhout and caſt ſtones at it. From its ſize one ſhould ſuppoſe it not adequate to encounter a ſtrong maſtiff.

*Beja*.

At one o'clock in the evening we reached the city of Beja, when I delivered the letters with which his Grace the Biſhop honoured me at my departure from Liſbon; his ſecretary informed me, that he had received orders to accommodate me in the palace, and to give every aſſiſtance in his power in facilitating the object of my journey.

This city is ſeated upon an eminence in the province of Alenteju, about three and twenty leagues South-eaſt of Liſbon. Julius Cæſar honoured it with the title of Pax Julia, and made it a Roman colony: the Moors had poſſeſſion of it from the year ſeven hundred and fifteen, till one thouſand one hundred and ſixty-two. Some remains of the walls, towers, and fortifications of the latter are ſtill extant, but none of the monuments of the former. The chief part of the preſent town was built by Alfonſo the Third. It contains one of the best constructed castles in the kingdom, founded by King Diniz. Two leagues from hence is the Guadiana, a celebrated river, which runs seven leagues of its course under ground, from the village of Argamasilla to the town of Daymiel. The ancient city of Beja was built a short distance to the East of the present. In digging there lately, several antique fragments were discovered. It must be regretted that these researches are not prosecuted; the process would not be attended with much difficulty or expence, as the pavement of the old city is not more than six and twenty feet beneath the surface of the earth: a speculator in this undertaking would, probably, be amply compensated for his trouble, if one may judge from the experiment already made. In a cave not exceeding thirty feet square by twenty deep, several fragments have been found, which are deposited among other ancient remains in the Bishop of Beja's Museum. The articles in the three following Plates, viz. XIV. XV. and XVI. are part of what I have copied from thence, except M and N, in Plate XIV. the prototypes of which are in the city of Evora.

## Reference to Plate XIV.

A and B. Monuments of marble.

C. A monument of solid stone, which appears by the inscription to have been deposited to the memory of a merchant (whose name is defaced) by his wife.

 D. D. Repre-

D. D. Represent one a sword, the other a dagger.

E. An Amphora.

F and G. Utensils of the Etruscan kind.

H. A vase copied from a sculpture on an ancient stone.

I. A Lachrymatory.

K. An ancient brick, such as were used in pavements.

L. An Ossuarium, or Sarcophagus, of an oval form. It is three feet long by one foot wide; the depth is the same as the width. In this were found petrescent bones of a brown colour, each piece of which appears to be as heavy as the same quantity of Carara marble. Whether this petrifying quality be inherent in the stone of which the Sarcophagus is formed, I could not learn; but it is not unreasonable to attribute it to that cause: for Theophrastus mentions, that *some stones have the property of petrifying or converting wholly into stone whatever is put into vessels made of them.* I shall add what Sir John Hill observes on this passage of Theophrastus.

" The stone *Theophrastus* next mentions, and of which he has recorded the petrifying power, but not the name, is the *Lapis Assius*, or *Sarcophagus*. The *Assian*, or flesh-consuming stone. The *Sarcophagus*, *Boet*. 403. *Assius vel Assius Lapis*; *Charlt*. 251. *Sarcophagus*, *sive Assius Lapis*, *De Laet*. 133. *Assius Lapis*, *Salmas*. *in*. *Solin* 847. *Plin*. book 36. chap. 17.

 " This

"This was a ſtone much known, and uſed among the Greeks in their ſepultures, and by them called σαρκὸ φαγος, from its power of conſuming the fleſh buried in it; which, it is ſaid, to have perfectly effected in forty days. This property it was much famed for, and all the ancient naturaliſts mention it: but the other, of turning into ſtone things put into veſſels made of it, has been recorded only by this author and *Mutianus*, from whom *Pliny* has copied it; and from him ſome few only of the later naturaliſts. The account *Mutianus* gives of it is, that it converted into ſtone the ſhoes of perſons buried in it, as alſo the utenſils, which it was, in ſome places, cuſtomary to bury with the body; particularly thoſe the perſons while living had moſt delighted in. The utenſils he mentions are ſuch as muſt have been made of many different materials; whence it appears, that this ſtone had a power of conſuming only fleſh; but that its petrifying quality extended to ſubſtances of very different kinds. Whether it really poſſeſſed this laſt quality, or not, has been much doubted, and many have been afraid, from its ſuppoſed improbability, to record it. What has much diſcouraged a diſbelief of it is *Mutianus*'s account of its thus taking place on ſubjects of different kinds and textures: but this, in my opinion, is no objection at all, and the whole account, very probably, true.—The place where this ſtone was dug was near *Aſſos*, a city in *Lycia*; from whence it had its name; and *Boethius* informs us, that in that country, and in ſome parts of the Eaſt, there were alſo ſtones of this kind, which, if tied to the bodies of living perſons, would, in the ſame manner, conſume their fleſh."

*Sir John Hill's Tranſlation of Theophraſtus' Hiſtory of Stones, page* 23. et ſeq. *in note.*

Plate XV. A. Is another monument of the ſame kind before-mentioned, C. Plate XIV.

B and C. Roman inſcriptional ſtones.

D. An ancient inſcriptional ſtone of the Chriſtian æra. The epitaph which it bears is written in all the ſimplicity of the apoſtolic ages. *Here lies Paul, the ſervant of God, who lived* 51 *years. He reſted in peace on the third day of the ides of March, Era* 582.

Plate XVI. The five inſcriptional ſtones repreſented in this Plate are alſo in the Biſhop of Beja's collection, except the one marked D, which is in the wall of the *praça* of the city of Beja. Several other Roman fragments have been found in the excavation above mentioned, among which was a mutilated ſtatue ſeated on a throne, ſuppoſed to have repreſented the Goddeſs Sybilla. The body of it is entire, but wants the head and arms; what remains of it, nevertheleſs, is very valuable, as the proportions of the members, the form of the drapery, and the delicacy of the ſculpture, clearly evince that it was executed when the arts were at their zenith. Near this ſtatue were found,

in

in the ſame cave, a hand holding a patera, and a buſt, which is ſaid to repreſent Auguſtus Cæſar.

Having taken ſketches of the moſt remarkable objects in this city and its environs, I ſet out with a guide and a mule for Evora, a city about twelve leagues diſtant from the former. As we could find no proper accommodation on the road, I reſolved to reach Evora that night; therefore I gave the mule to the guide, who was an old man, and walked after him the greater part of the journey. At eleven o'clock at night we reached

*Evora.*

This city is ſituated in the middle of the province Alenteju, upon an eminence; ſurrounded by a fine level country, which produces corn, wine, and oil. It is called in Latin *Ebora.* Some writers think that Ptolemy alludes to it when he writes *Ebura*, the name of a city in the province of Andaluſia. The Spaniſh antiquarians ſay Evora was firſt built by the Celti, about ſeven hundred and fifty-nine years before the birth of Chriſt. Pliny and others affirm, that it was inhabited by the Gauls, Phœnicians, and Perſians. Quintus Sertorius, the celebrated Roman Captain, made himſelf maſter of it about eighty years before Chriſt, and ſecured it with walls, fortifications, and ſubterraneous ways; he alſo ornamented

it

it with ſeveral public buildings, ſome of which exiſt to this day.

Julius Cæſar was the next that ſubdued *Evora*; he made it a municipal town, and gave it the name of *Liberalitas Julia*. The Moors took poſſeſſion of it in the year ſeven hundred and fifteen. It is not ſo large as Oporto, though conſidered as the ſecond city in the kingdom. The number of its inhabitants are computed at twenty thouſand, among whom are many families of diſtinction. It contains a college and a tribunal of inquiſition. The members of the latter may be conſidered as holding ſinecure places; for the power of this tribunal is greatly fallen, and likely never more to riſe again.

## *Aqueduct of Q. Sertorius.* Plate XVII.

Among the public buildings raiſed here by Quintus Sertorius, there exiſts a noble Aqueduct in good preſervation; the annexed View of it was taken about a mile and half to the North of the city. The piers are nine feet broad, by four feet and a half thick; the arched ſpace between is thirteen feet ſix inches, which is equal to the breadth and thickneſs of each pier added together. At intervals buttreſſes are ſuperadded to the piers, the better to ſecure the arcuation. The whole is formed of irregular ſtone, except the arches, which are of brick.

From

From the labour and expence required in building Aqueducts of this kind, many people have been led to conclude, that the ancients were unacquainted with the art of conveying water through unequal grounds by any other means, on account, as it is ſuppoſed, of their ignorance that water conveyed in tubes attained the level of its primitive ſource. Vitruvius, however, clearly ſhews the contrary: in b. viii. c. 7. he gives excellent rules for conveying water in tubes; rules which, if properly attended to, would prevent many blunders, in ſimilar operations, among us. Pliny alſo, in b. xxxi. c. 6. expreſsly mentions, that the ancients frequently conveyed water in this manner. It is a miſtaken notion then, to ſuppoſe that they were ignorant of the principles of hydraulics; becauſe they generally conveyed water in aqueducts, in preference to pipes.

Plate XVIII. is a perſpective repreſentation of a caſtellum, which is erected over the above Aqueduct at its termination in the city. In the centre of it is a ſmall reſervoir, from whence tubes are conveyed to the different fountains and ciſterns, agreeably to what Vitruvius recommends, b. viii. c. 7.

The plan of this caſtellum is circular; its greateſt diameter is twelve feet ſix inches, independent of the ſurrounding columns, which are eight in number, of the Ionic

Ionic Order. In each intercolumniation is a niche, with a ſtriated head; an aperture is formed in one of them to give acceſs to the inſide of the ſtructure. The ſecond ſtory is decorated with Ionic pilaſters, between which are apertures for ventilation; the top is crowned with an hemiſpherical dome.

What appear ſingular in this antique monument, are the acrotoires and depreſſed parapet over the entablature of the columns. It is probable that each of theſe acrotoires was formerly crowned with a vaſe: the remains of one is ſtill viſible, as expreſſed in the View; and the fragment of a pedeſtal to be ſeen in one of the niches, induces me to ſuppoſe that each of theſe alſo was decorated with a vaſe.

The whole is conſtructed of brick, incruſtated with cement, of ſo hard and durable a ſubſtance, that few parts of it appear to have failed by the natural decays of time. Conſidering it was built ſeventy years before the Chriſtian æra, we cannot but admire how ſuch an apparently delicate ſtructure has reſiſted the accumulated injuries of time. Upon the whole, it may be juſtly conſidered one of the beſt preſerved and moſt beautiful pieces of ancient architecture in exiſtence.

Here we have a ſtriking inſtance of what a good architect is capable of effecting with the meaneſt materials.

 Of

Of its dimenſions, nothing can be more elegant than this caſtellum, though formed of brick and cement.

The Greeks had many buildings conſtructed of the like materials *; and we find in Vitruvius, b. ii. c. 3. that the Romans alſo frequently built with bricks, as the remains of their edifices evince to this day. Palladio has left us a fine ſpecimen of this mode of building in an octaſtile portico at Venice; the columns of which are thirty-five feet high, formed of bricks that were caſt in circular moulds, and cut into quadrants before they were baked. From theſe, and many other examples that we could refer to, of elegant buildings conſtructed of brick, it appears evident that the meanneſs of our edifices, proceeds not from want of materials, but architects; for there is no country, however barren, but affords better materials than artiſts.

*Temple of Diana.* Plate XIX.

This Plate exhibits a view of another ſtructure, built by Sertorius, ſaid to be the remains of a Temple dedicated to Diana. The front of it preſents an hexaſtyle in the Corinthian Order; the diſtribution of which appears to be *pycnoſtylos*; for the intercolumniation is exactly one diameter and a half, like that of the Temple of the deified Julius, and of the Temple of Venus in Cæſar's forum, mentioned by Vitruvius, b. iii. c. 3.

* *Vide Remarques ſur l'Architecture des Anciens, par M. Winckelmann.*

The

The diameter of the columns is three feet four inches. The base is Attic, in height a semi-diameter of the column, or twenty inches, including the upper listle. The shafts are cut into channels and fillets; each channel is six inches and a half broad, and a semi-circle in depth; the number of channels in each column is but sixteen. Vitruvius assigns twenty-four channels to the Corinthian column, yet the appearance of these striæ is not unpleasing. For proportion and delicacy of sculpture the capitals are much to be admired.

The entablature is entirely destroyed, except part of the first facia of the architrave; the rest of the work is in a degree of preservation scarcely credible for a monument of its age. For this it is indebted to the durability of the materials, which is a species of granite somewhat asperous, but exceedingly hard. The rubble-work in the front and sides is evidently Moorisque, as may be inferred from the pinnacles with which it is crowned.

At one side of the hexastyle are five columns, including the angular one; at the other, I could discover but three.. From these and the columns of the front we may infer that it had been a *Peripteral* Temple; for, according to Vitruvius, b. iii. c. 1. Temples of this kind had six columns in the front, and as many in the *posticus*; the flanks had eleven each, including the angular columns, and a space equal to an intercolumn was left at every ſide between the ſurrounding columns and the cell or body of the Temple.

The elegance diſplayed in the remains of this Temple, have led many to conjecture that the architect had been a Greek, from a ſuppoſition that Rome at the time of Sertorius had not artiſts competent to deſign and execute ſo poliſhed a fabric. My firſt knowledge of it was derived from *Don Ignacia de Manique*, the Intendant General of Liſbon. In point of antiquity, as well as elegance, it is the moſt eſtimable ſtructure in Portugal; yet I am ſorry to add, that the ſtate of neglect in which it is left redounds little to the honour or diſcernment of the people of Evora. It is now converted into the meaneſt of offices—a meat-ſhambles. In this reſpect, however, it may be ſaid to have ſome affinity to its former deſtination; for then it flowed with the blood of victims, which were ſacrificed to appeaſe the Goddeſs Diana; whereas the like tragedies are now performed in it to appeaſe hungry mortals. Indeed, it appears to have been perpetually deſtined for a theatre of tragic exhibitions.

Several ancient inſcriptional ſtones have been found from time to time in this city and its environs, of which there are nine to be ſeen in an old wall contiguous to the priſon, with two modern ones. Copies of theſe inſcriptions may

 be

be ſeen in the following Plates; *viz.* XX. XXI. XXII. I cannot help obſerving that the inſcriptional ſtone D, repreſented in Plate XX. appears to be fictitious.

Plate XXIII. is a copy of an Arabic inſcriptional Stone at Evora.

The prototypes of the ancient vaſe M, and of the Doric frieze N, in Plate XIV. are alſo preſerved in the wall wherein the above inſcriptional ſtones are placed.

*Charnel Houſe.* Plate XXIV.

One morning, whilſt I was making ſome ſketches in the Praça, or Square, at Evora, a Franciſcan Friar accoſted me, and aſked, if I had ſeen the *Caſa dos Oſos* of his convent? On being anſwered in the negative, he replied, *Well then, Mr. Stranger, thou haſt ſeen nothing; come with me.* We paſſed through the Franciſcan church, and entered an arched-way, over which is this inſcription:

*Nos os oſos que aqui eſtamos,*
*Pellos voſſos eſperamos.*

Reader, reſpect each mouldering bone;
This ſacred cell await thy own.

The viſitant is ſtruck with ſurpriſe, mixed with terror, on entering this Golgotha. It is ſixty-ſix feet long, by thirty-ſix broad. The piers, which are eight in number.

ber, that is, four at each ſide of the nave, and alſo the walls, are lined with human ſkulls and bones, ſet in a hard cement. The obſcurity of the place, and the proſtrate poſture of the pious ſupplicants, render the whole a ſcene truly awful.

Dr. Young, who is ſaid to have compoſed his Night Thoughts by the light of a taper ſet in a human ſkull, would have ſaturated his melancholy had he ſtudied here; yet the Friars appeared to contemplate theſe mementos of mortality without the leaſt emotion of that awe incident to ſtrangers. Such is the effect of cuſtom, even death itſelf is diveſted of its terror in the idea of religious people, who are conſtantly ruminating on it, and alſo in the idea of thoſe men who are habituated to the ſight of dead bodies and ſanguinary ſcenes.

Montagne obſerves, "It was for this purpoſe that ſepulchres and cemeteries were made adjoining to the churches, and in the moſt frequented parts of the city, with a view to diveſt the people (ſays Lycurgus) of the idea of terror at the ſight of a corpſe, and to the end that the continual ſight of bones, graves, monuments, and funeral obſequies, ſhould put them in mind of their frail condition."

We may alſo add a cuſtom that obtained among the Mexicans, when the Spaniards firſt invaded their country, probably

bably with a view to inſpire courage, as well as to accuſtom their people to contemn the horrors of death. They frequently hung the ſkulls of their victims around their temples, and at other times piled them up in towers cemented with lime. In one of theſe towers *Andrea de Tapea* is ſaid to have counted an hundred and thirty-ſix thouſand ſkulls.

Hence, perhaps, the cuſtom of the ancient Romans, who at their banquets were wont to treat their gueſts with tragic exhibitions, making fencers fight in their preſence till ſtreams of blood guſhed over the tables and diſhes.— The Egpytians, in like manner, at their feaſts, had perſons who cried to the company whilſt they exhibited images of death; Drink, and be merry, for ſuch ſhall be thy fate at

THE END.

www.ingramcontent.com/pod-product-compliance
Lightning Source LLC
Chambersburg PA
CBHW020312240426
43673CB00039B/782
*9783337764104*